MANAGING
THE
OFFSHORE
INSTALLATION
WORKFORCE

MANAGING
THE
OFFSHORE
INSTALLATION
WORKFORCE

Rhona Flin and Georgina Slaven (Eds.)

PennWell Books
Tulsa, Oklahoma

Cover photo provided by Petroleum Helicopters, Inc.(Used with permission.)
Founded in 1949, Petroleum Helicopters, Inc. (PHI) provides helicopter transportation
to businesses engaged in domestic oil and gas, aeromedical, and international market-
place. Its helicopter fleet consists of 256 aircraft, which operates from 35 domestic and
4 foreign bases. The company employs a staff of 1,673, consisting of pilots, mechanics,
and personnel engaged in flight operations and administration. PHI is the world's
largest commercial helicopter operator.

Copyright (c) 1996 by
PennWell Publishing Company
1421 South Sheridan/P.O. Box 1260
Tulsa, Oklahoma 74101

Flin, Rhona H.
    Managing the offshore installation workforce / Rhona Flin and Georgina
Slaven.
        p.   cm.
    Includes bibliographical reference and index.
    ISBN 0-87814-396-3
    1. Offshore oil industry—Management.   2. Offshore oil industry—
Personnel management.   I. Slaven, Georgina.   II. Title.
HD9560.5.F545   1996   96-20367
622'.3382'0683—dc20   CIP

Printed in the United States of America

1 2 3 4 5 99 98 97 96

Contents

Acknowledgements

This book is the culmination of a decade of research conducted by staff and post-graduate research students at the Robert Gordon University. The editors would like to extend their thanks to two offshore managers in particular, Ronnie Compton (Shell Expro) and Maurice Ullman (Sun Oil) who provided the inspiration for our research into the OIM's role and responsibilities.

We would also like to thank Evelyn McLennan for providing excellent administration for our research team; David Sagar, Head of Aberdeen Business School for his encouragement of our endeavours, and Bob Miles of the Offshore Safety Division, Health and Safety Executive for his sponsorship of a number of our research projects. Our thanks also go to Marla Patterson at PennWell for her patience and advice during the editorial process and to an anonymous reviewer for his thoughtful comments.

The authors are grateful to the following for their advice and comments on draft chapters: Dom Bicocchi (OSD, HSE), Brent Curtis (OIM, Agip (UK) Ltd.), Dr Mike Doig (Senior Medical Advisor, Chevron UK Ltd.), George Fowler (Head of Personnel - Operations & Technical Support, Elf Enterprise Petroleum Ltd.), David John (Safety Manager, Total Oil Marine plc), Dr Alan Milne (Senior Medical Advisor, British Antarctic Survey Medical Unit, RGIT Ltd.), Malcolm Nicol (OIM, Amerada Hess Ltd.), Graham Norrie (Ninian Operations Advisor, Chevron UK Ltd.), John Ramsay (Chief Executive, OPITO), Alan Robinson (Platform Manager, Marathon Oil UK Ltd.), Bob Shields (Safety and Environment Manager, British Gas plc), Captain Ian Struthers (Chief Pilot, Bond Helicopters), Dr Alix Thom (Human Resources Manager, Wood Group Engineering), Doug Waterston (OIM, Texaco North Sea UK Co.) and Dr Zander Wedderburn (Heriot-Watt University). Any remaining errors and omissions are entirely the responsibility of the authors.

The views and opinions expressed in this book are those of the authors and should not be attributed in any way to the position or policy of any sponsoring organization.

Finally, the editors would like to thank all the offshore personnel in the North Sea who shared their feelings and experiences and contributed to the body of knowledge about what it is like to live and work in the offshore oil and gas industry.

Contributors

Jackie Burnett is a lecturer in Organisational Behaviour and Human Resource Management at Aberdeen Business School, The Robert Gordon University. A corporate member of the Institute of Personnel and Development, Jackie worked for two years in personnel management before starting her lecturing career in 1990. Her current research interests lie in employee motivation, in particular employees' needs and goal setting. She is currently working towards a Ph.D., examining employee motivation in the offshore oil and gas industry with a major UK operating company.

David Carnegie is a Personnel Manager with ICL Sorbus. His professional career began in 1990 with the oil service industry in Aberdeen, resourcing manpower for onshore drilling projects in Africa and Asia. In 1991 he registered for a Ph.D. at The Robert Gordon University, researching the role of the first line supervisor in the offshore oil and gas industry, working closely with oil industry leaders such as Shell Expro, Amerada Hess and BP. He is a member of the Institute of Personnel and Development.

Susan Coleshaw is Chief Research Officer and Head of Survival Research and Testing at RGIT Limited, Aberdeen. She has 16 years experience as a human physiologist, interested in occupational exposure to heat and cold, immersion hypothermia and problems relating to diving. She is responsible for research and consultancy projects relating to human performance, stress, offshore health and survival, as well as managing an accredited test laboratory for the approval of life-saving and personal protective equipment.

Mark Fleming is a Research Assistant at the Offshore Management Centre, Aberdeen Business School, The Robert Gordon University. He is working on a large scale study examining human and organizational factors in offshore safety. This is a continuation of a study measuring risk perception in the offshore oil industry. He has also been involved in a number of offshore consultancy projects and is investigating the role of the offshore supervisor in the management of safety for his doctoral thesis.

Rhona Flin is Professor of Applied Psychology at Aberdeen Business School and Director of Research at the Offshore Management Centre, The Robert Gordon University, Aberdeen. She is a Chartered Psychologist and has worked for 10 years with the UKCS offshore oil and gas industry on a variety of research and consultancy projects concerned with the management and safety of offshore installations. Her particular interests are offshore management skills, incident command in emergencies and human factors in industrial safety.

William Freeland is Medical Director at RGIT Limited., Aberdeen with responsibility for the occupational health business division, operating both onshore and offshore, as well as several remote overseas clinics. His clinical career began in Aberdeen where he gained experience of accident and emergency medicine, hyperbaric medicine and occupational health relating to the offshore industry. He then moved to a military appointment, specializing in preventive medicine and army community and occupational medicine.

Glyn David is a crew resource management (CRM) training captain with Bond Helicopters in Aberdeen. His professional aviation career began with the Royal Navy. He has both fixed wing and helicopter experience and has worked in oil and gas industry support aviation since 1987. Captain David is involved in training pilots, technicians, flight attendants, operations staff and aviation managers. He has served as a consultant on CRM training development for the Royal Air Force and the British Army Air Corps. He is a member of the Royal Aeronautical Society's Human Factors Group and is conducting post-graduate research in decision making by North Sea helicopter crews at the Offshore Management Centre, Robert Gordon University.

Rachel Gordon is a Research Assistant at the Offshore Management Centre. She is currently working on a large scale study examining the human and organizational factors in offshore safety. Her research interests include the human and organizational causes of accidents. She has also been involved in various human factors consulting projects for the offshore oil and gas industry.

Douglas Gourlay is an Honorary Research Fellow and previously Deputy Head of Aberdeen Business School, The Robert Gordon University. He has had experience as a personnel manager in the manufacturing industry and management education. He is an authority on industrial relations and has served as a member of the Industrial Tribunal (Scotland) and as an arbiter on the Advisory, Conciliation and Arbitration Service. Douglas is currently completing his doctorate on a history of industrial relations in the North Sea oil industry.

Rachel Harris is a Project Officer at the Robert Gordon University and was previously a Research Officer at RGIT Limited. She graduated in Physiology and Sports Science, and subsequently specialized in human psychological and physiological responses to stress. She has completed a study of stress responses in offshore survival course trainees and was awarded her doctorate in 1996.

Kathryn Mearns is a Senior Research Fellow at the Offshore Management Centre. After taking her doctorate in Norway in 1989, she returned to Aberdeen in 1991 and has since worked at Robert Gordon

University. Her research interests include the study of risk perception and safety attitudes; diet, health and fitness of offshore workers and professional women at work. She is currently managing a major research project on human factors in offshore safety, sponsored by several offshore organizations and the UK Health and Safety Executive.

Georgina Slaven is a Chartered Occupational Psychologist, currently employed as a Higher Scientific Officer at the Institute of Naval Medicine, Ministry of Defence, Gosport and formerly a Research Fellow at Aberdeen Business School, The Robert Gordon University. For five years she conducted research and consultancy within the UK offshore oil and gas industry on topics such as the role of OIMs, shift work, new technology in training, personality profiling, management competence and emergency command decision making. Her research interests focus on human factors and ergonomics in the workplace.

Jan Skriver is a Ph.D. student in applied cognitive psychology at the Offshore Management Centre, The Robert Gordon University, conducting research into emergency decision making. His research focuses on how experienced offshore installation managers make decisions in emergencies. This encompasses all aspects of the decision making process including information gathering, decision making strategies, execution, and identification of potential human errors.

Keith Stewart was formerly a Research Assistant at Aberdeen Business School, The Robert Gordon University, where he worked on projects relating to crisis command and control in the offshore oil industry. He has recently moved to the Centre for Human Sciences at the Defence Research Agency, Farnborough, UK.

Robin Tait has been a lecturer in Human Resource Management at Aberdeen Business School, The Robert Gordon University since 1991. He spent five years as a commercial diver in the North Sea, and four years as a Human Resources Representative for Marathon Oil (UK) in their Aberdeen and London offices. His research interests center on employee involvement and participation, specifically in the offshore oil and gas industry. Robin is a corporate member of the Institute of Personnel and Development.

Trudy Wagstaff is a sociology undergraduate student at the University of Bath. She spent the third year of her degree on placement at the Robert Gordon University, researching women employed in a science, engineering or technical capacity in the upstream oil and gas industry.

Chapter 1

Introduction
Rhona Flin and Georgina Slaven

"The oil installations are strange in the same way as the awkward, seemingly patched together contraptions NASA puts into orbit are strange. And the jobs in turn, are so complex that, to the outsider, the ingenuity required to do them seems like magic."[1]

Worldwide the offshore oil and gas industry employs about quarter of a million people who work more than 2,000 manned production platforms and drilling rigs.[2] This is a sizable workforce in an inhospitable and hazardous work environment, which makes a very significant contribution to the international economy.[3,4] There has been extensive and leading edge technological research and development in the upstream oil industry and as the above quote illustrates, this has been on a par with the efforts devoted to space exploration resulting in comparable achievements.

When we began to research the management of North Sea offshore oil and gas installations in the mid-1980s, we were struck by the lack of management research on the industry, despite the considerable experience and expertise which we encountered. There was a plethora of publications dealing with the technical aspects of offshore operations, yet very few discussed the contribution of the people who work offshore. Neither did they describe how to ensure a safe and productive work environment or how to create management systems which mitigate the effects of the high hazard environment.[5,6] In a review paper on working conditions and safety provision in the Canadian offshore oil industry, Doug House in 1985 stated,

> *Worldwide, there have been few systematic investigations of the offshore oil industry and its impact upon oil workers and their families. The dearth of empirical material has not been due to lack of interest by researchers, nor even primarily, by a lack of available funding. Rather, the main cause has been the successful resistance of the offshore petroleum industry to have itself investigated, and the reluctance of most governments that it be studied against its will.[7]*

This has not been our experience of the British and Norwegian oil and gas industry. Our first doctoral students were granted access to conduct research with the offshore industry more than a decade ago and since that time our research group has worked on a range of human factors and management projects.[8,9] However we would have to agree with U.S. researchers who commented in relation to the drilling industry, that this is "an occupational group with abundant folklore fueled by popular opinion and the press."[10] Myths and legends of the international offshore oil industry abound, in some cases willingly endorsed by the workers themselves who appreciate their frontier adventurer status. For example, in Scotland the offshore workforce has been characterized by the media as *the North Sea tigers* or *the bears*, and similar labels exist in other parts of the world.

One of the earliest studies to examine the psychosocial aspects of this unusual work environment was conducted by Lisandro Perez in the late 1970s in the Gulf of Mexico.[11] He asserted that the conditions and pressures associated with offshore employment were linked to accident rates. The four social factors he identified related to the inexperience of the workforce, competitive pressures in the oil industry, a *macho image* associated with offshore work, and political and administrative factors. There seems to have been little subsequent psychosocial research on offshore oil installations in the United States with the exception of accident and injury studies and work on offshore safety management.[12] In Canada, where there have been offshore drilling operations for a number of years, some research was carried out on drilling rig and supply boat workers by House and his colleagues, and there has been subsequent interest as a result of the Cohasset and Hibernia developments.[13] There have been few attempts to systematically describe and analyze the culture of the European offshore work environment. Exceptions include a very detailed study, which was sponsored by Statoil and Mobil, as well as several specific investigations such as studies of safety, diet, alcohol consumption, occupational stress, and personal accounts by journalists and workers themselves.[1,14-20] Elsewhere in the world, where there are offshore exploration and production operations, such as Indonesia, India, China, Australia, West Africa, and South America, almost no independent research of this kind seems to have been undertaken.

This book is an attempt to gather the existing research material and collective managerial wisdom into a single volume on how to manage an offshore workforce. We were guided in this endeavor by our professional curiosity about people (being psychologists we are naturally inquisitive) and by our contact with offshore managers, who have been unfailingly cooperative with our research. Over the years we have found that the problems that interest us as scientists are real problems for offshore managers. The aim of this book is to provide managers in the industry with the latest evidence from empirical research on the issues to address when managing an offshore workforce. We hope that providing such facts will enable managers and supervisors to make informed decisions about every aspect of the *human element* in their offshore operations.

Our knowledge of the industry is based predominantly on experience obtained within the European oil industry in the North Sea and Irish Sea, although we have also worked with Canadian researchers. In many respects, this area is at the forefront of technological offshore development, mainly due to the hostile environment, drilling depths, plus size and complexity of the installations. But we have tried to consider issues which could be of relevance to managers in any offshore location and to include the results of research from throughout the world. However, our efforts to locate research around the globe often reveal that few investigations of this type have been conducted on offshore installations outside Europe. We hope future editions of this book will include the results of more non-European research.

The chapters which follow are directed at offshore managers and supervisors, their onshore managers, and anyone involved in managing personnel offshore. Members of educational, professional, and trade union groups also may find information of interest. Managers and supervisors who are studying, or who share our curiosity in understanding human behavior in the offshore environment should find information to guide and inform their day-to-day work.

The book covers a diversity of topics. As a consequence, each reader may find certain chapters more relevant than others. The chapters are arranged in a sequence moving from a consideration of the factors involved in choosing suitable offshore workers, through daily management issues to emergency management, understanding accident and error reduction, through to management innovations from the aviation industry, to the increasing role of women offshore. Some may wish to dip into selected chapters and each chapter is written in such a way that it can be read in any sequence without the reader missing the thread of an argument. We have endeavored to include a comprehensive reference list for each chapter to provide full supporting evidence for readers interested in further exploration of a given subject.

The authors have all conducted research in their fields, and have experience in the offshore industry. They have written substantial and up-to-date summaries of the research on their topic. Chapter topics have been chosen because of their importance for managing the offshore workforce and in order to reflect current business and organizational developments. In general, the book attempts to increase managerial awareness of current issues concerning staff management and development by reviewing the following topics.

An increasing emphasis on competence and the more prevalent use of objective measures of candidate abilities are addressed in chapter 2, which considers staff selection and training.

Chapter 3 on health, discusses the need for medical services offshore, the requirement to assess medical fitness and the benefits of pro-active health management practices for an offshore workforce.

Chapter 4 examines the roles of the offshore installation managers and their supervisors. These personnel have considerable expertise developed over many years, but this is rarely formally recorded for the new generations of offshore managers and supervisiors.

In every industry workers are exposed to job pressures and demands, but when working offshore, there are aspects of the lifestyle which can cause additional stress. These are discussed in chapter 5 which considers the causes and effects of occupational stress on the offshore workforce and suggests how these may be managed.

Chapter 6 discusses shift work practices, explains the physiological basis for shift working problems, provides a summary of shift work studies conducted offshore and reviews the effects of time of day on an individual's capacity to perform.

The factors which should be taken into account when trying to understand people's motivation to work are reviewed in chapter 7 which highlights the key issues for offshore managers to consider when trying to improve employee motivation to increase productivity.

Chapter 8 focuses on the potential problems resulting from an offshore installation emergency and how to improve emergency management procedures and practices.

The role of human error in accident causation is considered in chapter 9. It includes an overview of accident and incident reporting systems and how they can be used to mitigate against the human contribution to accident causation.

This theme is continued in chapter 10 by considering risk and safety from the point of view of those who actually work in the hazardous offshore environment. As such, this chapter considers workers' feelings of safety and their attitudes toward safety and how these affect accident involvement.

Taking the example of the very different approaches found in Norway and the United Kingdom offshore industry, chapter 11 discusses human resource management from the viewpoint of industrial relations and traces the different historical traditions in these two countries and how they have influenced employers' approaches to governing employment offshore.

Chapter 12 describes the development of human factors appreciation in commercial aviation with particular reference to helicopter operations for the offshore industry. This includes the contribution of Crew Resource Management training as a means of reducing the problems posed by failures in human performance.

The book finishes with an overview of the increasing involvement of women in the UK, Norwegian, and Canadian offshore industries, both in the offshore environment and as partners of those who work offshore.

Each chapter concludes with practical guidance for managers on how they can apply the principles explored to their own installations. We hope that readers will share our enthusiasm for understanding human behavior and find this book a practical tool for managing the offshore workforce.

References

1. Alvarez, A. *Offshore: A North Sea Journey*. London: Sceptre, 1986.

2. ILO. *Safety and Related Issues Pertaining to Work on Offshore Petroleum Installations*. Geneva: International Labour Organisation, 1993.

3. Yergin, D. *The Prize*. New York: Simon & Schuster, 1991.

4. Harvie, C. *Fool's Gold. The Story of North Sea Oil*. London: Penguin, 1994.

5. Mather, A. *Offshore Engineering*. London: Witherby, 1995.

6. Barry, R. *The Management of International Oil Operations*. Tulsa, OK: PennWell, 1993.

7. House, J. D. *Working Offshore: The Other Price of Newfoundland's Oil*. St John's: Institute of Social and Economic Research, Memorial University, 1985.

8. Thom, A. *Managing Labour Under Extreme Risk: Collective Bargaining in the North Sea Oil Industry*. Unpublished PhD thesis. The Robert Gordon University. Aberdeen., 1989.

9. Sutherland, K. *Psychosocial Factors: An Investigation of the Offshore Oil Industry*. Unpublished PhD thesis. The Robert Gordon University, Aberdeen., 1994.

10. Mueller, B., Mohr, D., Rice, J. & Clemmer, D. Factors affecting individual injury experience among petroleum drilling workers. *Journal of Occupational Medicine*, 29, 2, 1987. 126-131.

11. Perez, L. *Working Offshore: A Preliminary Analysis of Social Factors Associated with Safety in the Offshore Workplace*. Sea Grant LSUT79001. Louisiana Centre for Wetland Resources, 1979.

12. Reber, R. A. & Wallin, J. A. Utilizing performance management to improve offshore oil field diving safety. *The International Journal of Organizational Analysis*, 2, 1, 1994: 88-98.

13. Storey, K. & Shrimpton, M. *Social, Psychosocial and Cultural Aspects of Health and Safety in the Offshore Oil Industry*. Newfoundland: ISER Offshore Oil Project, Memorial University, 1993.

14. Hellesoy, O. (Ed.) *Work Environment Statfjord Field*. Oslo: Universitetsforlaget, 1985.

15. Qvale, T. Design for safety and productivity in large scale industrial projects: The case of the Norwegian offshore oil development. In B. Wilpert & T. Qvale (Eds.) *Reliability and Safety in Hazardous Work Systems*. Sussex: LEA, 1993.

16. Ostgard, L. Food habits among Norwegian offshore oil workers: Adaptation to spectrum and abundance of food choice. In J. Somogyi & E. Koskinen (Eds.) *Nutritional Adaptation to New Life-Styles*. Basel: Karger, 1990.

17. Aiken, G. & McCance, C. Alcohol consumption in offshore oil rig workers. *British Journal of Addictions*, 77, 1982: 305-310.

18. Sutherland, V. & Cooper, C. *Man and Accidents Offshore*. London: Lloyds, 1986.

19. Punchard, E. *Piper Alpha: A Survivor's Story*. London: W. H. Allen, 1990.

20. May, J. *Divers. From Piper Alpha to the Gulf War*, London: Hodder & Stoughton, 1995.

Selecting and Training the Offshore Workforce
Georgina Slaven

Introduction

Selecting, training and developing the offshore workforce is concerned with finding the right people for the job and making the most of the human resources. This chapter provides an overview of common selection tools and their potential contribution to selection procedures for offshore personnel. The first section highlights some common attributes required for any offshore work (based on Alec Rogers' Seven Point Plan)[33] and how best to determine whether potential candidates possess such qualities. Illustrative examples from both industry and research studies are used to highlight potential pitfalls and provide empirical evidence to support the use of certain selection tools.

The second section discusses how to obtain the best performance from personnel once in position. In safety-critical industries such as offshore exploration and production, employers need to ensure that staff performance measures up to the standards required of employment. The current term to describe this attribute is *competence*. Techniques to determine competence are presented along with a cautionary note on the limitations of such an approach. The chapter concludes with some tips for managers on the most appropriate techniques for staff selection, training and development.

Selecting the Right Staff

Choosing the right person to work offshore is a critical management decision. Selecting the wrong person can result in poor individual and team performance and may affect the safety of both the individual and of all those on board the installation. Selection procedures can be expensive to conduct in the first place, and can cause significant problems if poor selection decisions are made and the process has to be repeated. When looking for the right candidate, an employer is trying to predict a person's suitability to do a particular job. In order to make such a prediction you need to understand the tasks of the job in question and have enough information about potential candidates to determine whether they possess the skills and abilities to undertake such tasks. The

following sections discuss the contribution of job analysis and how best to determine and measure key selection criteria relevant to offshore positions.

Job Analysis

The first step in designing selection criteria is clearly defining the job,
normally termed *job analysis*. This defines what the job involves and the criteria
for good performance. One needs to be able to distinguish between someone
who can do the job well and someone who cannot. Although job analyses are
often used for purposes other than selection (pay rates, training needs analysis,
etc.) they provide information about the characteristics required of the successful candidate.

A job description synthesizes the information from the job analysis into a
list of key tasks, duties, responsibilities and the required standards of the job.
From this list, it is possible to determine the key attributes for the job in terms
of a *person specification*, which details the qualities and skills a person needs to do
the job. This chapter will be structured around the key qualities in terms of
physical and psychological attributes which are required of personnel to work
offshore, and will discuss methods appropriate to determining whether a candidate possesses such characteristics.

Criteria

Physical Characteristics

Susan Coleshaw et. al. have already examined the medical criteria for
working offshore which organizations in some countries impose (see chapter
3). In remote work environments, employers obviously want the healthiest
workers available to reduce costly medical emergency evacuations onshore and
to minimize the potentially deleterious effects of ill health on performance and
safety. Such medical screening usually continues throughout an employee's
working life, not just at recruitment. In addition to general good health,
employers may want to ensure that potential employees are not addicted to
drugs or alcohol given the potential impact on performance and the increased
risk to the safety of others offshore which alcohol and drug abuse would pose.
Even though alcohol and drugs are usually prohibited offshore, drug use has
not been totally eradicated and employers have no control over employees'
alcohol consumption when on leave. To assume that individuals do not have a
drinking problem because they are not permitted alcohol for two weeks out of
every four would be naive. The loss of Exxon's tankship, *Exxon Valdez*[1] illustrates
the consequences of inadequate selection and monitoring procedures to deal
with alcohol dependency rehabilitation.

In addition to good health, organizations may wish to stipulate a specified proficiency in the common language used offshore. While this may sound obvious, it is an issue currently under debate by members of the International Maritime Organization. During day-to-day operations, individuals have the time to ensure their instructions are clearly understood. In an emergency, time is of the essence and under pressure, individuals often revert back to their native tongue. This obviously creates communication problems at a time when clear and effective communication is of paramount importance. The fire on board a Norwegian passenger ferry, the *Scandinavian Star* in 1990, which cost the lives of 158 people illustrates the problems which can arise with a largely non-English speaking crew.[2] The ship's emergency plan was in English, yet a large portion of the crew were Portuguese with a poor command of English. Thus they were unable to make themselves familiar with the emergency plan. In addition, many of the crew were unable to comprehend officers' orders or to communicate to officers. This had obvious implications for the ship's safety, and the official report of the investigation following the fire concluded that "the Committee does not consider that it was justifiable to sail with a crew consisting of so many persons with a poor command of English."[2] Oil companies operating with multinational crews need to bear in mind the demands of being able to work in another language, particularly in times of stress, and to work within a multi-cultural environment.

Attainments

The most typical qualities required of a candidate are education, training, experience and achievements. Evidence that a candidate possesses these are fairly straightforward to obtain. Certificates of qualifications can be easily presented to prove the candidate has the required level of education. However, such qualifications only demonstrate that the candidate possessed the relevant skills and often, theoretical knowledge to pass the examination at the time. Organizations are becoming increasingly concerned that candidates have the necessary skills and competence to perform the standards required of employment, i.e. the application of theoretical knowledge in the workplace.

In the United Kingdom, many organizations are assisting employees to obtain the relevant National Vocational Qualifications (NVQs) to demonstrate their competence at work. NVQs were first introduced by the United Kingdom government in 1981 to credit those in employment with a qualification which acknowledges their ability to perform the tasks required of a particular job to a nationally agreed standard. In the United Kingdom, the term *competence* refers to the minimum standards required, whereas in the USA the interpretation is more towards the *highest* standards required.[3] The United Kingdom now has

NVQs for various trade and craft jobs often found offshore including supervisory and personnel management standards, though few are specifically oriented to an offshore environment.

Aside from professional training, which can be easily determined and verified by the production of certificates, specialist training is normally required before working offshore (discussed more fully later in this chapter). The only other point of relevance for selection purposes is the necessity to determine what training is an absolute pre-requisite and what training can be provided after selection. For example, though offshore installation managers (OIMs) are required to be familiar with the relevant United Kingdom legislation for their role offshore[4], most companies would not consider it an employment disqualifier if a promising candidate had not already undertaken such training, but would provide it prior to their first trip offshore.

The offshore work environment is often considered unique, in terms of the location and specific hazards found offshore. Some employers prefer candiedates who have experience of working offshore or in related industries such as fishing, the armed forces and onshore petro-chemical plants, the assumption being that those who have are in a better position to determine whether they can adapt to the particular work environment. Offshore work experience is also usually considered a prerequisite for supervisory and managerial posts. In a survey of United Kingdom selection methods[5] the typical career development route for operating company OIMs was via offshore supervisory positions, whereas drilling company OIMs were almost exclusively Master Mariners (i.e. ship's captains). Given the demands of the job, one would expect experience of working offshore to be a pre-requisite for a managerial post, not just in terms of staff-management but in terms of technical experience and an appreciation of the particular demands of an offshore environment and the implications for the safety of personnel and the integrity of the installation.

General Intelligence

The concept of intelligence has been the subject of considerable research and debate (even to the extent that psychologists in the United States debate the existence of such a concept!), yet has remained almost impossible to define. Conceptually it usually refers to the ability to learn from experience. For the pragmatist, intelligence is usually inferred from an individual's score on a general intelligence test. Intelligence is probably the most generally recognized predictor of job performance and research has repeatedly shown that it is related to all types of jobs, from the simple to the most complex.[6] Intelligence is one of the main determinants for the ability to learn. When selecting offshore personnel, one certainly hopes to find individuals with the ability to learn from their mistakes and a degree of problem solving ability. One might reasonably expect to ascertain general intelligence level during a personal interview with the candidate and to infer intelligence from a candidate's educational achievements. As the term *general intelligence* is rather difficult to define, it may be more appropriate to define the specific skills and abilities which are required for a particular job.

Special Aptitudes

Many offshore jobs require specialist skills and abilities to perform them well. For example assistant drillers need numerical ability to calculate mud weights and working with machinery requires manual dexterity. Such skills are usually inferred from an individual's work experience, though job history only tells us what jobs have been done and not how well they have been done. Other, more reliable methods of determining whether a candidate possesses certain essential skills and abilities are psychometric tests (discussed more fully later in this chapter). They include tests of manual dexterity, verbal and numerical reasoning, problem solving and spatial relations to name a few.

The drilling company Smedvig Ltd. provides an illustrative example of how such tests are used for offshore workers, as they conducted an in-house analysis of the competencies necessary to work offshore.[7] The competencies they identified included work ethic, learning and ambition, thinking, planning and organizing, team focus and confidence. As part of their selection procedure, candidates undertook a battery of psychometric tests to measure their mathematical, verbal reasoning skills and mechanical comprehension. Electricians and mechanics also completed a test measuring their fault- finding abilities.

Interests

It is not uncommon for employers to assume that certain interests and hobbies outside work are related to good performance on the job. A common assumption for offshore work is that if candidates play sports they are likely to be fit and healthy. Another factor is an individual's interest in the particular job offer. Vocational interest blanks and work style inventories can be used to assess individuals' preferences for different types of work in a systematic way. They are an efficient way of obtaining a comprehensive picture of an individual's attitudes towards various jobs. Though they tend to be poor predictors of job success, they are good predictors of job choice and tenure. If individuals are interested in their jobs, they tend to have greater job satisfaction and tenure.

In the mid-1970s the then United Kingdom Petroleum Industry Training Board (PITB) investigated the selection criteria that predicted success (namely job tenure) for roustabouts and roughnecks.[8] They were concerned about a high turnover rate for these positions; typically 50% of new employees left before completing three months of service. Their research was based on extensive interviews with those in position, and those who had left the industry (*stayers* and *quitters*). Of those who stayed in the industry "the majority emphasized the work itself, and related it in preference to any other factor, relegating money to third position."[8] As offshore work involves long hours and living at one's place of work, interest in one's job would be a distinct advantage. Hobbies are also often a source of valuable information about an individual's latent skills, abilities and preferences.

Disposition

Not everyone can adapt to the long hours, isolation, and harsh environment of offshore working life. It requires individuals with certain personal qualities to enjoy, though some might say endure, such working conditions. Two studies have examined the particular personal attributes of those who are successful offshore. In the earlier mentioned PITB study of roustabouts and roughnecks,[8] the authors identified teamwork ability, cooperation, and physical determination as key criteria in predicting job success (defined as tenure). Teamwork was rated the highest quality necessary for the job by those employed, followed by physical fitness. Assessment of these qualities consisted of a combination of structured interviews and practical, situational, leaderless group exercises.

A recent survey of selection methods in the United Kingdom offshore industry[9] found that companies emphasized maturity, reliability and the ability to work well in a team as key characteristics they sought in prospective candidates. Given the close physical proximity of work areas and living quarters, the latter is hardly surprising. A more detailed study of one particular offshore group, OIMs,[5] found that a number of personal qualities were sought by employers, particularly in relation to the ability to manage an offshore emergency. Specific personal qualities sought included :

- Ability to stay calm
- Leadership
- Decisive under pressure
- Ability to assess the overall situation
- Ability to communicate
- Self-confidence

Most companies tended to appoint from internal candidates for the OIM post, using appraisal reports, personal recommendations, and interviews to determine whether candidates possessed the desired qualities. At the time of the study, few organizations used more formal selection techniques such as psychometric tests or assessment centers, which is surprising given the highly responsible and safety-critical nature of the OIM's job.

Circumstances

Many companies require personnel to be flexible with respect to relocation and international travel for offshore operations. Personnel may also be required to work on short notice. Not everyone can adapt to offshore life: having to spend long periods away from home and family plus living and working in a remote and sometimes hostile marine environment. The main attractions to the job have been good pay and a work pattern with long periods of rest.[10] It is difficult to screen personnel for the possession of qualities which would suggest a propensity for adaptability to such an environment. A good indication of whether someone can adapt to the life is to choose those who have worked offshore before. Without prior experience, it is difficult to know how an individual will adjust. The Livy and Vant study[8] identified that of those who had left offshore work as roughnecks and roustabouts, the main reasons for leaving were shift work and difficulties with home life. Whether the individual candidate can cope with the offshore work cycle is not the only consideration. His or her family also needs to be able to adjust to the long absences. (see chapter 13 for a discussion of such issues.)

Measurement Tools

Once the relevant criteria are defined for the particular offshore position, there remains the task of determining the appropriate tools to measure such criteria. Traditionally, employers have used a combination of interviews, application forms and personal references, though modern selection procedures now usually include work samples, psychometric tests and may even combine a range of selection tools into an assessment center.[11] The advantages and limitations of each method are discussed in greater detail below.

Interviews

Regardless of job, probably the most prevalent selection tool is the interview. Despite the inherent biases and poor figures for predictive validity, employers continue to use interviews to screen prospective candidates. Numerous research studies have demonstrated the limited value of face-to-face interviews as they are subject to the various biases of the interviewers. One's perception of an individual is more complex than perceiving an object as there is more information to interpret and understand and one is actually interacting with the person being perceived. It is important for the interviewer to be aware of his or her own personality, values, attitudes, past experiences, current mood, expectations, and interviewing skills and the effects these may have on the candidate and ultimately the success of the interview. Other factors which can affect the interview are the physical location and the social context. While it is practically impossible to remove every source of potential bias, a well trained interviewer will be aware of his or her own prejudices and take steps to ensure they exert a minimal effect on the candidate and the outcome of the interview. Structured interviews tend to provide greater validity for predicting job success than unstructured interviews.[12]

References

The testimony of referees and personal associates is another traditional source of information about potential candidates, yet referees tend to reveal only a candidate's positive characteristics. Individual referee's opinions are also subject to similar biases as interviewers. Their views about an individual will, in part, be a reflection of their own personalities, attitudes, values and experiences of dealing with the candidate. Referees are not known for their objectivity, yet personal recommendations, often referred to as the *buddy* system can carry considerable weight when assessing a potential candidate. Selectors should consider the potential costs of selecting the wrong candidate and the difficulty of being able to justify to external authorities the importance one attached to a reference should the successful candidate subsequently be found unsuitable.

Biographical Inventories

Biodata refers to information on an individual's life-history, such as the amount and nature of education, job experiences, special skills, hobbies and recreational activities.[13] Application forms are examples of biographical inventories, though few forms have been systematically designed to determine whether the information obtained is directly related to key job criteria and job performance. This is the distinction between application forms and biographical inventories. Items on the latter have been selected and weighed against job criteria.

In the Livy and Vant study of roughnecks and roustabouts[8] they found that the following biographical details predicted both job satisfaction and job tenure:

- basic formal education
- previous employment in an outdoor job
- outdoor hobbies
- stable employment records
- average age of 26

The main problems posed by biographical inventories are that some bio-data items might predict job success, but have no rational relationship with the job.[14] Biodata also seems to have greater predictive validity when it is designed for clearly defined uses. It can be designed for use with a specific job within one company, but the same form would probably prove of limited value for a similar job in another organization. Its applicability tends to be limited not only to a particular job, but also to a particular organization.[14]

Job Sample Exercises

Job samples are examples of specific tasks involved in the job to be performed, though the circumstances under which the tasks are taken are carefully controlled to ensure the task remains the same for each candidate. A close fit between the job sample and job tasks which are carefully designed provide an ideal way to determine whether the candidate can perform the required work. The drawbacks to this method are that not all jobs can be broken down to specific tasks which represent the range of duties involved. However, some tasks are considered so crucial, that it is essential to ensure the successful candidate can perform them.

One such example is the ability of an OIM to deal effectively with an emergency, as he/she has sole responsibility (at least in the initial stages) for dealing with an incident. Since the *Piper Alpha* disaster, the United Kingdom offshore industry has devoted considerable resources to ensure OIMs (both prospective and in position) are *competent* to deal with an offshore emergency. In 1992, the Offshore Petroleum Industry Training Organization (OPITO) devised units of competence for OIMs,[15] one of which: "Controlling Emergencies" details the performance standards required to demonstrate competence in this area. Though the standards are not compulsory, many organizations use them to assess OIMs' competence. The standard includes a form of job sample in that managers must demonstrate their ability to handle at least three emergency scenarios chosen from the following:

- Well control incident
- Explosion and fire
- Accommodation fire
- Helicopter incident
- Collision or wave damage causing structural collapse
- Loss of stability

In addition, managers may be assessed in relation to endorsements specific to the installation's operations (such as production or drilling operations).

Assessment of competence is usually conducted in a simulated offshore emergency control room. While both employers and training regulators appreciate that performance in a simulator cannot accurately predict 100% how an individual will react in real life, this type of exercise enables employers to identify those who are unlikely to be able to cope in an emergency.

Assessment and training in this aspect of an offshore manager's job was considered of such vital importance, that a research report for the United Kingdom Health and Safety Executive (HSE) recommended:[5]

> *1. In terms of emergency command responsibilities, a satisfactory assessment of competence to take command in an offshore emergency is required in the selection criteria and this must be stipulated.*
>
> *18. Simulated emergency exercises are essential to the training and competence assessment of OIMs and other key personnel.*
>
> *20. The competence of an OIM to take command in an offshore emergency should be assessed prior to his appointment. This should be judged on the basis of his ability to manage three simulated emergencies of different types as outlined in the OPITO (1992) unit of competence for OIMs entitled "Controlling Emergencies.*

Not all offshore positions can be broken down into key tasks which can be presented to candidates. However, for some posts, particularly those with safety-critical responsibilities, job samples, as illustrated with the OIM post though applicable to drilling, diving and production operations, provide a useful method of determining a candidate's suitability.

Psychometric Tests

Psychometrics is the study of individual differences by using specific types of tests called *psychometric* tests. Psychometric tests have become increasingly popular to screen prospective job candidates. Their main advantage is the reliable and valid measurement of candidates' skills, abilities, and personal qualities compared with other selection techniques. Psychometric tests are not a recent introduction and their use is well documented for both civilian and military occupations.[16]

Psychometric tests have certain defining features such as reliability and validity which can discriminate between individuals with reference to group norms. A reliable test can produce similar scores for the same individual on two separate occasions. If a test gives different scores each time an individual takes the test, one can have little faith that either score is correct, unless the individual has significantly changed between test sessions (for example, has learned a new skill or new information relevant to the test questions).

Validity refers to a tests ability to measure what it claims to measure.

There are three types of validity commonly ascribed to tests. A test which looks valid (i.e. the questions seem to measure what the test says it measures), particularly to the individual being tested, is said to have *face validity*. *Predictive validity* refers to a test's ability to predict a relevant outcome. For example, if a group of engineering apprentices were given a test measuring mechanical aptitude, the apprentices could be followed up at the end of their apprenticeship to determine how successful they had been. If their test scores were positively related to success, the score would have predictive validity. Finally, the test items must be closely related to whatever is being tested. Termed *construct validity*, it refers to whether the test items capture the hypothetical quality or ability being measured. To illustrate, if a test purports to measure mechanical aptitude, one should ask what abilities characterize mechanical aptitude and whether the test measures these.

As part of a larger study for the HSE, a survey of oil and gas companies' selection methods[5] found a number of organizations in both the United Kingdom and Norway using psychometric tests (principally personality profiling) for selecting OIMs. The study also examined whether personality profiling was a useful predictor of an OIM's incident command ability.[17] The types of psychometric tests being used included the Predictive Index, Cattell's 16PF, the Wonderlic Personnel Test, the Occupational Personality Questionnaire (OPQ); and in Norway the GARUDA personality questionnaire and the DAPA (Data Assisted Personality Analysis).

In the United Kingdom, two further studies have examined the role of personality for success offshore. Henry Steenbergen correlated 42 offshore workers' scores on the Occupational Personality Questionnaire (OPQ) with ratings of their job performance.[18] A total of six OPQ dimensions were significantly correlated with performance ratings, though the two strongest predictors were high scores on the dimensions *Decisive* and *Optimistic*. The author concluded that "certain OPQ dimensions might function as valid predictor variables."[18]

The second study aimed to identify the personal qualities associated with close-knit diving teams.[19] Again, using the OPQ, the author found that the divers had higher scores than a norm group on the dimensions: *Affiliative, Democratic, Modest, Active* and *Change-oriented*, though with a small sample size (N=43) .

Finally, Karen Sutherland identified an ideal personality profile as part of a PhD project.[20] She asked 10 oil industry managers which qualities they felt were the most important for the ideal offshore worker, using the OPQ profile chart (Concept 5). Their mean scores were combined to produce the ideal profile for offshore work. The profile shows the ideal offshore worker to be very practical, rather than an intellectual and very tough-minded. The individual would not be prone to worry and would tend to remain calm under pressure. The person would be active, enjoy managing others, tend to plan ahead, and generally adopt a conscientious and methodical approach to work. This may represent an idiosyncratic view of the *ideal* offshore worker, but it highlights the potential value of using personality profiling to articulate what are often unspoken assumptions about the type of person sought for offshore work.

Case Study Smedvig[7]

Smedvig Ltd. has drilling and production interests in Europe employing about 1300. As part of an organization program change their United Kingdom operations base analyzed the abilities, personal qualities and skills required for a competent offshore workforce. The resulting competency profile included work ethic (displayed by effort, reliability, concentration, problem solving and loyalty), learning, ambition, confidence, the ability to think, plan and organize and team focus. Their recruitment and appraisal procedures were restructured to ensure their key competencies were reflected in current and future staff.

Their recruitment procedure now has three stages. First, a six-page application form is used to determine personal adjustment factors, abilities, work ethic, learning and ambition. Second, candidates complete a battery of psychometric tests to measure their mathematical and verbal reasoning skills and mechanical comprehension. Specific job categories also may undertake additional tests measuring abilities related to the position. Candidates also complete a work style inventory to determine their preferences for different types of work. Finally, a structured interview is designed for each job to determine an individual's team focus, self confidence, technical knowledge, safety-awareness, and personal adjustment. The interview schedule is designed such that each candidate is asked the same range of questions.

Recruitment practices are conducted by personnel department staff who have received training in these selection techniques, with line management participation in the structured interview. The company has also ensured that ethical standards have been set for candidate feedback on their results. The company now considers that these revised selection and recruitment procedures ensure they obtain competent staff.

Training and Development

Once the ideal candidate has been selected, offshore work requires specialist training to live and work on an installation. An area of increasing importance to employers is the requirement to ensure individuals are competent to carry out their work. Being competent is not simply a matter of training, experience and knowledge are also important. An employer needs to determine that a candidate has sufficient skills, experience, knowledge, and other qualities to carry out tasks. In order to do this, an employer needs to have a clear understanding of the tasks involved in the job (from job analysis), what competencies are required to deal with them (from selection criteria) and what action is necessary for workers to demonstrate the required level of competence (from assessment criteria). This includes safety critical competencies such as knowledge of their role and how to work within the permit to work system. Employers have a duty to ensure the health and safety of their employees. Adequate training and instruction is an important part of this responsibility, especially in a hazardous environment. Individuals require training to be both technically competent and to apply safe working practices. It is beyond the scope of this chapter to discuss the full range of training required for all offshore positions, therefore three examples: general offshore training, permit to work, and well control will serve to illustrate.

General Offshore Training

The offshore environment is a unique workplace, given its geographical isolation combined with hazardous operations and the close proximity of living quarters. To ensure the work force's safety, it is usual to provide not only an induction to the workplace (installation geography, location of their muster stations and explanations of platform emergency alarms), but also some form of training in emergency evacuation and survival, often completed prior to personnel going to an installation for the first time. The death of the radio operator on the *Ocean Odyssey*[21] emphasizes the potentially tragic consequences of failing to provide training in installation geography and escape routes.

In the United Kingdom, OPITO produces guidelines for the minimum safety induction and emergency training for new offshore workers.[22] This comprises a basic safety induction, helicopter safety and escape, sea survival, fire fighting and self rescue. Personnel with specialist duties during an emergency receive additional training pertinent to their role, e.g. lifeboat coxswain and members of the fire and emergency management teams. OPITO maintains a central training register containing accurate records of survival training certificates (following a recommendation from the inquiry into the *Piper Alpha* disaster)[23] to enable employers to ensure that prospective offshore workers possess valid certificates. The American Petroleum Institute has devised similar guidelines for offshore safety training.[10]

While the training media for undertaking survival training are now well established, the range of training content and length of course have recently been reviewed by OPITO.[22] The review was driven by a need to ensure that training met industry requirements following legislative changes as a result of the

Cullen Inquiry.[23] To what extent this will impact offshore safety is yet to be determined, though companies, certainly in the United Kingdom, are devoting increased attention to tangible training outputs. Performance appraisal was incorporated into the design of the revised OPITO guidelines.

Permit To Work

To prevent accidents offshore, it is vital that organizations lay down safe working practices. The operations carried out on a production platform or drilling rig involve hazardous chemicals and processes, which necessitate a system of authorizing any work on the installation, usually termed a permit-to-work system. In many countries a permit to work (PTW) system is a legal requirement, in the United Kingdom it comes under Section 2(1) of the Health and Safety at Work Act (1974).[24] It is a formal system used to control certain types of work identified as potentially hazardous, to ensure that full consideration is given to minimize the risks posed by a particular job. In addition, the Offshore Installations (Safety Case) Regulations (1992)[25] require that particular attention is given to the design of PTW systems to minimize the risk of working offshore, and to the arrangements for the instruction and training of all who use permits. This regulation particularly refers to the training and competence requirements for contractors' supervisors required to implement the PTW system and the documentary proof they should carry of having completed the relevant training.

> *When incidents do occur, human factors, such as failure to implement procedures properly, are often a root cause. These failures may in turn be attributable to a lack of training, instruction or understanding of either the purpose or practical application of the permit-to-work systems.*[26]

The importance of ensuring that staff carry out work according to the written permit to work procedures cannot be overstated.[23] In many countries legislation now requires that such training is not only provided, but also that evidence exists that it has been completed and to a specified standard (determined by the individual company).

Well Control

Due to the dangers of blowouts while drilling, workovers, and other drilling activities, some countries have established regulatory standards of competence for certain drilling personnel. In Europe, the European Well Control Forum (EWCF) has introduced training standards for the drilling industry. It is an industry-driven organization, therefore none of its recommendations carry statutory obligations. Its Well Control Certification Standards[27] specify that for well control training purposes, the trainee requires a fully structured and integrated training program, combining computer simulations, written tests and assessments by experienced trainers. The simulator should resemble, as far as is reasonably practical, the rig environment. Following successful examination, the EWCF certificate is valid for two years. In its members' manual the EWCF states that it views this certificate as the first move towards a single international well control certification standard. Certainly the certificate is accepted as the standard across Europe and many EWCF member companies have instructed their operating companies to accept the certificate worldwide. Regulations covering similar training in well-control and drilling operations apply in the U.S.[10]

Training Media

The way in which training is presented must facilitate the successful transmission, retention and comprehension of information. The offshore environment places a number of constraints on training opportunities. Due to their geographical location, it can be costly to transport a trainer to the installation, and the physical constraints offshore mean that there is often little space to create a training room. Workers are also understandably reluctant to sacrifice any of their leave time when they return onshore to attend training courses. In the 1980's the proposed solution was to provide on-the-job training as: "The trainees can continue to engage in productive work while they are learning, their motivation is likely to be high because they can see the significance of what they are learning."[29]

Increased regulation and company's preferences for competence-based training have resulted in a need for more formal and verifiable training which on-the-job training cannot fulfill. While it enhances training transferability to the workplace, on-the-job training is often delivered by staff who are not trained in how to train, it is difficult to standardize training content and to assess trainees to provide evidence of training completion to a specified standard. This has culminated in a search for alternative delivery mechanisms.

In 1995, Georgina Slaven et. al. evaluated the introduction of computer-based training for permit to work training within seven United Kingdom offshore operating companies and well control training with post-graduate students and two drilling companies.[30] Computer-based training systems are expected to positively enhance trainee learning because they are assumed to provide unique practice opportunities and contain certain instructional features to aid the retention of information.[31] These include self-paced instruction, immediate feedback, having a wide range of interactive practices and the computer's graphic display. Computers are also particularly suitable for training workers offshore, as they can be easily installed in a small space on the platform or drilling rig. Training content and delivery style are consistent and auditable, along with software advances which permit a controlled ingress and egress from the system and automated assessment to audit individual's training outcomes.

However, although studies have shown that computer-based training can enhance the immediate recall of information[32], CBT's impact on long-term retention had not been measured until the Slaven et. al. study.[30] For a permit-to-work training package, they found that almost every group sampled within each of the seven participating companies exhibited an immediate improvement in their knowledge of the PTW system. In addition, this improvement was largely maintained four weeks after training. The design also incorporated a classroom trained sample, who although they showed an immediate improvement in knowledge of the PTW system, did not maintain this improvement after four weeks following training delivery. The findings suggest that computer-based training may exert a greater, positive long-term effect on training outcomes than classroom-based training, though this would obviously need to be confirmed by further similar studies. Other benefits claimed for computer-based training include lower costs (due to reduced training time, no travel or accommodation costs for trainees, less time away from work), and particularly for global operations, consistency of training content, delivery and assessment of competence regardless of the installation's location. Computer-based training can also be made available in multiple language packages to tailor training delivery to the workers' native language.

Improving Selection and Training Procedures

Effective selection procedures for offshore work conform to a similar framework as that for any position, though as in any safety-critical industry, the requirement for ensuring only competent personnel are selected is paramount. Offshore disasters, such as *Piper Alpha* have emphasized the need to check the veracity of candidates' qualifications and training certificates, though it is all too easy to be wise after the event. It has always been good professional practice to ensure that personnel are qualified to make selection decisions, for example, by providing training in interviewing skills, to improve the quality, quantity and validity of the information obtained. The increasing use of psychometric tests requires further specialist training to ensure personnel are qualified to administer and interpret psychometric instruments. The importance of determining a candidate's competence and monitoring competence on the job brings additional training demands to ensure that assessors are qualified to assess competence, particularly for technically complex and demanding posts such as an OIM.

The acid test of any selection procedure is to determine its validity, either by monitoring the future progress of successful candidates, or by comparing successful candidates with existing exemplary performers. Such validity checks determine whether the selection procedure actually measures a candidate's qualities which are strongly related to on-the-job performance.

To obtain the most from an investment in training, one first has to identify the information to be learned, the most appropriate medium and who the trainees are. The basis of any training program is an identification of the training needs of the target population, industry guidelines and legislative requirements. Once the training content has been established, the most appropriate method of presenting the information can be chosen. The best delivery medium depends on the information to be learned and how this relates to work tasks. If the method of instruction is not appropriately matched to actual work tasks, training will be ineffective. The geographical isolation of many offshore platforms presents certain logistical difficulties to training provision. Information technology provides a novel solution to such difficulties and to the challenges of assessing trainee's competence following training completion and will no doubt become an increasingly prevalent training medium.

Further Reading
> Smith, M. & Robertson, I. T. (Eds.) *Advances in Selection and Assessment.* Chichester: John Wiley, 1989.

References
1. National Transportation Safety Board *Grounding of the US Tankship Exxon Valdez on Bligh Reef, Prince William Sound Near Valdez, Alaska 24 March 1989.* Marine Accident Report PB90-916405. Washington: NTSB, 1990.
2. Norwegian Official Report *The Scandinavian Star Disaster of 7 April 1990.* Oslo: Norwegian Government Printing Service, 1991.
3. Silver, M. *Competent to Manage.* London: Routledge, 1991.
4. Offshore Petroleum Training Organisation *The Offshore Installation Manager's Manual.* (3rd Ed.) Montrose: OPITO, 1991. (Update December 1991; July 1992; February 1993; December 1993 & September 1995.)
5. Flin, R. & Slaven, G. *The Selection and Training of Offshore Installation Managers for Crisis Management.* Report for the Offshore Safety Division, HSE. OTH 92 374. Sudbury: HSE Books, 1994.
6. Schmidt, F. L. & Hunter, J. E. Employment testing: Old theories and new research findings. *American Psychologist, 36,* 1981: 1128-1137.
7. Ramsay, J. *Creating the Right Culture for Flexible Team working.* In collected papers of the Empowering Flexible Work Team Offshore conference, Aberdeen, February. London: IIR, 1994.

8. Livy, B. & Vant, J. Formula for selecting roughnecks and roustabouts. *Personnel Management,* February, 1979: 22-25.

9. Whyte, F., Slaven, G. & Flin, R. The selection of staff for North Sea petroleum installations. P*etroleum Review,* February, 1995: 72-73.

10. ILO *Safety and Related Issues Pertaining to Work on Offshore Petroleum Installations.* TMOPI/1993. Geneva: International Labour Office, 1993.

11. Woodruffe, C. *Assessment Centres: Identifying and Developing Competence.* London: Institute of Personnel Management, 1990.

12. Weisner, W. H. & Cronshaw, S. F. A meta-analytic investigation of the impact of interview format and degree of structure on the validity of the employment interview. *Journal of Occupational Psychology, 61,* 1988: 275-290.

13. Hunter, J. E. & Hunter, R. F. Validity and utility of alternative predictors of job performance. *Psychological Bulletin, 96,* 1984: 72-98.

14. Stokes, G. S., Mumford, M. D. & Owens, W. A. *Biodata Handbook: Theory, Research and Use of Biographical Information in Selection and Performance Prediction.* Palo Alto, CA: CPP, 1994.

15. OPITO. *OPITO Units of Competence Governing the Management of Offshore Installations.* Montrose, Scotland: Offshore Petroleum Industry Training Organisation, 1992.

16. Furnham, A. *Personality at Work.* London: Routledge, 1992.

17. Flin, R. & Slaven, G. Personality and emergency command ability. *Disaster Prevention and Management, 5, 1,* 1996: 39-45.

18. Steenbergen, H. D. C. Determination of selection criteria and techniques for establishing the suitability of candidates for employment in the offshore environment of the North Sea oil industry. Unpublished MBA Dissertation, Strathclyde Business School, Scotland, 1989.

19. Blewett, P. R. The relationship between diving team effectiveness and individual differences. Unpublished MBA Dissertation, The Robert Gordon University, Aberdeen, Scotland, 1993.

20. Sutherland, K. Psychosocial factors: An investigation of the offshore oil industry. Unpublished PhD dissertation. The Robert Gordon University, Aberdeen, Scotland, 1994.

21. Ireland, Sheriff Principal. *Fatal Accident Inquiry into the Death of Timothy John Williams on Board Ocean Odyssey.* Aberdeen Sheriff Court, Scotland, 1991.

22. OPITO. *Basic Offshore Safety Induction & Emergency Training and Further Offshore Emergency Training.* Montrose, Scotland: Offshore Petroleum Industry Training Organisation, 1995.

23. Cullen, the Hon Lord. *The Public Inquiry into the Piper Alpha Disaster.* Vols. I & II. CM 1310. London: HMSO, 1990.

24. HSC. *Health and Safety at Work Act.* HMSO: London, 1974.

25. HSE. *A Guide to the Offshore Installations (Safety Case) Regulations (1992).* London: HMSO, 1992.

26. Offshore Industry Advisory Committee. *Guidance on Permit to Work Systems in the Petroleum Industry.* London: HMSO, 1991.

27. European Well Control Forum. *Well Control Certification Standards.* Montrose: EWCF, 1992.

28. European Well Control Forum. *Well Control Certification Standards - Members Manual.* Montrose: EWCF, 1993.

29. Hayes, J. & Vant, J. Better training in the workplace, *Training Officer,* October, 1984: 296-298.
30. Slaven, G., Boyle, J., Charnley, L., Hunt, A. & Murton, B. *The Application of Information Technology to Safety Training.* Report to the Offshore Safety Division of HSE. OTH 94439. Sudbury: HSE Books, 1996.
31. Schlecter, T. M. Computer-based instruction and the practical aspects of memory. *Applied Cognitive Psychology, 7,* 1993: 653-664.
32. Kulik, C.C. & Kulik, J.A. Effectiveness of computer-based training: an updated analysis. *Computers in Human Behaviour, 7,* 1991: 75-90.
33. Roger, A. *The Seven Point Plan.* Windsor: The National Institute of Industrial Psychology, 1974.

Chapter 3

Health and Medical Fitness
Susan Coleshaw, Rachel Harris and William Freeland

Introduction

Health can be defined as the physical and psychological capacity of the individual. Work can have both positive and detrimental effects on health, due to the conditions imposed by the work environment and performance effects influenced by work load. The offshore workplace is an extreme and hostile environment. The location generally is very remote (even inshore installations generally require the use of helicopters to transfer personnel to the mainland). It is the responsibility of the employer to make the working environment as safe as possible, reducing the risks to acceptable levels. However, some hazards cannot be avoided completely. Workers may be exposed to chemicals, high levels of noise, and the extremes of climate. Working hours tend to be long, while sleep patterns may be disturbed by shift work. In an emergency situation, the health and medical fitness of employees may have a profound influence on the outcome, where a quick response, or something as simple as the ability to swim may save lives.

In many parts of the world, employees will be required to meet a minimum level of medical fitness prior to working offshore. This requirement applies to both permanent staff and visitors (the high cost of evacuation is the same in both cases).

In the event that an employee falls ill, or is injured, then provision must be made to supply skilled primary care and first aid, followed by evacuation to onshore medical services as appropriate. In the event of a major accident offshore, with the worst case scenario being a mass evacuation of casualties, backup will be required from a range of emergency and rescue services. The psychological well-being of personnel while offshore and onshore must not be forgotten, having a major impact both on the health of the individual and on the group dynamics of the isolated community in which that individual operates.

This chapter will discuss issues such as the provision of medical services, the need for the assessment of medical fitness to work offshore, the benefits to be gained from health promotion programs and specific problems relating to the working environment. Special attention will be given to the medical implications of a major accident. Finally, consideration will be given to measures which can be taken by offshore managers to maintain and improve the health and well-being of their workforce.

Medical Support Services

The range of services required to maintain the health and medical fitness of the offshore population includes the provision of an occupational health service, whose role is primarily preventative, plus topside medical cover to facilitate the evacuation of ill and injured workers, stabilizing their medical status until they can be transferred to a hospital, or rehabilitated, as appropriate.

Occupational Health Services

The level of occupational health care provided for the offshore workforce may vary depending upon the location, size, and type of operation. Larger companies have full-time onshore medical staff, nursing staff, and occupational hygienists. A few even have specialists such as dentists and physiotherapists. The smaller companies tend to rely on nursing staff backed up by the part-time services of primary health care physicians. It is normal practice for each installation to have a *sick bay*, equipped with medical supplies and operated by a rig medic or nurse, who will gain specialist help and advice from the onshore medical support as appropriate.

The objective of an occupational health service is primarily preventative, thus covering activities such as,

- assessment of medical fitness to work
- promoting the continuing health of the employee
- protecting the employee from hazards and risks while at work.

The occupational health service also will be responsible for maintaining medical records to identify general health trends, problem areas, and take legal responsibility for actions such as the notification of accidents.

The Role of the Rig Medic/Nurse

The offshore medic plays a first aid and primary health care role, being the first point of contact for both ill and injured patients. This requires the ability to act independently and to assess the patient, making a decision as to whether external assistance is needed or not. Where support is deemed necessary, the medic must be able to accurately describe symptoms and signs to the onshore physician, and carry out medical procedures with remote supervision. The medic must be able to splint fractures, remove foreign bodies and dress open wounds. The medic may have to set up an infusion or administer oxygen.

In an emergency the medic may need to carry out cardiopulmonary resuscitation (CPR), and arrest bleeding, thereby maintaining the patient until back-up arrives. Medics are occasionally required to help with diving problems requiring further specialized knowledge.

Due to the wide range of essential skills and the responsibility carried, the offshore medic normally will be required to hold a nursing qualification as a minimum. In some circumstances, paramedics with advanced first aid training may be acceptable. A worldwide audit of rig medics and sickbay resources demonstrated a wide variation in the background training and medical knowledge of the medics.[1] The need for medical audits was demonstrated by a lack of standardization in the provision of medical equipment and supplies.

When not involved in nursing activities, the medic also has a role to monitor environmental and occupational hazards. Many now run health promotion programs to improve the well-being and fitness of offshore personnel. Other functions such as clerical work may be carried out as time allows.

Topside Medical Cover

Emergency cover for the offshore medic ideally is provided by a team of on-call physicians. At least one person in this team must be available at all times to go offshore in the event of an emergency, carrying emergency medical equipment and being prepared to escort the patient onshore. A "second on-call" is needed to cover the responsibilities of the first during the emergency call-out. A medical evacuation requires careful logistical planning, coordinating with the operating company, the helicopter operator, local hospitals, and in some cases others including the police. In urgent cases a dedicated helicopter flight may be deemed necessary. In very remote or underdeveloped regions the cost of providing such a service will be very high. Decision support systems have been developed in which sophisticated telecommunications networks are used to link the rig medic at the remote site with the company physician or hospital services.[2,3] Such assistance will help to prevent unnecessary evacuations.

In the event of a major disaster, a team of doctors and specialists may be needed, including surgeons and anesthetists. The medical team must be able to cooperate and coordinate their activities with other rescue organizations. In the worst case it may be necessary to set up a temporary mortuary.

Diving operations may require medical cover which is separate from the normal topside cover. Some of the specialist problems associated with diving are described later in this chapter. The diving medical team will require access to a decompression chamber.

Assessment of Medical Fitness to Work

The main purpose of an employment medical examination is to ensure that the employee is medically suited to offshore work. Certain specialist groups such as divers and catering staff are subject to additional medical requirements due to the nature of their work. These two groups are discussed in greater detail later. All offshore workers must be able to work at full capacity at all times. The cost of sickness and injury is high, such that anyone who is incapacitated for more than 24 hours is likely to be evacuated, to make space for a replacement. For this reason a medical history and examination are required periodically, to ensure that the employee is medically fit, that ill-health is prevented and avoided where possible, and to provide occupational health surveillance. Age is not a bar to fitness to work offshore, although it is advised that the frequency of medical examinations be increased for older age groups.

Conditions which may affect medical fitness to work offshore include,
- infectious diseases
- diseases of the digestive system (including dental problems)
- cardiovascular and circulatory problems (including pacemakers and poorly controlled high blood pressure)
- cerebro-vascular disorders (including strokes and dementia)
- diseases of the blood
- mental disorders (including psychoses, phobias, chronic anxiety states, depression, alcohol or drug abuse)
- diseases of the nervous system (including epilepsy)
- musculoskeletal or recurrent skin problems
- hormone and metabolic disorders (diabetes may be a problem, with insulin dependence considered to be an unacceptable risk)
- respiratory problems (including asthma)
- ear, nose, throat and eye disorders (chronic or debilitating).

As mentioned previously, the medical status of a visitor may be as important as that of the offshore employee if any medical conditions prevail which could be exacerbated by an offshore trip. Factors to be considered include the mode of travel, the environmental and climatic conditions, and the sheer number of stairways and sea walkways requiring a certain amount of physical stamina. While fear of flying may be low in regular workers due to self-selection, it may prove to be more of a problem to an employee only required to go offshore for occasional short visits.

Specialist Job Groups

Catering crew are regarded as a special group due to the role they play in preparing food. Care is needed to ensure that they do not suffer from any form of communicable disease. The carriage of infections carries a high risk, requiring laboratory screening of samples taken from catering staff at least annually. Further care must be taken in regions with known endemic or epidemic disease.

Crane operators require specialist examination of their vision and mobility. The nature of their job means that visual acuity, visual field, stereoscopic vision and color perception must all be good. Unrestricted mobility and full coordination are also necessary attributes for carrying out skilled maneuvers while working within a restricted space.

The diver carries out what is undoubtedly a physically and mentally demanding job, with all the potential risks posed by exposure to pressure, the gases breathed, and other dive related medical disorders. For insurance reasons if nothing else, divers in most countries are required to possess a medical certificate of fitness to dive. Many countries require a statutory examination of medical fitness carried out by an approved physician. Specific areas which a diving medical may cover include skin infections, the ability to clear the ears, adequate lung function, a high degree of dental fitness, initial chest and long bone radiographs, a neurological assessment, an electrocardiogram to assess cardiac function, an exercise tolerance test, and an assessment of body composition to exclude obesity. Regular medical histories and examinations are used to detect any long-term effects of diving.

Physical Fitness

Physical fitness is not normally assessed during an offshore medical examination, the diving medical being an exception. However, in some occupations, fitness certainly is desirable to meet the demands of the job. The fast rescue craft (FRC) crews are a good example. When called out in an emergency, these individuals must be able to demonstrate rapid decision making and cope with short bursts of physical activity such as the retrieval of a casualty over the side of the craft. Recently concern has been raised that medical examinations do not fully assess fitness for the specific demands made upon individuals such as FRC crew.[4] It is often the ability to undertake training which results in crew selection.

Training courses in offshore survival and fire fighting, conducted around the world, are acknowledged to be both physically and psychologically demanding. All age groups, whatever their level of fitness, participate. An investigation of stress during training[5] showed that anxiety levels tended to be lower in the older age group, perhaps due to their greater experience. However, the older age group found the water exercises, involving such actions as climbing into a life raft, to be more physically demanding than did their younger colleagues. In a real survival situation, physical fitness will be of significant benefit, particularly in situations where self-rescue is necessary.

Medical Status of Oil and Gas Workers

A number of investigations have been conducted to determine the incidence of illness and injury in populations of oil and gas workers, the majority in the offshore environment. Certain trends have been identified, although many of the problems encountered are not specific to the industry.

An extensive investigation of the health of offshore workers was carried out on an installation in the Statfjord field in Norway.[6] Approximately half of those questioned perceived that their own health was excellent. The most common reasons for visiting the sick bay were digestive symptoms, chest pains, and respiratory complaints. Consultations were also made regarding personal matters, for routine check-ups and following injury.

During a three-year seismic and drilling operation onshore in a remote region of northern Canada,[7] the major complaint presented to the medic was infection, followed by soft tissue injuries. Throughout this project there were a number of lost time accidents. Some patients were able to stay in camp and continue work after 24 hours. The majority of those evacuated had non-work related injuries or illnesses. Two medical emergencies are cited, one being unstable blood pressure with angina and chronic chest disease, the other presented as a blood disorder later diagnosed as malignant disease. Both patients were contractors who had not undergone pre-placement medicals, demonstrating the need for assessing medical fitness to work. The closest evacuation point was 350 km (217 miles) away, with the nearest specialist hospital 2,000 km (1,250 miles) further. The cost for such evacuations is obviously high.

Medical evacuations from a sample of installations in the United Kingdom sector of the North Sea have been studied over recent years, the aims being to identify trends in illness and injury and assess the effectiveness of their management.[8,9] During the period from 1987 to 1992, 3,979 medical evacuations were reported, the majority being from production or accommodation installations. Just over half of the evacuations were due to illness, with digestive and respiratory problems occurring most frequently.[9] The occurrence of dental problems has decreased since dental screening was introduced into the routine medical in 1992, as a result of this ongoing study. A higher incidence of illness was found on the first day of the tour, suggesting either that workers may be commencing a tour of duty while medically unfit, or that the stress of travel may provoke ill health.

The most common forms of injury were musculoskeletal problems, including upper limb fractures, sprains and strains.[9] Injuries tended to peak on the fourth and fifth days of a tour, but did not appear to be linked to any shift in the work schedule which would explain this consistent finding. Traumatic injuries encountered offshore are similar in nature to those found in the heavy engineering and construction industry onshore, the main difference being the remote site.[10] Cases of acute trauma thus require a high level of skill in the rig medic/nurse so as to stabilize the patient until a medical evacuation is effected.

All of the evacuations were made by helicopter, of which 10% required a dedicated flight due to their urgency. The cost of providing topside medical cover and dedicated medical evacuation flights is high. The overall message is that serious medical events should be avoided where possible. This study demonstrates how the investigation of health trends can be used to improve screening methods, decrease the number of lost work days, hopefully improve the health of the workforce and overall benefit both the employees and the operating company.

In developing countries, health problems are caused by poverty, malnutrition, a shortage of health workers, limited supplies of drugs, poor training, and illiteracy. Diarrhea and gastroenteritis constitute a major health problem, often associated with contaminated water supplies. It is recommended that suspect drinking water be tested at least once a month. Techniques have been developed so that this task can be performed by the rig medic on site.[11] Special medical problems may be experienced by offshore oil workers in tropical regions of the world. A study of accident and illness trends in Burma showed malaria to be the major cause of illness.[12] Immunity within the local workforce was found to be very specific to a given area and was lost when the worker moved to a new area only 30 km (19 miles) away. Preventative measures for the entire workforce therefore is advised in regions where malaria is endemic. C.E. Moore and D.R. Hudgins describe measures taken when faced with a malaria epidemic during operations in Chad.[13] A malaria consultant was brought in to help improve diagnosis, increase employee and contractor compliance with preventative regimes, and establish an environmentally safe program to control contamination and spread of the disease.

Mental Health

Life in a remote and isolated environment will always challenge the mental equilibrium of an individual. Working in the oil industry may have adverse effects on both mental health and well being due to the confined living and work space, the shift schedules, the continuous emphasis on safety in what is potentially a high risk environment, the lack of privacy, and peer group pressure. Poor physical working conditions, shift work and physical danger are all recognized to be factors leading to work stress.[14] Whereas acute mental disturbance will necessitate medical evacuation, less acute problems such as anxiety and depression may remain undetected and severely affect performance in the work place. These mental outlooks have implications for safety and productivity. The families of those involved also will be affected. A study of shift work and alertness in the United Kingdom oil industry has shown significantly higher levels of anxiety in offshore control room operators compared to a matched group working onshore, while both groups demonstrated low neuroticism scores.[15] However, no comparison was made with other onshore groups making it difficult to assess which group represents a normal population.[16] Offshore employees demonstrated sleep problems, dissatisfaction with the patterns of shift work and a perception that their workload was greater than it would be if onshore.

Job underload associated with boring and under-stimulating work has also been associated with ill health. This factor should be considered when looking at standby vessel crews who have to cope with long periods of relative inactivity while being prepared to act quickly and on very short notice when the need arises.

Travel to and from an offshore installation by helicopter can cause stress in some individuals as can the training in helicopter underwater escape carried out in many countries including Canada, U.S., United Kingdom, and Norway.[5,6] However, as with the other environmental stressors, the work force may be self-selecting, with some who find it difficult to cope choosing to seek employment onshore.

Involvement in or observation of an accident or disaster is likely to have long-term effects on the health and well-being of an individual. Post-traumatic stress disorder is a well-documented problem where victims may show symptoms such as anxiety, depression, uncertainty and insomnia many months after the event. Nine months after the *Alexander Keilland* oil rig disaster in Norway, poor mental health was reported in 24% of the rescuers, with those who experienced the most extreme stress reactions during the rescue work showing severe long-term symptoms of restlessness, uncertainty, apathy, and anxiety.[17] This group of rescuers benefited from systematic debriefing and sharing their reactions and feelings with others, demonstrating the beneficial role of counseling.

Drugs

Drugs and alcohol are generally forbidden offshore due to the safety implications inherent in their use. However, while abstinence is enforced offshore, it cannot be enforced during periods of leave and holiday. This situation may pose problems when the employee returns after an onshore trip involving heavy drinking, where the drying out process results in withdrawal symptoms. The rig medic may have a role in raising awareness of drug and alcohol problems. Depending upon whether or not the operator has a thorough misuse of substances policy in place (including information to employees, appropriate systems of screening, chain of custody, defined disciplinary, counseling and rehabilitation measures), the medic may play a part in managing cases of misuse.

The costs of not having a substance abuse screening program may be high. The following case report demonstrates the impact of alcohol abuse, and the responsibility of employers for screening, treatment, and follow-up. On March 24, 1989 the U.S. tankship *Exxon Valdez* ran aground on Bligh Reef, Prince William Sound, Alaska. The accident report stated, "The Safety Board concludes that the master of the Exxon Valdez was impaired by alcohol at the time the vessel grounded on Bligh Reef and that impairment of his judgment owing to alcohol consumption caused him to leave the bridge at a critical time."[18] The master apparently had a history of alcohol abuse for which he had received hospital treatment four years before the accident and had been recommended to receive outpatient treatment. The employer could provide no records to show that the recommended treatment had been followed or that they had provided guidance, advice, or support on dealing with alcohol abuse to either the master or his supervisor. The report concluded, "the Exxon management and the medical department were unprepared or unwilling to deal with an alcoholic master."[18] Their oversight undoubtedly contributed to the ensuing accident which resulted in the loss of cargo ($25 million), significant damage to the ship ($3.4 million), and catastrophic damage to the marine and shore environment caused by the spilled oil costing $1.5 billion to clean up. This dramatically illustrates the costs of failing to enforce an alcohol and drugs policy.

Health Promotion Programs

As mentioned previously, one objective of the occupational health service is to promote the continuing good health of the employee. Educational programs have been shown to play an important promotional role. This work in part falls to the rig medic who has daily contact with the employees while offshore.

A recent survey assessed the number and types of health promotion programs currently in operation on Norwegian and United Kingdom installations.[19] While health promotion was seen to be an important aspect of health and safety offshore by both the British rig medics (66%) and the Norwegian platform nurses (72%), health promotion programs were limited to one third (39%) of the installations manned by British rig medics in this sample. The relatively poor lifestyle offshore (caused by a general lack of exercise, overeating and easily accessible, duty free tobacco) and the aging population were cited as the major health issues facing the offshore workers. The most common type of program was *stop smoking*, closely followed by *healthy eating* (United Kingdom) and *fitness/exercise* (Norway).

Other health promotion programs currently in operation in the United Kingdom and Norwegian sectors include weight loss, general lifestyle, low cholesterol/blood pressure, a *well man* clinic, looking after the heart, alcohol, drugs, dental health, awareness of chemicals, ergonomics and backache, cancer of the colon, HIV and AIDS information, and skin and hygiene. The rig medics felt that such programs would have more impact if they themselves were better trained to provide the advice on such topics as exercise, fitness and diet.[19]

The need for weight reduction and fitness programs is brought about by two problems, a lack of exercise and a ready and plentiful supply of food around the clock. While some workers have physically demanding jobs resulting in a considerable expenditure of energy, others will be relatively sedentary, where the most exercise they gain is to climb the large number of stairways and negotiate narrow gangways. Obesity may be a health problem for the oil and gas worker in an emergency situation, where speed and the ability to escape through a narrow opening may be lifesaving factors. The overweight worker may hinder others as well as reducing personal chances of escape. High food intake and little exercise are both risk factors associated with heart disease. A further lifestyle risk factor is smoking, exacerbated by the fact that there are few relaxation activities, and a duty free supply of tobacco while offshore. All these factors must be considered a high priority when we consider that the United Kingdom offshore workforce is aging.

Special Problems

A number of health problems are specifically related to the offshore environment and therefore require special attention.

Gas

Inadvertent exposure to one of several noxious gases may occur during the process of exploring and drilling for oil and gas. Hydrogen sulfide (sometimes known as *sour gas*) found in some natural gas reserves, is acutely toxic. It may cause sudden asphyxia with collapse, followed by coma and a rapidly fatal outcome.[10] The characteristic smell of hydrogen sulfide (bad eggs) can be smelled at low concentrations, when it causes eye irritation, blurring of vision, and photophobia. Continuous monitoring for this gas is necessary, with an automatic warning system which will activate when levels start to rise. Where high risks of exposure are known "all the workers on a rig may need to wear respirators and they must be medically fit to do so."[10] Hydrogen sulfide may be formed in stagnant water, such as that found in the legs of offshore installations, due to the action of sulfate reducing bacteria. This risk should be recognized and suitable care taken when entering such areas.

Methane, the principal component of natural gas, is not toxic, but it may cause problems if the concentration reaches such a high level that it reduces the concentration of inspired oxygen below an acceptable level. Methanol, used in gas production, is only toxic if ingested. It is unlikely to be a risk to workers as it cannot be inhaled in sufficiently high levels to be hazardous and it is not absorbed through the skin in normal usage.[10]

Protection should be provided for those exposed to dust, whether from activities such as sandblasting or the compounding of drilling mud from its dry constituents.

Adequate ventilation and respiratory protection is required for workers involved in welding to protect them from the fumes of the process. Foreign bodies in the eye are common from spattering molten metal where eye protection is not being used.

Noise

A high level of noise is a continual problem on an offshore installation. Excessive levels of noise may and do cause permanent hearing loss. In the workplace, it may seriously impair communication, leading to errors and accidents. In accommodation areas, if the individual cannot get away from the noise, it may prevent sleep leading to stress and fatigue. As the rig is worked for 24 hours per day there is no respite in the noise levels. Accommodation areas may also need to be protected from vibration caused by heavy plant and machinery.

Consideration should be given to limiting and controlling noise levels wherever possible. A noise control program should place initial emphasis on engineering controls, identifying hazard areas and including the substitution or modification of equipment and plant where necessary. Regular noise surveys are an essential component of the program. Regular hearing assessments will determine potential problems. Care can then be taken to ensure the safe deployment of employees. Hearing protective equipment should be used as a last resort (as failure will result in immediate exposure).

Heat and Cold

Extremes of temperature are a problem in any working environment. High air temperatures may reduce performance when an individual is carrying out hard physical labor. Problems are also found when personal protective clothing must be worn, particularly if the clothing is not or cannot be (chemical protection) breathable.

Cold is a more obvious problem for offshore installations, although adequate protection can be provided under most circumstances. Under arctic conditions, the extremities (hands, feet, face) are the most susceptible to freezing injuries.

Immersion in cold water is a much greater potential threat in areas where sea temperatures are low. An initial *cold shock* response causes gasping and an inability to control breathing, often resulting in drowning. Hypothermia, a fall in the core temperature of the body to below 35°C, can develop after a period of immersion of only 20 to 30 minutes under severe circumstances. As body temperature falls, consciousness gradually is lost. Injury, an inability to swim, and panic will all reduce the chances of survival. Survival time will be increased by the insulation provided by body fat and by the level of clothing worn.

The 50% survival time (based on experimental data and case histories of shipwreck and aircraft survivors) for adult males wearing conventional clothing, immersed in water at 5°C is approximately 1 hour, while at 0°C it is approximately 30 minutes.[20] These times may be doubled by the use of an uninsulated suit such as those used for helicopter transfer, while insulated abandonment suits will provide in excess of 6 hours protection from the cold.[21]

When immersion suits are used it is important that they are correctly donned, and sealed where appropriate. As before, the extremities are least protected. Cold impairs manual dexterity which may hamper or even prevent self-rescue attempts if the victim is unable to grip ropes or other objects. While drowning is the greatest hazard of accidental immersion, the development of hypothermia always should be suspected and investigated in cases where the patient was immersed for some time. Hypothermia victims may appear dead (due to an undetectable pulse, very shallow breathing and loss of reflexes) when they are, in fact, still alive and capable of being revived. Therefore it is necessary to rewarm any victim who is known to have been immersed for some time. In some countries it is mandatory to provide an immersion bath on off-shore installations for the rewarming of hypothermia patients.[10]

Drowning

There are three main scenarios which may lead to accidental immersion offshore: a helicopter ditching, a major emergency requiring some individuals to escape into the water, and a man overboard incident. In the case of a man overboard or jump into water, the victim may suffer impact injuries after falling from heights of up to 50m (165 feet). In most waters, cold shock will be a prob-lem during the first few minutes of immersion. A lifejacket, if worn, will turn the unconscious or injured victim into a stable, face-up position and hold the mouth above water, helping to prevent water being swallowed. High and break-ing waves pose the greatest hazard due to water washing over the face and being swallowed. The mouth can be protected by the use of a splash guard fit-ted to the lifejacket. High seas will also impair the location and rescue process. For this reason, standby vessels with fast rescue craft always should be at close hand when any over-the-side work is being carried out. In a helicopter ditch-ing, victims may be required to egress from a capsized cabin. The effects of cold shock impair the ability to breath-hold, allowing very little time for escape. The victim may be injured, panicking, and disorientated. If safe egress is made, passengers and crew normally will be wearing a manually inflated lifejacket, thus aiding survival. However, the ditching may well occur in a remote loca-tion, such that it may be some hours before the rescue services reach the scene. During this time, exposure of the open mouth to wave splash for just a few sec-onds may result in drowning.

Drowning is caused by suffocation, when water entering the windpipe causes spasm. This stops both water and air from entering the lungs, thus pre-venting oxygen uptake. Individuals who have survived a period of submersion are described as being victims of *near drowning* or *partial drowning*. The period of oxygen lack may or may not lead to injury of the central nervous system. Approximately one third of near drowning cases are fatal.

Survival from near drowning is more likely if water has not entered the lungs. When water does enter the lungs, complications can occur up to four days later due to a condition known as *secondary drowning*. Contaminants such as bacteria, vomit, mud, and sand cause irritation and damage to the lung lining, resulting in breathing difficulties. All near drowning patients should therefore be monitored for some days before being pronounced fit.

Diving

Diving medicine is a complex subject covering problems which include decompression sickness (*the bends*), caused by bubble formation in the bloodstream and the various forms of barotrauma, including lung damage due to a rapid decrease in pressure.[22]

More general problems are caused by long periods of water immersion or high humidity in a dive chamber, leading to an increased chance of skin and ear infections. Divers must be able to clear their ears following a pressure change, while good hearing is also essential. Any respiratory condition is undesirable and may be hazardous during a diving operation.

Divers face high physiological demands, with diving which is surface orientated and surface supplied being as equally challenging as saturation diving. A high standard of mental as well as physical fitness is required for diving, with individuals relying heavily on their *buddy* diver. In saturation diving, the living space is cramped with little privacy and no escape route. Attention to the mental well-being of divers is therefore especially important.

The Offshore Emergency—Medical Implications

The management of an offshore emergency will depend upon the severity and size of the problem (see chapter 8). In the event of a cautionary evacuation, the main medical requirement will be to maintain control so as to minimize the level of stress and anxiety experienced and ensure that the less fit and healthy are able to cope.

When a major incident results in casualties, triage procedures are required to differentiate minor injuries requiring no treatment, those where first aid will be of benefit, and serious cases where immediate evacuation is necessary. In cases where the installation is itself unsafe, priorities may be changed to ensure the safety of those with a chance of survival.

The primary evacuation route is likely to be by helicopter. This will depend on the time taken for helicopter support to be scrambled and reach the emergency site, weather conditions which may prevent flying, and the state of the installation as a major fire hazard could prevent landing.

The secondary evacuation route from an offshore installation is by lifeboat, either davit-launched or freefall. Totally enclosed lifeboats provide cramped accommodation and generally are not designed to carry stretcher cases. Motion sickness is an immediate problem, that while not likely to be life-threatening, can cause great discomfort and lead to dehydration.[23,24] The sight of others being sick is a significant trigger, as are diesel fumes, vibration, heat and an upright posture.[25] Most of the drugs used to treat nausea and vomiting are given prior to exposure to prevent the development of symptoms. Usually this is not possible in an offshore emergency. Drugs are required with a rapid onset of action, which will be effective prior to the onset of vomiting.[26] Various options are available which include self-administered injections (difficult in a cramped and dirty lifeboat), tablet medications which may be vomited up and transdermal patches which act too slowly to prevent early sickness, but which last for more than 24 hours. Extremes of heat and cold may pose further problems to occupants of a lifeboat, depending upon the environmental conditions, level of clothing, and their medical status.

Escape into the sea should be considered only as a last resort due to the previously discussed problems of cold shock, drowning, and hypothermia. It may take some hours for victims to be located, particularly in the dark, while recovery may not be immediate if severe wind and wave conditions are prevalent. Survival may depend on the performance of lifejackets and immersion suits (if worn), on the ability to swim, and the will to survive. Injured victims will be potentially disadvantaged due to their inability to swim towards the help of a lifeboat or another survivor, difficulty maintaining stability in large breaking waves and possibly impaired metabolic shivering mechanisms. Panic is likely to result in useless physical activity, which may only serve to fatigue the victim more quickly. Following successful rescue, all victims should be assessed for the possible effects of drowning and hypothermia.

The Management of Health Offshore

The maintenance of a healthy workforce is thus dependent upon a range of measures encompassing all aspects of work and living offshore. These include,

- medical risk analysis to identify all health risks, occupational hazards associated with the offshore operation and the availability of treatment resources
- medical screening of all offshore personnel, including visitors
- health trend monitoring to identify and minimize special problems and ensure the continuing health and well-being of the offshore workforce

- provision of health promotion programs to educate and increase the awareness of employees on topics which may include smoking, diet, and physical fitness
- provision of personal protective equipment for the head, eyes, hands, feet and body (types of clothing used for body protection include chemical suits, flame and heat resistant suits, thermally insulated suits, high visibility clothing, and personal buoyancy equipment)
- implementation of audits and management review of the health care system.

If illness and injury can be prevented, then the number of lost days will be reduced and the number of medical evacuations limited. Measures can thus be taken which will reduce health insurance and decrease the chances of litigation. The desired overall outcome is that preventative medical and health promotion programs will improve the physical and mental capacity of the workforce.

Further Reading:

Cox, R.A.F. *Offshore Medicine - Medical Care of Employees in the Offshore Oil Industry.* New York: Springer Verlag, 1982.

Norman, J.N. & Brebner, J. *The Offshore Health Handbook - A Practical Guide To Coping with Injury and Illness.* London: Martin Dunitz, 1985

Bennett, P.B. & Elliot, D.H. *The Physiology and Medicine of Diving.* (4 Ed) Philadelphia: Saunders, 1993.

References

1. Barbey, A., Bobillier, A. & Pelat, F. *Worldwide training of rig medics.* Paper in Proceedings of the Second International Conference on Health, Safety & Environment in Oil and Gas Exploration and Production; Jakarta, Indonesia: Society of Petroleum Engineers SPE 27192, 1994.

2. Armstrong, I. & Haston, W. *Decision support for remote medical practitioners.* Paper in Proceedings of the World Congress on Telemedicine, for the Development of the Global Information Society for Health; Toulouse, France, 1995.

3. Norman, J.N. & Brebner, J.A. *A system of remote medicine.* Paper in Proceedings of the Second International Conference on Health, Safety & Environment in Oil and Gas Exploration and Production; Jakarta, Indonesia: Society of Petroleum Engineers SPE 27200, 1994.

4. David, G.C. & Fernandes, A.F. *Physical Selection for Rescue Craft Crew.* OTH 93 408. Suffolk: HSE Books, 1995.

5. Harris, R.A., Coleshaw, S.R.K. & MacKenzie, I.G *Analysing Stress in Offshore Survival Course Trainees.* OTH 94 446. Suffolk: HSE Books, 1996.

6. Hellesøy, O.H. (Ed.) *Work Environment, Statfjord Field - Work environment, health and safety on a North Sea oil platform*. Bergen: Universitetsforlaget AS, 1985.

7. McDougall, J.D. *Evaluation of a health care program for a remote oil and gas exploration project*. Paper in Proceedings of the First International Conference on Health, Safety & Environment in Oil and Gas Exploration and Production; The Hague, The Netherlands: Society of Petroleum Engineers SPE 23190, 1991.

8. Norman, J.N., Ballantine, B.N., Brebner, J.A., Brown, B., Gauld, S.J., Mawdsley, J., Roythorne, C., Valentine, M.J. & Wilcock, S.E. Medical evacuations from offshore structures. *British Journal of Industrial Medicine*, 45, 1988: 619-623.

9. Horsley, H.D. *Study of Medical Evacuations from Offshore Installations - Five Year Report 1987 - 92*. Offshore Technology Report. Suffolk: HSE Books, (in press).

10. Cox, R.A.F. *Offshore Medicine - Medical care of employees in the offshore oil industry*. New York: Springer Verlag, 1982.

11. Barbey, A. & Bobillier, A. *Proposed method for testing drinking water on rigs and remote seismic camps*. Paper in Proceedings of the Second International Conference on Health, Safety & Environment in Oil and Gas Exploration and Production; Jakarta, Indonesia: Society of Petroleum Engineers SPE 27205, 1994.

12. Dawson, D.G., O'Donnell, B. & Hursey, M. *Accident and illness trends over a 15-month seismic survey period in Myanmar (Burma)*. Paper in Proceedings of the Second International Conference on Health, Safety & Environment in Oil and Gas Exploration and Production; Jakarta, Indonesia: Society of Petroleum Engineers SPE 27203, 1994.

13. Moore, C.E. & Hudgins, D.R. *Exploration site medical problems in a remote African country*. Paper in Proceedings of the First International Conference on Health, Safety & Environment in Oil and Gas Exploration and Production; The Hague, The Netherlands: Society of Petroleum Engineers SPE 23188, 1991.

14. Cooper, C.L. The stress of work: an overview. *Aviation Space and Environmental Medicine*. 56, 1985: 627-632.

15. Parkes, K.R. *Human Factors, Shift Work, and Alertness in the Offshore Oil Industry*. OTH 92 389. London: HMSO, 1993.

16. Flin, R.H. & Sutherland, K.M. *Occupational stress and health in the UK offshore oil industry*. Paper in Proceedings of the 9th European Health Psychology Conference, Bergen, Norway, 1995.

17. Ersland, S., Weisæth, L. & Sund, A. The stress upon rescuers involved in an oil rig disaster. "Alexander L. Keilland" 1980. *Acta Psychiatrica Scandinavica*. Suppl.355; 80, 1989: 38-49.

18. National Transportation Safety Board. *Grounding of the US Tankship Exxon Valdez on Bligh Reef, Prince William Sound, Near Valdez, Alaska, March 24, 1989*. Marine Accident Report PB90-916405. Washington: NTSB, 1990.

19. Mearns, K.J. & Fenn, C.E. *Diet, Health and the Offshore Worker - A Pilot Study*. OTH 93 399. Suffolk: HSE Books, 1994.

20. Golden, F.St.C. Hypothermia: a problem for North Sea industries. *Journal of the Society of Occupational Medicine*. 26, 1976: 85-88.

21. Allan, R. Survival after helicopter ditching: a technical guide for policy-makers. *International Journal of Aviation Safety*. 1, 1983: 291-296.

22. Bennett, P.B. & Elliot, D.H. *The Physiology and Medicine of Diving.* (4 Ed) Philadelphia: Saunders, 1993.

23. Landolt, J.P., Light, I.M., Greenen, M.G. & Monoco, C. Seasickness in totally enclosed motor propelled survival craft (TEMPSC): five offshore oil rig disasters. *Aviation Space and Environmental Medicine.* 63, 1992: 138-144.

24. Landolt, J.P. & Monaco, C. *Seasickness in occupants of totally-enclosed motor-propelled survival craft (TEMPSC).* Report 89-RR-14. Downsview, Ontario: Defence and Civil Institute of Environmental Medicine, 1989.

25. Light, I.M. & Coleshaw, S.R.K. *Survivability of occupants of totally enclosed motor propelled survival craft.* OTH 92 376. London: HMSO, 1993.

26. Coleshaw, S.R.K. *Review: Medications for the treatment of motion sickness during evacuation, escape and rescue offshore.* OTH 94 462. Suffolk: HSE Books, (in press).

Managers and Supervisors on Offshore Installations
Rhona Flin, Georgina Slaven and David Carnegie

Introduction

The roles of the managers and supervisors on offshore installations are considered in this chapter, with particular reference to exploration and production in Northern Europe. Most of the issues relating to the management and supervision of an offshore workforce are international and will apply to rigs, platforms, and support vessels around the world. Obviously, differences in the size, function and location will determine the level of managerial expertise required and cultural differences present in work ethic, attitudes and business practice will influence the optimal style of management. The following discussion does not deal with the technical and financial responsibilities of managing offshore installations, although it is acknowledged that these are a significant part of the job. Rather it is concerned with the unique features of the offshore environment and their impact on the management of the offshore workforce.

The first section of the chapter looks at the role of the installation manager and the unusual combination of environmental and operational features of offshore operations which create particular managerial challenges, such as multiple roles, work patterns, and emergency management. The second part of the chapter reviews the position of the first line supervisors, how their role has evolved into a critical part of the management structure, and what characterizes the most effective supervisors. In contrast to the extensive research by business schools worldwide into the performance of onshore managers, there appears to have been virtually no research into the offshore management positions. The extant research from the few European studies which have been undertaken regarding managers and supervisors of offshore installations will be outlined below.

The Offshore Installation Manager

On the waters of the United Kingdom Continental Shelf (UKCS), the most senior manager of a petroleum installation (production platform, drilling rig, or support unit, e.g. flotel) is termed the Offshore Installation Manager (OIM), responsible for the operation of the installation as well as the health, safety and welfare of the personnel on board. The acronym OIM will be used throughout to refer to the senior manager on an installation, although other titles may be more common in other countries. (The pronoun he will be used as there have never been any female OIMs in the United Kingdom, although there have been several in Norway.)

The OIM's job is an amalgam of a plant manager and a ship's captain. He is responsible for production and/or drilling targets, the well-being of the crew, the maintenance of order, and discipline; in an emergency he acts as the incident commander. An OIM is essentially in the role of overseer. He must remain aware of all installation activities and ultimately must ensure that production, drilling and marine operations run safely and efficiently. His level of financial and strategic control will vary across companies depending on their management philosophy and the size and function of the installation he is managing.

In the United Kingdom recent emphasis on operating cost reductions has increased the level of budgetary responsibility and accountability placed on the offshore management team. One OIM told us that he was a production manager, a hotel manager, an industrial relations manager, a safety manager, a personnel manager, a heliport manager, a harbor master, and everybody's mother. There is no doubt that the job can require a broad range of managerial expertise as illustrated by the following fictitious job description, penned by an experienced OIM:

> *Young graduate required for managerial position with a willingness to travel and demonstrating complete computer literacy, applicants must have experience in all aspects of personnel administration and possess excellent all round communication skills. Some first hand counseling in marriage guidance skills would be advantageous. . . . Almost certainly a qualified Process or Production engineer, the aspirant will also be expected to have detailed knowledge of meteorological forecasting, while a background in logistics planning is also required. Although not considered essential, membership of a body of chartered accountants is preferred to ensure the successful production and execution of accurate budgets for the multi-million pound assets under his/her control. . . .This position carries with it the unique opportunity, under certain conditions, for the incumbent to take life and death decisions. Therefore a certain degree of interest in people and their welfare may be an advantage.[1]*

In an increasingly competitive oil market, the OIM has an influential role as a catalyst and change manager. In the words of Dick Parker, Shell Expro's Production Director,

> *With regard to leadership, the OIM must establish direction— developing a vision of the future, and strategies for producing the changes needed to achieve that vision. The OIM must communicate direction by words and deeds to all those whose cooperation may be needed, so as to influence the creation of teams and coalitions that understand the vision and strategies, and accept their validity. The OIM must motivate and inspire— energizing people to overcome political, bureaucratic and resource barriers-to-change by satisfying human needs. The OIM can produce change, often to a dramatic degree, and has the potential to produce extremely useful change (e.g. new approaches to labor relations, helping make a company more competitive.)[2]*

The OIM has a significant influence on the production, safety, well-being and mood of the installation and its crew. Recent empirical studies of offshore safety culture and risk perception in British and Norwegian offshore workers have highlighted the impact of organizational and managerial factors in the safety management of offshore installations.[3-6] Not all managers have the combination of knowledge, management skill, and leadership ability to perform successfully in this position and OIMs have to be selected, trained, and assessed with great care to ensure that the individual has the capacity to meet the rigorous demands of this unusual management position. However, the OIM does not work alone. He is supported by a team of departmental supervisors as shown in a typical production platform organogram (see figure 4-1), thus his job is to oversee and orchestrate the activities which actually are directed and managed by the superintendents and supervisors.

Unique Aspects of Offshore Management

The first study of OIMs was carried out in 1991, when Flin and Slaven sent out a questionnaire to 337 OIMs on United Kingdom installations which asked for information on their careers, principal roles, and responsibilities.[7,8] A total of 134 OIMs replied giving detailed answers, with many writing additional comments explaining the nature of their job in more depth. A more specific study was subsequently commissioned by the Offshore Safety Division of the United Kingdom Health and Safety Executive, to examine the selection and training of OIMs, with particular reference to crisis management.[9]

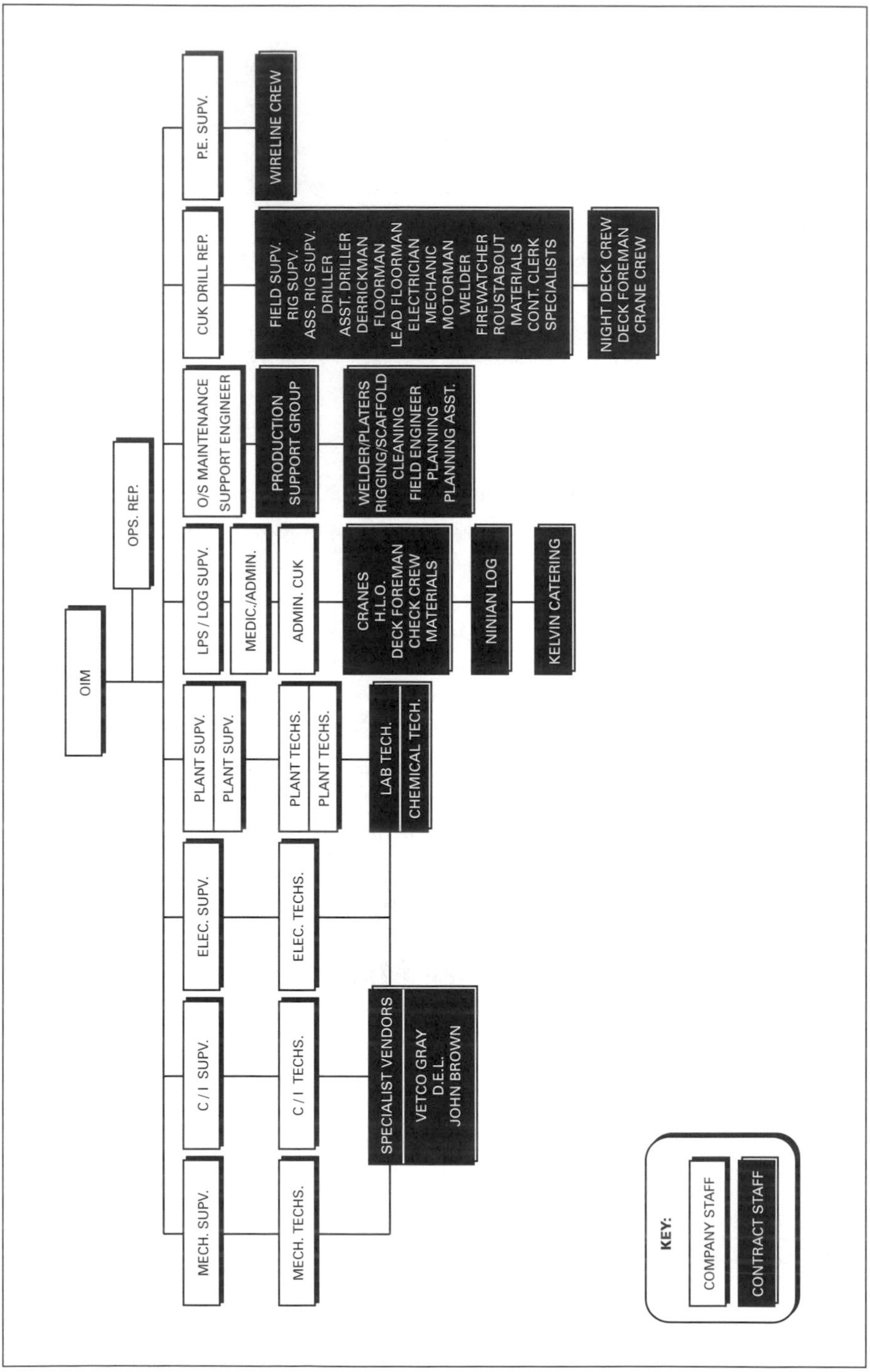

Figure 4-1 Organization chart for Chevron's Ninian Central platform *(Reprinted with permission of Chevron North Sea Ltd.)*

In Norway there has also been interest in the unusual aspects of offshore management. Reidar Mykletun examined the effect of OIMs' rotating work patterns for platform safety and efficiency, by studying four managers with different leadership styles who were sharing the same position on a Norwegian platform.[10] Drawing on these research findings, the next section considers the special features of the offshore environment which have implications for managers and supervisors.

Geographical Isolation

Offshore installations may be located from a few miles to over a hundred miles from shore. This means that OIMs are effectively physically isolated from their onshore line management and support services, resulting in considerable responsibility, not only for the multi-million dollar installation under their control, but for the lives of everyone on board. The geographical isolation also provides a degree of freedom from onshore line management interference, providing a high level of autonomy with respect to day-to-day operational matters. It is not a job to suit everyone, yet these conditions have a special appeal for some managers. In Flin and Slaven's survey of United Kingdom OIMs, 25% of respondents mentioned the levels of autonomy and responsibility as their main source of job satisfaction.[7]

Work Patterns

Like most managerial posts, OIMs have to work long hours. In common with other marine occupations and remote mining operations, this work schedule may be maintained for up to 28 days without a rest day, due to the work patterns dictated by their remote location. Flin and Slaven's first survey of United Kingdom OIMs found that rather than working a 12- hour day (the usual shift length offshore), many OIMs worked 14 to 16 hours a day which could often stretch to even longer hours (e.g. for rig moves or in severe weather).[7,8] Norwegian job descriptions specify this demanding aspect of the OIM's job:

> *The position requires full concentration on work without periods of sleep, in total 24 hours state-of-readiness. Daily rhythms and work routines must be adapted to the work. The level of stress is affected by disturbances in operation and other factors (weather, sea, accidents, etc.).*[9]

The long hours can take their toll on an individual's stamina. As one offshore worker reported, "Long disjointed working hours can cause havoc with sleeping patterns. Most people are physically worn out at the end of a 14-day trip".[11]

Offshore work patterns (discussed in chapter 6) mean that two or three individuals will act as the manager for a given installation, although only one of them will be offshore at a time. These managers may differ in their work experience, competence and managerial style which can impact organizational effectiveness. Having more than one manager for an installation has implications for the continuity of work across the rotations. Mykletun in his study of four Norwegian OIMs identified some potential problems relating to having four incumbents in the same management position, such as the crew exploiting differences in the managers' attitudes, but he also found positive aspects, such as the opportunity for the managers to learn from each other and to apply corrective action if one manager was a poor performer.[10]

The four managers he studied were perceived by the rest of the crew as quite different in their leadership and communication styles when dealing with daily platform activities. Such differences could cause problems for developing good working relationships between the managers, but they were aware of the importance of being on good personal terms with each other. Each offshore trip necessitated a changeover from the previous manager to obtain an update on what had happened in his absence. These transfers briefings which took at least three hours are critical to ensure the continuity of work offshore and Mykletun found that each manager had a different approach to changeovers. For example, one manager was unconcerned about activities conducted while he was away as he fully approved of what his back-to-back had done. Another Norwegian company, Statoil, has tried to address this problem of continuity between OIMs by providing leadership training. Their main objective is to develop

> . . . a common uniform leadership throughout the group where a common culture is very important. A common culture is the basis for how to judge on the same information and make correct decisions according to corporate strategies. Further, a common culture is the basis for being able to communicate and respond effectively.[12]

One potential problem these managers faced was the fact that their crews also rotated jobs, and offshore managers rarely worked on the same schedule as their crews. Mykletun found that this negatively affected communication processes and impeded overall crew cooperation. In effect, managers were rarely able to get to know their crew and vice versa, thus personnel were constantly trying to create work teams when staff rotated. He proposed that this might actually have positive consequences, in that the constant social adjustment might create a stimulating work environment and relieve the monotony at work. His recommendations included the need to provide team building training for offshore staff so that "it is possible to know how the fellow worker or leader will think and act in different situations."[10] Total Oil Marine also has found that team building training produced considerable benefits for their small crew on the recently completed Dunbar platform.

> *A high level of trust, commitment and enthusiasm was generated within the team and with onshore personnel. . . . Our experience has been that: all personnel have a positive open attitude to offshore colleagues and onshore personnel; barriers with management are reduced; there is an integrated approach to problem solving; there is evident pride and ownership of the installation operation.[13]*

Like any manager, OIMs rarely find the time to complete all their work tasks while offshore. As their work is shared across at least one other manager, one might expect them to forget about work while at home on leave. Mykletun found that some of the managers in his study took paperwork home with them, while others left unfinished work for the next manager to complete.[10] He found that the type of work most likely to remain unfinished at the end of a trip concerned staff issues, including social, welfare and medical problems. OIMs in the United Kingdom reported that the major hassles they encountered were dealing with onshore management and paperwork, and almost half of those sampled in an early survey reported that their job was considerably or extremely stressful.[8] This echoes concern previously expressed by Michael Gann et. al. who compared the levels of anxiety and depression in onshore and offshore staff in a major operating company.[14] He noted: *"this group of men [OIMs] carry the ultimate responsibilities for the safety of their installations and the possibility of excessive stress warrants careful attention."* (see chapter 5) for a review of occupational stress in the offshore oil industry.

Hazardous Process

Offshore operations present particular hazards to the workforce. To minimize capital expenditure, installation size is kept to a minimum, resulting in confined spaces for drilling and production operations. Personnel not only work but live offshore, in quarters close to drilling, production, and process plant. The hazards inherent in hydro-carbon operations are intensified by the risk of oil and gas leaks and potential sources of ignition which could lead to a rapidly escalating emergency. Such risks are exacerbated by the remote marine location of installations and the difficulties of safely evacuating personnel. Offshore operations therefore require a management system to closely monitor and control all work conducted on board. As a result, the installation manager will often be involved in the day-to-day details of work operations and their control to a greater degree than many onshore management positions. A key aspect of his job will be managing by walking about, to be seen, lead by example, meet his staff and discover their views and concerns first hand.

In the United Kingdom, operating companies legally are required to devise Safety Management Systems (SMS) which identify and quantify the principal risks on board an installation and the systems of control which minimize those risks to As Low As Reasonably Practicable (ALARP). Some companies (e.g. Shell International Petroleum) have realized the value of such operating and control systems and have decided to implement SMS and Safety Cases throughout their world wide upstream operations.[15] Essential to the successful implementation and operation of the SMS is management commitment and involvement. "Managers must show personal interest in how it is going and in what is being learned and not just in how well the program for completing the safety case is being met."[15] The change in safety performance as a result of introducing such systems is partly because, in the words of one OIM,

> . . . *instead of him influencing the platform on an ad hoc basis, we now have a safety plan. Our job is to perform duties within the plan and most importantly, by way of audit, personal example, coaching and encouragement, ensure that all others are also fulfilling their contract within the plan. And it is this last point that is most important. The Safety Management System is all about the team and the environment in which they work.*[16]

In chapter 10 Mearns and Fleming discuss the management of risk, safety, and the need for workforce involvement in greater detail.

Emergency Response

The remote location of installations, in combination with the hazardous nature of extracting and processing hydrocarbons have implications for the management of major problems, such as blowout, fire, marine collision, explosion. In an emergency, the installation needs to be self-sufficient in its ability to control or mitigate the effects of a serious incident as the emergency services normally called upon to deal with an onshore industrial incident, are simply unavailable offshore. In such an emergency, everyone is looking to the OIM to remain calm and make the decisions necessary to effectively handle the incident. This requires a level of command ability clearly outwith the range of typical managerial responsibilities. Central to the OIM's capacity to successfully manage emergencies is the ability to take critical decisions when under pressure. This was highlighted by Cullen in his report following the *Piper Alpha* disaster:

The post of OIM calls for decisions which may make the difference between the life and death or personnel on board. The remoteness of installations, the requirement for installations to be self-contained in the means of dealing with a rapidly developing incident, the need to obtain, verify and consider data communicated to him from various sources for immediate decision on which the lives of those on board depend demands a level of command ability which is not a feature of normal management posts.[17]

The OIM is undoubtedly the key figure in an offshore emergency, though he does not operate alone, but with the support of his emergency command team. As the senior manager, he is effectively the incident commander, ultimately responsible for any decisions and their implementation, particularly the order to evacuate the installation, which in a hostile and remote environment is a high risk option. His job is to direct and coordinate his ER team to ensure a prompt and efficient response which will ensure the safety of all those on board the installation. (See chapter 8 for more details on emergency command.)

Given their incident command responsibilities, one would expect OIMs to receive some form of specialist training to prepare them to deal effectively with an offshore emergency. In Flin and Slaven's first study they asked OIMs whether they had received any training to undertake the role of incident commander in an emergency.[8] At that time, 28% had received no specific emergency command training, which was surprising given the level of command which could be required. Some of the drilling OIMs in the sample reported receiving such training earlier in their careers from the Merchant Navy or Armed Forces. Indeed the subsequent study of selection and training procedures revealed that many companies chose candidates for the OIM post from the Merchant or Royal Navy or armed forces due to their managerial experience.[9] Such a career has involved progressive responsibility, training, experience of emergencies, and the ability to be self-reliant in an emergency. It is now common, certainly in the United Kingdom, to provide specific emergency response training for OIMs and their teams in specially designed onshore simulators, supplemented by drills and exercises on the installation. Flin and Slaven commented that simulated emergency exercises are essential training for OIMs and recommended that OIMs should participate in at least one offshore drill or simulated emergency exercise per year.[9]

The most important characteristics and skills needed to deal with off-shore emergencies were obtained from speaking to OIMs themselves and their onshore line managers.[7-9] The list included

Leadership ability

Stable personality

Communication skills

Delegating

Team working

Decision making, under time pressure, especially under stress

Evaluating the situation

Planning a course of action

Remaining calm and managing stress in self and others

Preplanning to prepare for possible emergencies

Some quotes from managers who had actually managed a serious off-shore emergency are given from Flin and Slaven's 1994 study.[9]

- *OIM should . . .know plant and effects of actions and levels of shutdown. Develop control team ruthlessly to what you want them to be. Always keep personnel informed*
- *Be conversant with his emergency procedures manual but only to the point that he is confident that eventualities are covered. If he has any doubts about it's completeness then raise them immediately. Always use the manuals during drills and actual occurrences. Not to refer to manuals in an emergency is not macho, just stupid*
- *Run a major exercise involving all members of your team at least every month. Think outside of the environment outside your platform, what can damage you? help you? Review your offshore team - have you the right people in place to handle a crisis?*
- *Make your own judgments - go with your gut feelings in those situations. Forget about everything apart from your vessel at the time (e.g. other peripherals). As OIM [you] are best qualified to assess - if based on other's judgment, he is making decision.*
- *Have to keep calm or you lose it straight away. Must have performed contingency plans in own mind i.e. thought out possible scenarios and responses before incidents occur*

Finally, the last word on emergency management should go to Maurice Ullman, an OIM who, when asked in a survey of OIMs to respond to criticisms made by Lord Cullen, wrote,

Having read the report I believe that he, and now the HSE are look-ing for the perfect being, somebody like Clark Kent, who will sit in his office chair carrying out mind numbing admin for 364 days with a wry grin on his granite hewn features, only to disappear into the closet on hearing the general alarm and to reappear in a trice with a flowing cape, a pair of tights, complete with modesty knickers over them and a huge OIM emblazoned on the chest. Ready to take on the world. Where they are going to find him God only knows and when they do I want to be there to read the job description and see the salary grade.[9]

Advice from OIMs

This section will conclude with some general advice for recently appoint-ed offshore managers. These are not the ideas of the authors, but are quotes from United Kingdom OIMs who were surveyed by Flin and Slaven in 1991.[18] It is hoped that their cumulative experience may be of some value to future off-shore managers.

- *Try and be strong-willed because if you are not there are plenty of people to take advantage of any weaknesses you may have.*

- *Do not be pressured into taking actions unless sure in your own mind.*

- *A manager gets work done through others. Use the expertise on board, learn when and when not to delegate. You cannot do it all by yourself.*

- *Accumulate knowledge of the crew and equipment as the highest priority, continually update this knowledge.*

- *Know legislative requirements and company policy. Review plat-form operations and safety appliances until they become memory.*

- *Never stand aloof to the others on the rig.*

- *Read about accidents and crises and how they were or should have been coped with.*

- *Don't be afraid to shut down the platform if you think it is neces-sary.*

- *Do not hesitate to bring the total commitment and authority in use if required to achieve full protection of the facilities.*

Offshore operations create many challenges for managers and supervi-sors in relation to human resource management. The next section deals with supervisors and their contribution to maximizing the performance of the off-shore workforce.

Supervisors

The first-line supervisor is an integral and critical part of the management team on an offshore oil and gas production platform or drilling rig and he or she plays a key part in determining the efficiency of the exploration and production arm of the oil and gas industry. In many countries, rising operating costs, aging installations, and a declining field life are necessitating a particularly high level of supervisory skills to maximize performance and minimize costs while maintaining offshore safety standards. While innumerable management books are available for supervisors dealing with topics such as motivation, discipline, and leadership, and extensive research has been undertaken on supervisors working in onshore industries, there is no generally accepted theory of what makes an effective offshore supervisor.[19,20] Nevertheless, many leadership models such as Adair's three circle model (which encourages the supervisor to focus on the individual, the team, and the task) remain popular, if unproven.[21]

One of the reasons for the failure of general models to apply universally is that the work demands and organization culture require and foster particular styles of leadership. That is, the characteristics and processes of effective supervision may be specific to a particular industry rather than being universally applicable. This may be especially true for the offshore oil and gas industry which has an unusual working environment and lifestyle as discussed above. Notwithstanding the lack of a general theory, there is unanimous agreement across industries and cultures, that the supervisor has an important role to play in the success or failure of the organization. In the words of a director at Nissan:

> It is critical that we in the manufacturing industry realize that the first-line supervisor, if carefully selected, well trained, highly motivated and given the status and pay appropriate to being what I call 'the professional at managing the production process' can make more difference to the long term success of the company than any other group other than top management. And even here it is the supervisor who delivers top management policies.[22]

The supervisor is the key link between management decisions and their implementation; the job involves simultaneously satisfying the potentially conflicting goals of both superiors and subordinates. As the first person responsible for the work performance of nonmanagement employees, the supervisor allocates tasks and is accountable for work done. The traditional view of the supervisor as that of an *overseer*, inspecting work and maintaining discipline is beginning to change with a new emphasis on participative management, empowerment, autonomous work groups, computerized control systems, and the influence of staff specialists.[23,24] These factors also may be observed in the offshore industry with additional changes due to multi-skilling, work rotation patterns, down manning, and the increasing status of the contracting companies. As a result, the offshore supervisor must adopt a leadership style that reflects not only the changing demands of the role, but also addresses the special dimensions of installation life such as living with their work group, the intensive work, and rest patterns. Many of the aspects of the offshore environment that affect the OIM's job (discussed above) will also have an impact on the supervisor. This section of the chapter reviews the limited research which has specifically studied the job of the offshore supervisor, in relation to stress, job satisfaction, performance management, and safety. Again the only published material is drawn from the North Sea but it is anticipated that many of the principles will apply equally to supervisors in other offshore locations.

Odd Hellesoy, Leonard Moss, and Barry Milcarek (1985) studied a group of Mobil's offshore supervisors on the Statfjord A platform as part of their investigation of occupational stress.[25] The supervisors tended to be dissatisfied with the time available to do their job properly and the degree of pressure and stress in their work. They placed considerable importance on opportunities to take responsibility and to use their abilities. There was some indication that the effects of job pressure may have more impact on the supervisors' onshore life than on their time spent on the platform. Managing differences in language and culture between supervisors and the workforce did not appear to be a difficulty on this platform (probably due to the high percentage of Norwegian employees), although there was a range of fluency in English and Norwegian. However in other parts of the world, cultural and language barriers can be a significant problem and an added burden for the supervisors and managers.

David Carnegie carried out an interview study with 29 supervisors on a United Kingdom production platform in 1993 and asked them about the differences between the job of a supervisor onshore and offshore.[26] He found that while 48% thought there was no difference, the others felt that personal working relationships were different, that they were more flexible offshore, and that jobs had to be completed more quickly offshore. Particular problems of being an offshore supervisor had to do with relationships and personalities, discipline, and that little problems appeared larger. When asked what motivated them they replied that job pride, bonuses, promotion prospects, and praise were effective in encouraging them to perform better. They were asked what training they required and 57% said personal/behavioral training, such as motivation, team leadership and communication.

What Makes an Effective Offshore Supervisor?

In a subsequent study, Carnegie interviewed 100 first line supervisors on one Norwegian and two British platforms with the aim of describing the non-technical aspects of the supervisor's job and identifying the characteristics of high performing supervisors.[27,28] He used a structured interview as well as standard questionnaires to assess personality, leadership style, job satisfaction and perceptions of the work environment. The supervisors' effectiveness was assessed by a job performance appraisal form completed by their superiors. Supervisors were defined as those at the first level of the organizational hierarchy on a platform who were responsible for the work performance of their team.

The 100 supervisors (99 male) were not all direct employees of the platforms' operating companies; the majority worked for contracting companies and were an experienced group both in terms of their time as supervisors and their offshore experience. A total of 91 of the supervisors were appraised by their immediate superiors on six aspects of their job performance, the highest mean score was for the scale *technical/specialist ability* and the lowest mean score was for *change oriented*. Overall the supervisors were rated as good performers. The biodata variables (age, offshore experience, and specific supervisory experience) did not predict the performance ratings.

In terms of personality, they appeared to be a fairly heterogeneous group which is similar to an earlier study of OIMs' personality profiles (see chapter 2). There is some indication that they are more imaginative, methodical, and ambitious than a population norm group but this is only a preliminary finding. Their job satisfaction scores were comparable with an onshore sample but were higher than studies of offshore workers' job satisfaction undertaken in the mid-1980s. (The latter were general samples and not specifically first line supervisors, so it is not possible to judge whether this represents a status difference or an improvement over time). The supervisors were most dissatisfied with the management and industrial relations on their platforms and most satisfied with their fellow workers and their own level of responsibility. This indication of the importance of relationships with fellow workers has been shown in all previous offshore studies and is a reflection of the lifestyle and team work culture on offshore platforms.

They were asked to report how they perceived their work environment in relation to its social and management aspects, using a standard North American scale.[3] This type of assessment had not been made previously for off-shore platforms. In general they felt a strong emphasis on rules and procedures (more than onshore workers) which is not surprising given the emphasis on safety, standard operating procedures, and permit-to-work systems on European production installations. Similarly they felt that there was not a high emphasis on autonomy (this was rated significantly lower than onshore workers). This is an interesting finding given the empowerment initiatives being introduced by a number of companies (see chapter 7). They also perceived a higher degree of work pressure and time urgency in comparison to onshore workers, which echoes the earlier Norwegian finding.[25] In relation to the social atmosphere, they felt that *peer cohesion*, the extent to which employees were friendly and supportive of each other, was high.

Their management style was assessed by a standard leadership questionnaire developed by Bernard Bass at the Center for Leadership, New York which measured transformational, transactional, and laissez faire behaviors.[29] Bass argues that in order to produce exceptional performance, supervisors must go beyond the typical transactional style of "you do this for me and I'll do that for you" which only results in expected performance levels. To achieve performance beyond expectations, supervisors (and managers) need to use a transformational style. Bass has identified four characteristics of transformational leaders from his work in the United States, Canada and Europe:

> *Leadership is* charismatic *such that the follower seeks to identify with the leader and to emulate him or her. The leadership* inspires *the follower with challenge and persuasion providing a meaning and understanding. The leadership is* intellectually stimulating, *expanding the follower's use of his or her abilities. Finally the leadership is* individually considerate, *providing the follower with support, mentoring and coaching.*[30]

The supervisors in Carnegie's study felt that they used a style which was primarily transformational, particularly focusing on individual consideration of their subordinates' needs.[27] They did not see themselves as adopting a laissez faire approach, that is, only managing in a reactive fashion when corrective action was required. These of course are the supervisors' perceptions of their style; their subordinates may have held a different view.

An attempt to use these quantitative measures of supervisors' characteristics as predictors of job performance was not very encouraging. Very few dimensions functioned as effective discriminators of supervisory performance. That is the scores on the leadership style questionnaire, job satisfaction scale, personality scale, and perceptions of the work environment did not significantly differentiate the more effective from less effective supervisors. However, these data were combined from three platforms, one of which was Norwegian; and platform, company, and national cultural differences may be masking underlying trends. Further analyses indicate that there were different patterns of responses for the three installations, which is not surprising given the common recognition that installations belonging to the same company can have quite distinct cultures. Additional qualitative data from the interviews suggest that issues relating to communication, business training, and the supervisor's role definition should be explored in greater depth.

David Carnegie's research also showed that while superiors and peers could provide reasonably consistent judgments of supervisors' performance, measuring the essential ingredients that determined the more effective supervisors proved to be more difficult. As with the earlier studies of OIMs, he found that half the supervisors surveyed found their jobs to be stressful. The supervisors believed that the most important skills were related to man management, communication, and motivation. A number of operating and contracting companies are now establishing systems to develop the training of their offshore supervisors, particularly in management and business techniques as well as technical and financial skills. Recently in the United Kingdom, companies have also begun to formally assess their supervisors' competence against national vocational standards and this is encouraging the development of formal supervisory qualifications (see chapter 2). However, Richard Coonen carried out a study of offshore supervisors employed by a major United Kingdom-based contracting company and he found that the new British standards of management competence had limited application for their offshore staff.[32] Given the atypical work conditions, he argued that supervisory training and competence assessment should be tailored to fit the offshore environment.

Supervisors as Safety Managers

The critical role of management and supervision in offshore safety management has been emphasized in a number of studies and in a recent series of 18 discussion groups on drilling rigs and production platforms, Mark Fleming asked what the key skills were that a supervisor ideally should have to manage safety effectively.[4,32,33] Five themes emerged:

1. *Concern for safety* - good supervisors should be more concerned about safety than the average worker; they should ensure that the work group performs their tasks safely and leave the worksite in a safe condition;

2. The supervisor should be *technically competent* and explain the work clearly;

3. Supervisors should be able to *communicate effectively* with their work force; the workers should not feel the supervisor is going to attack them if they are having difficulty. "Knows how to speak to someone, does not shout", " Someone you can go to and they won't jump down your throat. ";

4. Being *interested in their work group* was seen as a key attribute of the good supervisors. "A good supervisor has got time for you. . . . Is tolerant, willing to wait for people to learn.";

5. *Strength of character* - supervisors should be able to stand up to management and refuse to take chances with safety. They should also be strong enough to take the blame for their mistakes.

Fleming has now begun an interview study with offshore supervisors from both operating and contracting companies to determine in more detail the characteristics and skills that supervisors use to achieve both high safety and high productivity in their work groups.

Conclusion

Offshore operations present offshore installation managers and their supervisors with an unusual package of job challenges. Remote rig and platform locations can result in isolation from onshore line management which provides the opportunity for considerable autonomy. Work patterns require long periods of concentration resulting in physically and mentally demanding working conditions, and job sharing with more than one back to back can bring problems as well as benefits. The high risk and hazardous process operations can add to the stressful nature of the manager's job, including the demands to lead personnel in an emergency and to take decisions under pressure. It is not a job to suit everyone, though the challenges are a source of considerable job satisfaction for those who stay in the post.

The supervisor is a key figure in establishing and maintaining a safe and productive team work culture on an offshore installation. Identifying how they do this and why some supervisors perform better in this environment than others remain fundamental questions. While offshore managers will readily identify those who are their best supervisors, and which ones they would choose to have with them for a maintenance shutdown, pinpointing the common characteristics or leadership style of these individuals is more difficult. It seems that high performing supervisors need to be flexible, with a range of styles at their disposal and to be able to judge which style is appropriate for a given situation or subordinate. Team leaders, whether drillers, foremen, supervisors, camp bosses, or managers must have a good understanding of human behavior and the Crew Resource Management techniques now used by the international aviation and shipping industries offer a valuable approach for the enhancement of supervisory and team performance in the offshore oil industry. [34] As installations move to lower manning levels the emphasis on team working appears ready to increase. A recent case study of the selection and training practices for the new generation of North Sea platforms shows that companies such as Phillips Petroleum are investing in careful selection and team building practices to enhance their platform teams' performance.[35] The transformational approach to leadership appears to capture the critical components which organizations are attempting to instill into their offshore culture. Future research will determine whether this is indeed the most appropriate leadership style for the supervisors and managers on the rigs and platforms for 21st century exploration and production.

References
1. Ullman, M. A funny thing happened to me on the way to the forum. Paper presented at the Third OIM conference, *Law and Practice*, The Robert Gordon University, Aberdeen, Scotland, April, 1994.
2. Parker, R. Opening Address to the Fourth OIM conference, *Effective Team Working*, The Robert Gordon University, Aberdeen, Scotland, April, 1995.
3. Alexander, M. The concept of safety culture within a United Kingdom offshore organisation. Paper presented at the conference *Understanding Risk Perception*, The Robert Gordon University, Aberdeen. February, 1995.
4. Flin, R., Mearns, K., Gordon, R. & Fleming, M. Risk perception and safety in United Kingdom offshore oil workers. *Safety Science* (in press), 1996.
5. Rundmo, T. Risk perception and safety on offshore petroleum platforms. *Safety Science*, 15, 1992: 39-68.
6. Rundmo, T., Mearns, K., Flin, R., Fleming, M. & Gordon, R. *A Comparative Study of Risk Perception and Safety in European Offshore Personnel*. Report prepared for the Norwegian Petroleum Directorate and the Offshore Safety Division of the United Kingdom Health and Safety Executive, 1996.
7. Flin, R. & Slaven, G. Selecting and training offshore installation managers. In collected papers from the First SPE conference on *Health, Safety and Environment in Oil and Gas Exploration and Production*. The Hague, November (SPE23256), 1991.
8. Flin, R. & Slaven, G. Managing offshore installations. *Petroleum Review*, 47, 1993: 68-71.
9. Flin, R. & Slaven, G. *The Selection and Training of Offshore Installation Managers for Crisis Management*. Report OTH 92 374 for Project P2719 to the Offshore Safety Division of the Health and Safety Executive. Sudbury: HSE Books, 1994.
10. Mykletun, R. Safety hazards related to the rotation of Norwegian platform managers. Paper presented at the Second OIM conference, *Managing Offshore Safety*,

The Robert Gordon University, Aberdeen, Scotland, April, 1993.

11. Sutherland, K. *Psychosocial Factors: An Investigation of the Offshore Oil Industry.* Unpublished PhD thesis, Robert Gordon University, Aberdeen, Scotland, 1993.

12. Lynghaug, E. Positive power by team management. Paper presented at the Fourth OIM conference, *Effective Team Working,* The Robert Gordon University, Aberdeen, Scotland, April, 1995.

13. Ling, M. Developing a team to operate Dunbar. Paper presented at the Fourth OIM conference, *Effective Team Working,* The Robert Gordon University, Aberdeen, Scotland, April, 1995.

14. Gann. M., Corpe, U. & Wilson, I. The application of a short anxiety and depression questionnaire to oil industry staff. *Journal of Society of Occupational Medicine, 40,* 1990: 138-142.

15. Bentley, P. D., Jones, M. G., & Geert de Jong. Development and implementation of an HSE management system in exploration and production companies. In collected papers of the Second SPE Conference on *Health, Safety and Environment in Oil and Gas Exploration and Production.* Jakarta, January. Richardson, Texas: Society of Petroleum Engineers. (SPE 27075), 1994.

16. Everest, P. A view from a bridge: An OIM's personal view, pre and post Piper Alpha. Paper presented at the Third OIM conference, *Law and Practice,* The Robert Gordon University, Aberdeen, Scotland, April, 1994.

17. Cullen, The Hon. Lord. *The Public Inquiry into the Piper Alpha Disaster. Vols. I & II.* London: HMSO. CM1310, 1990.

18. Flin, R. & Slaven, G. *Managing Offshore Installations: A Survey of UKCS Offshore Installation Managers.* Oil Industry Report, Robert Gordon University, 1992.

19. Moseley, D., Megginson, L. & Pietri, P. *Supervisory Management* (3rd ed.). Cincinnati, Ohio: Southwestern Publishing, 1993.

20. Child, J. & Partridge, B. *Lost Managers. Supervisors in Industry and Society.* Cambridge: Cambridge University Press, 1982.

21. Adair, J. *Effective Leadership.* London: Pan, 1983.

22. Wickens, P. *The Road to Nissan.* London: Macmillan, 1987.

23. Harrison, E. The impact of employee involvement on supervisors. *National Productivity Review,* Autumn, 1992: 447-452.

24. Kerr, S., Hill, K. & Broedling, L. The first-line supervisor: Phasing out or here to stay? *Academy of Management Review,* 11, 1986: 103-111.

25. Hellesoy, O., Moss, L. & Milcarek, B. The supervisor - stress and coping. In O. Hellesoy (Ed.) *Work Environment Statfjord Field.* Oslo: Univeristetforlaget, 1985.

26. Carnegie, D. First-line supervisors in the offshore oil industry. In collected papers of the Second SPE Conference on *Health, Safety and Environment in Oil and Gas Exploration and Production.* Jakarta, January. Richardson, Texas: Society of Petroleum Engineers. (SPE 27295), 1994.

27. Carnegie, D. The role of the first line supervisor on an offshore platform. PhD thesis, The Robert Gordon University, Aberdeen, (in preparation).

28. Carnegie, D. Effective supervisors on offshore petroleum platforms. In collected papers of the Fourth OIM Conference, *Effective Team Working.* Robert Gordon University, Aberdeen, April, 1995.

29. Bass, B. & Avolio, B. *Improving Organizational Effectiveness Through Transformational Leadership.* New York: Sage, 1994.

30. Bass, B. Implications of transformational leadership for teamwork. In collected papers of the Fourth OIM Conference, *Effective Team Working*. Robert Gordon University, Aberdeen, April, 1995.

31. Moos, R. & Insell, P. *Work Environment Scale*. Palo Alto: Consulting Psychologists Press, 1974.

32. Coonen, R. Supervisory competence. Unpublished Master of Personnel Management Sciences thesis. University of Tilburg, Netherlands, 1994.

33. Fleming, M., Flin, R., Mearns, K. & Gordon, R. The offshore supervisor's changing role in safety management: From law enforcer to risk manager. In collected papers of the Third SPE Conference on *Health, Safety and Environment in Oil and Gas Exploration and Production*. New Orleans, June. (SPE 35906), 1996.

34. Flin, R. H. Crew Resource Management for teams in the offshore oil industry. *Journal of European Industrial Training, 19, 9,* 1995: 23-27.

35. Boyd, R. Preparing a team to operate the Judy platform. Unpublished MSc thesis, The Robert Gordon University, Aberdeen, 1996.

Chapter 5

Occupational Stress: Identification And Management
Rhona Flin

Introduction

Occupational stress (and consequent costs to individuals and to organizations) has become an issue that managers can no longer afford to ignore. The United Kingdom Health and Safety Executive recently published guidelines for employers on the identification and management of stress within their workplaces, the European Foundation for the Improvement of Living and Working Conditions have prepared similar advisory material and the United States National Institute for Occupational Safety and Health have sponsored a series of major conferences on the subject[2-4]. In addition, there is growing concern at the apparent incidence of mental health problems in the workforce and the inability of operational managers to detect and deal with staff showing symptoms. While extensive research into occupational stress and psychological well-being has been carried out in a wide range of onshore organizations, comparatively little work has been carried out in offshore industries.[1,6,7] This chapter first explains what is meant by the term occupational stress and then considers the causes and effects of stress for offshore oil industry workers. The final section outlines a risk assessment and management approach for dealing with stress in the offshore environment.

The upstream oil and gas industry offers a unique combination of working conditions, job demands, and challenges for those employed on the production platforms, drilling rigs, and support vessels. The environment is remote and the operations involving the extraction and processing of high pressure hydrocarbons are potentially hazardous. Moreover, the work scheduling is unusual and is not found in comparable onshore occupations. Workers on offshore installations typically spend two to four weeks on the installation working a minimum 12-hour shift each day, with no rest days (this is followed by a period of one to four weeks onshore). For the period on the installation, the crew are away from family and friends but they also escape from commuting, domestic chores and some of the day-to-day family responsibilities. They regularly are screened for medical fitness, and no alcohol is permitted on offshore installations in most countries. Is this then a work environment which would produce a greater experience of occupational stress than a similar onshore workplace? Are there particular aspects of the offshore work environment likely to cause or exacerbate stress? No major study of this issue has been undertaken. Michael Gann et. al. commenting on the lack of research into occupational stress, (even though the psychological demands of offshore work are taken into account during routine health screening), suggest that offshore oil companies may have "an inherent suspicion of psychologists in a traditionally hard nosed industry."[8] This chapter reviews findings from the handful of psychological studies designed to measure occupational stress and mental health in the offshore workforce. These allow us to develop our understanding of the psychosocial demands and possible benefits or negative consequences from working in a remote and hazardous environment.

What Is Stress?

The word *stress* (probably from the Latin *stringere* meaning to "draw tight") is the label now widely used to describe psychological distress and discomfort. If we consider work-related stress, it is important to distinguish between two types, and using a medical analogy, these can be labeled *chronic stress* and *acute stress*. Chronic stress, usually called occupational stress, is related to conditions in the workplace and the individual's reaction to these, usually over a protracted period of time. Employers are beginning to treat this subject seriously given the threat of litigation, and stress-related mental health claims to the workers' compensation schemes for *cumulative trauma* are very common in the U.S.[9] A recent article reported that North American job-related stress claims were "proliferating out of control", and that some states (e.g. Oklahoma) will not compensate workers for *mental-mental cases*, that is where a mental trauma like stress causes a mental problem such as depression.[10] Other costs of occupational stress to industry can include reduced productivity, increased errors, accidents, sickness absence, early retirement, staff turnover, and industrial disputes.

The other type of stress, which is discussed elsewhere (see chapter 8) is acute stress, called emergency stress or critical incident stress. At its most extreme, this occurs where the individual is suddenly exposed to a threatening situation, such as a life endangering event or a traumatic scene and begins to experience a pronounced physiological and psychological reaction, which in many situations is a highly adaptive, valuable response. Individuals exposed to very high levels of acute stress may suffer long term effects, sometimes in the form of Post Traumatic Stress Disorder (PTSD). For example, Norwegian psychiatrists studied 134 rescue personnel who were involved in the *Alexander Keilland* oil rig capsize (123 fatalities) and found that nine months after the disaster, 24% of the rescuers reported poor mental health due to the impact of the disaster.[11]

The physiological basis of both acute and chronic stress is the flight/fight response, so called because of the need to flee or fight the threat, produced when the brain perceives a threat in the immediate environment and signals the rest of the body to be ready to produce an energy surge to allow the animal to quickly flee the situation or to fight the aggressor. Any situation perceived by the individual to be demanding or challenging can produce this effect, and most people will have experienced heightened arousal (acute stress) in situations of alarm, such as having a near miss when driving or flying in an aircraft that starts to produce peculiar engine noises. Less intense tension can also be experienced in difficult work situations such as a disagreement with a boss, a tight deadline, or fear of redundancy. The advantage of this reaction is a surge of energy to deal with the threat, and running or fighting are useful responses when in physical danger. They are less valuable behaviors when disagreeing with your boss or struggling to meet an unrealistic deadline. Moreover, this tension is an expensive state for the brain and body to maintain and if prolonged (chronic stress), it can result in short term and longer term physical and psychological side effects.

If we look at the psychological process of occupational stress at its simplest, stress occurs (and for the purposes of this chapter, the term stress will be taken to represent negative, unpleasant effects) when the perceived demands (stressors) exceed the perceived resources to cope with these demands. Thus the key element of this model is the person's judgment of the degree of demand in the environment (workload, time pressure, responsibility) and whether their personal resources (knowledge, skills, coping mechanisms, time, support from others) can match these. The critical appraisal of demands and coping resources is based on a host of factors, such as their previous experience, training and personality, thus resulting in distinct individual differences in the onset and extent of stress reactions. A worker faced with an increasing workload or a domestic problem may feel calm, confident, and totally in control, while another in the same circumstances could be uneasy, irritable, and suffering from sleep loss. This theoretical model can be portrayed as a balance mechanism as shown in Figure 5-1.

When the available resources are judged as equal to the demands, then the individual feels in control and comfortable, and in this state moderate levels of demand may increase motivation and performance. When the demands are judged to outweigh the resources then the stress response (distress) begins to occur, with a complex and interacting package of mental, physical, behavioral and emotional effects. Tom Cox offers a more precise definition: "The experience of stress is defined by, first, the realization that they are having difficulty coping with demands and threats to their well being, and, second, that coping is important and the difficulty in coping worries or depresses them."[1]

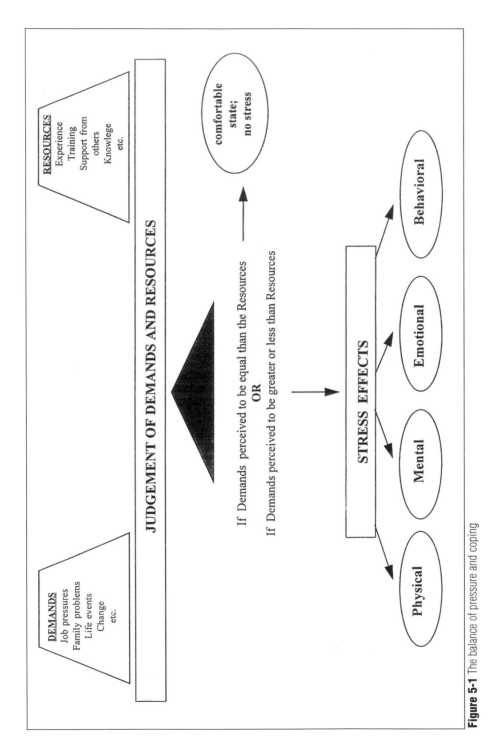

Figure 5-1 The balance of pressure and coping

Any attempt to remove the sources of stress, to manage the stress reaction, and to mitigate negative effects needs to be based on a proper understanding of the likely causes and symptoms of stress in a given situation, in this case, the offshore workplace. It should be emphasized that, "There is no such thing as a pressure-free job. Every job brings its own set of tasks, responsibilities, and day to day problems, and the pressures and demands these place upon us are an unavoidable part of working life."[2] The following section briefly reviews the relevant studies and then presents a summary framework of stress in the offshore oil industry which provides a number of pointers for stress management.

Studies of Occupational Stress in Offshore Work

The Norwegians have long been interested in the psychosocial effects of working life offshore and the first European investigation of offshore working life was carried out in the early 1980s by a team from Bergen University led by Odd Hellesoy, sponsored by Mobil Norway.[12,13] They collected data from 465 employees on the Statfjord A platform (operators, drillers, caterers and flotel crew) and found that the majority were satisfied with their jobs offshore, but that certain environmental and social factors could function as stressors. Heat, noise, and ventilation were judged to be the most unsatisfactory aspects of the work environment on the platform, and concern about events at home was the most prevalent personal worry. No standard instruments were used to assess the incidence of clinical cases of anxiety or depression, but employees were asked about mental problems and irritability. They found that depression and loneliness affected 8-10% of the crew. They, and later Torbjorn Rundmo in a subsequent study of risk perception in 900 Norwegian offshore workers, pointed out the critical role of occupational stress and job strain in relation to workers' well-being, feelings of safety, job performance and accident involvement.[14]

In the United Kingdom sector, the first large-scale psychological study of offshore life was published by Valerie Sutherland and Cary Cooper.[15,16] Having conducted a series of interviews, they designed a comprehensive questionnaire which measured sources of stress for offshore workers, as well as personality (Type A behavior; locus of control; extraversion and neuroticism), job satisfaction, mental health and self-reported accident rates. In the initial study (1986) they surveyed 194 men employed by a contractor (Dietsmann) on platforms and rigs in the British and Dutch sectors of the North Sea. They reported that this group were less satisfied with their jobs than their onshore counterparts and that levels of anxiety were significantly higher than the general population norms. (Katherine Parkes criticized their method and argued that this comparison should be interpreted very cautiously).[17]

The top three causes of stress were financial (lack of paid holidays, rate of pay, and pay differentials between operating and contracting staff). Apart from pay and conditions, workers were most concerned about problems involving relationships at work and home, as well as site management problems. Levels of stress associated with relationships at home and at work were found to predict both job satisfaction and mental health. They also found those who had been accident victims reported reduced mental well-being and lower job satisfaction, but acknowledged that it was impossible to determine cause and effect.

In a follow-up study (1991) they surveyed a further 310 men sampled from a North Sea contracting company and union organization mailing lists on three occasions over 18 months and again found that the principal factors perceived as potentially stressful by offshore workers were understimulation; home-work interface; career prospects and reward; safety and insecurity. They concluded,

> Although it is accepted that cost cutting, safety and the need to meet production figures are probably antagonistic goals, many companies have shown that stress management can be a cost saving exercise. In the offshore environment the benefits could extend to improved safety standards, accident reduction, improved productivity and a much needed boost to morale in general.[17]

The second British study was carried out by Karen Sutherland who was the first psychologist to be granted research access by U.S. oil companies onto their North Sea production platforms.[18,19] Three operating companies and one contracting company participated in the study which involved a series of interviews conducted offshore followed by two questionnaire surveys (n=212; n=191) which were carried out with a 15-month interval (before and after the *Piper Alpha* disaster in 1988). The first questionnaire collected information on sources of stress, demographic factors, personality (Type A behavior), job satisfaction, mood state, physical, and mental health.

The second questionnaire did not include the mood and physical health sections, but at the request of the participating companies included a special section on offshore safety. The principal sources of stress were pay and lack of job security for contractor staff and management issues for the operating staff. The contractor staff reported higher levels of stress and lower job satisfaction than the operating staff, but levels of mental and physical health were similar. In general the level of mental health appeared to be comparable with that of relatively demanding onshore occupations such as the police and the fire service, with around 12% of the sample reporting symptoms of anxiety and 2% symptoms of depression, at a level of clinical significance. Those individuals experiencing more stress also reported poorer mental health and lower job satisfaction.

The levels of stress reported in the studies described above indicate that a number of personnel do perceive their work offshore as stressful and this was endorsed in more recent research into managerial occupations on offshore installations. For example, a survey of 134 United Kingdom offshore installation managers found that 32% of them reported that their job was *mildly stressful*, 42% found it *considerably stressful*, and 5% found it *extremely stressful*.[20] The main hassles were reported to be dealing with onshore management, paperwork, legislation, and problems with personnel. For drilling rig OIMs, relations with the operator was most frequently mentioned. Similar results were found in an interview study of 100 first-line supervisors on British and Norwegian platforms where 47% said they found their job to be considerably or extremely stressful.[21]

Little research appears to have been carried out to examine stress and mental health in other offshore locations. In the Gulf of Mexico, Lisandro Perez in 1979 argued that psychosocial factors were related to high accident rates and more recently Clemmer and Mohr studied offshore drillers in this location and found an association between lower-back injuries and economic factors e.g. layoffs and high turnover rates, and suggested that, "psychogenic stress engendered by poor market conditions may have played a role."[22,23] The available data on direct links between the causes and effects of stress in offshore workers are somewhat limited but following a standard approach and drawing on earlier models, the main causal factors, possible buffer factors and associated effects from the above studies were organized into a diagram which is shown in Figure 5-2.[12,23]

It should be emphasized that this is simply a descriptive framework and does not provide evidence for direct links between factors, because at present there is insufficient evidence to predict precise causal relationships. The main causes of stress (or stressors) are shown on the left-hand side These include both offshore workplace stressors and onshore home stressors (major life events, e.g. bereavement, divorce) and many of these elements would apply equally to onshore workers. The right-hand side shows possible effects of stress which can manifest as physiological, behavioral, emotional symptoms, for example tension, sleep disturbance or irritability. There may also be organizational outcomes such as poor morale, an increase in grievances, absenteeism, but these have not been displayed in the diagram. Whether exposure to the causes of stress actually results in the experience of stress, depends on a number of intermediary or buffer factors shown as the middle box of the model. These include individual characteristics, such as personality and offshore experience as well as social support and management factors.

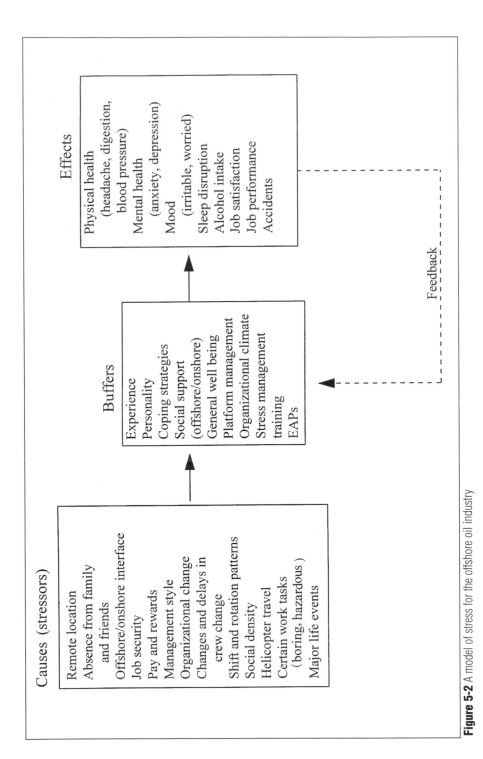

Figure 5-2 A model of stress for the offshore oil industry

Causes of Stress (Stressors)

A recent guide for employers on occupational stress states that

In general, harmful levels of stress are more likely to occur where pressures pile on top of each other or are prolonged; people feel trapped or unable to exert any control over the demands placed upon them; people are confused by conflicting demands made on them.[2]

These general conditions will obviously apply offshore as well as onshore, but if we examine the studies mentioned above, a number of more specific factors have been reported as causing stress to offshore workers. The *remote location* of most offshore oil and gas installations means an *extended work rotation* with minimum 12-hour shifts, night shifts, and a trip of one to four weeks on the installation. Worldwide a variety of rotation systems are used and while it appears that workers vary in their preference and adjustment to particular schedules, there are no guidelines on the optimal offshore rotation and shift patterns for worker well-being. The International Labor Organization has commented, "it seems doubtful that the hazards of current offshore working time practices have been properly researched."[24] Certain aspects of particular work patterns may well be stressful and adequate rest periods must be provided to avoid fatigue effects, for example midhitch rollovers (changing from day shift to night shift mid-trip) can produce jet lag effects.[26] (see chapter 6 which considers shifts and rotation patterns in greater depth).

An *absence from family and friends* for periods of several weeks at a time, which inevitably means missing birthdays, festivals and important family events can be stressful. For workers who have partners and children this can produce additional pressures for all family members.[27] (see chapter 13 for a discussion of how wives cope with husbands working offshore). A number of respondents in Karen Sutherland's study reported feeling depressed and withdrawn two or three days before their leaves were up and experiencing feelings of guilt at "deserting my wife and children again". While workers rank "worry about my family" as a source of stress, many claim to deal with the offshore routine by trying not to think about home for the duration of the trip. One man commented, "When you come offshore, you undergo a personality change and have to switch off to what is going on at home; otherwise, you would be unable to cope".[18]

With experience, both the offshore workers and their partners can learn to adjust to this lifestyle although it can remain a difficulty for some individuals, particularly when domestic problems arise. Irrespective of occupation, *coping with major life events* such as bereavement or divorce, presents problems of adjustment which will often require help and support to resolve. For offshore workers these can be even more difficult to manage when they are away from home and do not have the immediate contact of close friends and families.

The remote location can also add pressure to normal work operations due to the *offshore/onshore interface,* manifested as communication problems between onshore and offshore, logistical difficulties, and delays with the transport of equipment and personnel. There can be a sense of detachment from what is happening elsewhere in the company. In the words of one worker, "Sometimes I get a feeling of isolation and not being involved in the everyday run of things onshore."[18] However for some offshore managers and supervisors this is precisely the joy of working offshore rather than onshore.

Another aspect of the location which can cause stress is the uncertainty element of the work environment, particularly last minute *changes and delays in crew change arrangements.* The non-arrival of one's *back to back* (relief) can mean an extended stay on the installation until a replacement is sent out. The expression "waiting on weather" refers to a window of calm conditions required to conduct a particular operation, but the phrase becomes a definite stress trigger when helicopter flights are on an extended delay due to fog or high sea conditions and personnel are required to spend additional days on the installation or at the heliport. For a number of offshore personnel, *traveling by helicopter* represents a source of stress which they must tolerate in order to travel to their work. In Norway special courses are held for workers who have a fear of flying, which is not an uncommon phobia in the general population.

Prime stress factors in the United Kingdom studies carried out in the 1980s were *pay and rewards,* particularly for the contracting population who constituted the majority of the offshore workforce and who were generally on poorer rates and contract conditions than the operating company staff. Some leveling appears to have taken place over the last decade and contracting company staff are now holding increasingly senior supervisory positions on many United Kingdom production platforms, which can improve career prospects (*lack of career opportunities* had been found as a cause of stress in the British samples). Job security was also a major concern in the initial studies following the oil price crash in the mid-80s.

With cost-cutting and rationalization now a prominent aspect of worldwide petroleum operations in the mid 1990s, *job security* is likely to be a current stressor for many workers, although this is also true for many onshore employees in the oil business as well as other industries.

Organizational change is generally reported as stressful and this requires careful management not just in terms of down-manning but also as new methods of working such as autonomous teams and multi-skilling are introduced. Organizational and management factors appear as principal causes of stress, with items such as *management style, company communication, company organization, consultation about working issues* featuring among the highest rated stressors for both operator and contractor staff.

One employee from a United Kingdom production platform in the mid-80s commented, "I feel the biggest problem is the company's outmoded managerial views and their rule by fear attitude."[16] Again such organizational features are commonly found to be stressors in onshore studies and there is some evidence that management style has been changing to a more consultative, democratic mode in western industry including the offshore sector, but whether this has altered levels of stress remains to be seen (see chapters 4 and 7). Differences between parent company culture, operators versus contractors, production platforms versus drilling rigs, size and function of installation, country of location, and economic climate all have to be taken into account when considering the impact of organizational factors on occupational stress. This would certainly appear to be a topic worthy of further investigation given the implications for safety and production.

The *social density* of the living accommodation on an installation can be a source of stress with limited opportunities for rest and recreation, particularly for those who like space to be alone in their time off. The similarity of an offshore installation to an institution such as a prison has been noted by a number of observers and the lack of opportunity to escape from one's workmates at the end of a shift requires a degree of adjustment. Limited personal space is also a potentially stressful aspect of life for those working on ships or in remote mining and forestry camps.[28] The atmosphere on many petroleum installations is characterized by banter and camaraderie but this requires some degree of management and workplace frictions need a degree of self control in order to maintain a harmonious social environment.

The *nature of the work* offshore can be a source of stress but this varies markedly across the wide range of occupations represented and so generalizations are difficult. Valerie Sutherland and Cary Cooper found that unstimulating work causing boredom was a feature of some offshore occupations and this emerged as a cause of stress in their research. Katherine Parkes found that offshore and onshore production control room operators reported similar concerns when asked about the most demanding aspects of their work. These were pressure and responsibility, interruptions, maintaining concentration, and keeping their knowledge up to date.[25] For some jobs, the offshore location involves exposure to particular hazards such as working at heights, over the side, under the sea, in confined spaces, with high pressure or heavy equipment, with toxic chemicals or radioactive materials.

Studies of European offshore workers show that they are aware of the risks and are generally confident with regard to safety procedures.[29] (see chapter 13). For an experienced and highly trained workforce, workplace hazards do not seem to be a significant stress factor, and while the risk of a major accident may have an immediate impact on feelings about offshore work, this does not seem to be a pervasive stressor. In the study of stress carried out just after the *Piper Alpha* explosion and the *Ocean Oddysey* blowout, the danger of offshore work and recent events in the North Sea were ranked among the highest stress factors, but overall levels of stress, mental health and job satisfaction were found to have changed little from an earlier sample.[19] Richard Fuchs et. al. were able to make a similar comparison in their study of Canadian offshore drilling workers after the loss of the *Ocean Ranger* rig with 84 fatalities.[30] According to Fuchs, this event had a traumatic effect on Newfoundland but, "We were surprised to learn from our respondents that the Ocean Ranger tragedy had little influence on how they saw their jobs and their future in the oil industry". One of their respondents commented, "I always thought it was dangerous working offshore. Anyone who thinks otherwise is foolish."[30] This quotation illustrates that awareness of risks does not necessarily mean that this causes stress and in this context, it is worth noting that the offshore workforce are a self selected group who have chosen to work in this environment.

Buffer Factors

Studies of occupational stress have repeatedly shown that there are marked individual differences in the experience of stress, primarily due to a number of moderating or buffer factors. These include prior *experience* in the offshore oil industry or occupations with similar demands, such as fishing, remote mining, merchant marine, or armed forces. Many companies use this as a one of their selection criteria when recruiting offshore staff. The *age* of the worker can be a mediating factor with older workers more concerned about personal fitness, new technology and job security.[16] *Personality* also plays a role in susceptibility to stress but the research findings are not clear cut. There is some evidence that those offshore workers with a Type A disposition (time pressured, competitive) may be more likely to experience stress (although they may also opt for stress-inducing work) than those with the Type B (more easy going) disposition. Personal *coping strategies* for identifying one's stress level and for using techniques to relax or switch off are a buffer factor as some individuals have acquired skills to unwind, such as systematic relaxation techniques, a fitness regime or a hobby which can be pursued offshore. *Fitness and general well being* also can provide a good buffer against stress. It is well known that feelings of tiredness or common ailments such as colds and flu can increase sensitivity to stress.

One of the most significant buffer factors is the presence of *social support*, having trusted others for company or to share problems with, either onshore during leave or offshore. In the Statfjord study, the authors commented

Social support is clearly an area with both positive and negative possibilities. Poor social support makes the individual and organizations vulnerable to a number of disagreeable and harmful effects of environmental demands and limitations. Good social support protects against health and safety risk factors, improves learning and coping and clearly contributes to improving the quality of work life in the offshore environment.[13]

Paradoxically the presence of 200 fellow crew members does not guarantee social support while offshore. In one study 8% of workers on large platforms reported that a source of stress was "not having anyone to talk to".[19] Service company personnel who travel to different platforms and rigs can feel especially isolated and lonely on unfamiliar installations where they do not feel part of the crew. The addition of TV sets to cabins, while a welcome amenity, can reduce off duty interaction and one Norwegian OIM successfully improved the social atmosphere on Statoil's *Statfjord* A platform (POB 295) by installing a bar (serving only non-alcoholic drinks).[31] Formal systems for improving social support and counseling, such as Employee Assistance Programs are discussed.

The *management style* and *organizational climate* on an installation can act to enhance or reduce the effects of stress in the offshore environment. A supportive, caring supervisory approach will serve to assist those experiencing personal difficulties. A new guide on occupational stress for employers states,

Problems at work can be triggered or made worse. . . where there is a lack of understanding and leadership from managers and supervisors. This does not mean they have to be easy-going and undemanding. People usually welcome clear direction and will often feel less stress if they can see that the boss at least understands the problems they are under and will do what he or she can.[2]

An open, trusting, good-humored atmosphere on an installation will moderate stressful aspects of the lifestyle. Good communication both on the installation and from the onshore base will facilitate job performance and can help to reduce unnecessary anxieties particularly in times of change.

Effects and Symptoms of Stress

Stress effects appear in different guises, although there is generally a complex package of physical, emotional, cognitive, and behavioral reactions. These may produce different kinds of symptoms and those easiest to detect are changes in behavior patterns. The effects on *physical health* which have been identified include elevated blood pressure, headaches, and digestive problems, contributing to more serious complaints, such as heart disease in the longer term. A direct relationship between stress and physical ailments is difficult to prove, although workers reporting higher levels of stress often report more physical symptoms. These can be difficult to detect due to extensive use of self medication for head pain and digestive upsets, although the presence of an installation medic who can be readily consulted may make these symptoms more apparent than on an onshore work site.

The effects on *mental health* are also recognized and this has been examined for the offshore population where two investigations found that workers who reported experiencing more stress also reported poorer levels of mental health in terms of anxiety and depression.[15,19] Due to limitations in the self report methodology of these studies, this does not necessarily imply a causal relationship, for instance those already suffering from anxiety could find more aspects of their work environment to be stressful.

The question of whether offshore work affects mental health has been examined in two studies which compared the mental well-being of offshore and onshore workers in operating companies. The first was carried out by Shell Expro medical staff who administered a mental health questionnaire to 403 offshore and 393 onshore personnel who were undergoing routine medicals and found that the numbers of offshore staff at risk from depression was 10% and from anxiety was 4%.[8] No significant differences with onshore staff were found. In a subsequent project supported by BP Exploration, Katherine Parkes compared the mental health of 84 offshore and 88 onshore control room operators.[17] There were no significant differences between the onshore and offshore groups in physical symptoms or social dysfunction scores but onshore workers showed significantly lower scores on the anxiety scores. (No comparison with other published norms for this anxiety subscale are reported so it is difficult to determine whether the onshore or offshore group is closer to the population norm.)

The general mental health of the offshore sample was not significantly different from the reported onshore norm data (engineering). While it is apparent that a small number of offshore workers do suffer from mental health problems, there is no strong evidence to suggest that incidence rates are any higher than the general population rate. Thus saying, it must be acknowledged that certain mental health conditions can present serious problems in terms of treatment and safety offshore and those identified with symptoms should be medivaced onshore without delay. Studies in the United Kingdom of causes of medical evacuations from offshore installations show that those of a psychiatric nature are very infrequent; of 1509 evacuations over a two-year period, only 29 (2%) were due to mental conditions.[32]

Stress may also produce changes in *mood* state, such as irritability, worry or withdrawal, these are most likely to be identified as *behavior changes*, such as avoidance of others, ill temper or interpersonal friction in a work group. Other behavior changes may appear as *work related problems*, poor time keeping, carelessness, slow pace of work or difficulty in decision making. The possibility of stress resulting in *accidents* was raised by Sutherland and Cooper, and Rundmo from a recent Norwegian study argues that stress may have an indirect role in accident causation.[14,15] *Sleep* is easily disrupted by stress in the form of difficulty getting to sleep, disturbed sleep, or early waking; the consequent tiredness does nothing to help the individual. Other observable behavior effects are changes in eating patterns, increased cigarette or caffeine consumption. Some effects of stress only may be evident when the individual is onshore, such as *relationship problems* or increased *alcohol consumption.*

Stress Management on Offshore Installations

There is a range of approaches to stress management, in the short term they involve identification and treatment of cases, but for longer term prevention, a *risk assessment and management strategy* is required, in line with the control of other workplace hazards affecting health and safety. The initial stage requires a *stress audit* which charts the sources and effects of stress within the company in general or on a given installation.[33] Specific causes of stress require to be tackled directly which may involve *job redesign, organizational culture change or shifts in management style.* Obviously there are elements of the offshore industry that cannot be altered, such as the location in a remote marine environment with long work rotations, and the *selection procedures* for offshore workers need to ensure that they are prepared for this lifestyle.[34]

In a traditionally *macho* culture, such as the oil industry, armed forces or emergency services, it is sometimes necessary to openly address the issue that stress or mental health problems may be regarded as a weakness which individuals will therefore strive to conceal. This has been tackled in a number of organizations, such as police forces, by instigating a *program of stress awareness* involving promotional materials and short courses which acknowledge that stress is a common problem which most people will experience at some time in their lives. Participants in the training courses and seminars are taught to identify both the causes and effects of stress and are informed of the support systems available within the organization. Also they can be given training in personal stress management techniques, such as relaxation skills or time management.

Dealing with cases of stress can present difficulties for busy managers and supervisors who are rarely trained in counseling. As offshore rig medics are often the first detect or to be told of an employee's problems, then they should be provided with appropriate training in counseling. They are very conscious of their support role and are already involved in physical health promotion campaigns on their installations.[35] Another widely adopted solution within the oil industry has been to introduce *Employee Assistance Programs* (EAP) which were originally designed to deal with alcohol and drug dependence but which now deal with a wide range of personal problems. The employer pays an annual per capita charge to the EAP company, which in return provides confidential counseling services (telephone and face-to-face) on demand for all staff, and sometimes also for their immediate family members.

One such EAP was introduced by Mobil in 1989 and they reported,

There is no doubt that an EAP has much to offer by way of helping people cope with psychological worries at an early stage, usually before they become more deeply ingrained or start leading to mental ill-health. Because of special and unique stress factors it is especially appropriate in the offshore environment.[36]

Shell Canada found that,

Adaptation, flexibility and responsiveness are critical to the success of assistance programs. At the very least, availability of an EAP is increasingly being regarded by the courts in Canada as a requirement, if addressing employee problems such as impairment, safety issues and performance problems.[37]

Chevron and Conoco not only use their EAPs for routine counseling services but also for Critical Incident Debriefing following an emergency.[38]

To summarize, having systems to deal with problems once they are manifested can only be part of the solution and will do nothing for the incidence rate of occupational stress if there are serious stressors present in the organizational environment. Employers must realize that they are responsible for assessing risks to mental health as well as to physical health and that this includes the identification of stressors within the work environment. Systems then should be put in place to either remove the stressor or at least to reduce the risks from exposure to such stressors. Identification of the main sources of stress in the offshore environment can enable offshore managers to determine which of these conditions can be modified in order to reduce the risks to personnel. Some factors cannot be altered such as the remote location and the need to travel by helicopter, but other aspects of the social and work environment can be addressed, such as supervisory style, organizational climate, provision of support through an EAP, facilitating communication links with home, and providing good quality privacy, rest and relaxation facilities on the installation. Ensuring the well-being of your workforce is the basis of effective performance and safety management for offshore operations.

References

1. Cox,T. *Stress Research and Stress Management: Putting Theory to Work.* HSE Contract Report 61/1993. Suffolk: HSE Books, 1993.

2. Health and Safety Executive *Stress at Work. A Guide for Employers.* Suffolk: HSE Books, 1995

3. Kompier, M. & Levi, L. *Stress at Work: Does it Concern You?* Luxembourg: Official Publications of the European Communities, 1994.

4. Quick, J., Murphy, L. & Hurrell, J. (Eds.) *Stress and Well-Being at Work.* Washington: American Psychological Association, 1992.

5. Health and Safety Executive *Mental Health at Work.* Sheffield: HSE Information Centre, 1993.

6. Murphy, L., Hurrell, J., Santer, S. & Kerta, G., (Eds.). *Job Stress Interventions.* Washington: American Psychological Association. 1995.

7. Sutherland, K. & Flin, R. Stress at sea: A review of working conditions in the offshore oil and fishing industries. *Work and Stress,* 3, 3, 1989: 269-285.

8. Gann, M, Corpe, U. & Wilson I. The application of a short anxiety and depression questionnaire to oil industry staff. *Journal of Social and Occupational Medicine, 40,* 1990: 138-142.

9. Earnshaw, J. & Cooper, C. Employee stress litigation: the United Kingdom experience. *Work and Stress, 8, 4,* 1994: 287-295.

10. Clay, R. Job stress claims spin out of control. *American Psychological Association Monitor,* November, 36, 1995.

11. Ersland, S., Weiseath, L. & Sund, A. The stress upon rescuers involved in an oil rig disaster. 'Alexander L. Kielland' 1980. *Acta Psychiatra Scandinavia Supplement 335, 80,* 1989: 38-49.

12. Sunde, A. Psycho-social aspects of offshore work. Paper presented at the Safety and Health in the Offshore Oil and Gas Extractive Industries Conference, Luxembourg, April, 1983.

13. Hellesoy, O. (Ed) *Work Environment Statfjord Field.* Oslo: Universiteforlaget

14. Rundmo, T. (1992) Risk perception and safety on offshore oil platforms. *Safety Science, 15,* 1985: 39-68.

15. Sutherland, V. & Cooper, C. *Man and Accidents Offshore.* London: Lloyds, 1986.

16. Sutherland, V. & Cooper, C. *Stress and Accidents in the Offshore Oil and Gas Industry.* Houston: Gulf, 1991.

17. Parkes, K. Mental health in the offshore oil industry: A comparative study of onshore and offshore employees. *Psychological Medicine, 22,* 1992: 997-1009.

18. Sutherland, K. & Flin, R. Psychosocial aspects of the offshore oil industry. In *Proceedings of the First SPE Conference Health, Safety & Environment in Oil and Gas Exploration and Production.* The Hague, November. Richardson, Texas: Society of Petroleum Engineers. (SPE 23517), 1991.

19. Sutherland, K. Psychosocial factors: An investigation into the offshore oil industry. Unpublished PhD Thesis, The Robert Gordon University, Aberdeen, 1994.

20. Flin, R. & Slaven, G. Managing offshore installations. *Petroleum Review,* 47, 1993: 68-71.

21. Carnegie, D. First line supervisors on offshore oil installations. PhD Thesis. The Robert Gordon University, (in preparatiion).

22. Perez, L. *Working Offshore: A Preliminary Analysis of Social Factors associated with Safety in the Offshore Workplace.* Sea Grant LSUT79001. Louisiana Centre for Wetland Resources, 1979.

23. Clemmer, D. & Mohr, D. Low-back injuries in heavy industry II: Labour market forces. *Spine,* 16, 1991: 831-834.

24. Flin, R. & Sutherland, K. Occupational stress and health in the United Kingdom offshore oil industry. In collected papers of the 9th European Health Psychology Conference, August. Bergen University, Norway, 1995.

25. International Labour Office *Safety and Related Issues Pertaining to Work on Offshore Petroleum Installations.* Geneva: ILO, 1993.

26. Parkes, K. *Human Factors, Shift Work and Alertness in the Offshore Oil Industry.* Report OTH92389 Offshore Safety Division, HSE. London: HMSO, 1993.

27. Clark, D., McCann, K., Morrice, K. & Taylor, R. Work and marriage in the offshore oil industry. *International Journal of Social Economics, 2,* 1995: 36-47.

28. International Labour Office *Workers in Remote Areas. The Petroleum, Mining and Forestry Industries.* Geneva: ILO, 1996.

29. Mearns, K. & Flin, R. Risk perception and attitudes to safety by personnel in the offshore oil and gas industry: a review. *Journal of Loss Prevention in the Process Industries, 8,5,* 1995: 299- 305.

30. Fuchs, R., Cake, G. & Wright, G. *The Steel Island. Rural Resident Participation in the Exploration Phase of the Oil and Gas Industry, Newfoundland and Labrador.* Department of Rural, Agricultural and Northern Development, Government of Newfoundland and Labrador, 1983.

31. Lynghaug, E. Positive power by team management. Paper presented at the Fourth Offshore Installation Management conference. The Robert Gordon University, Aberdeen, April, 1995.

32. Gauld, S. Illness and injury in the offshore workforce. Unpublished M.Phil Thesis, The Robert Gordon University, Aberdeen, 1993.

33. Sutherland, V. & Davidson, M. Using a stress audit: the construction site manager experience in the United Kingdom. *Work and Stress,* 7, 3, 1993: 273-286.

34. Flin, R., Slaven, G. & Whyte, F. Selection for hazardous occupations: Offshore oil installations. In M. Smith & V. Sutherland (Eds.) *International Review of Professional Issues in Selection and Assessment,* Vol. 2. Chichester: John Wiley, 1996.

35. Mearns, K. & Fenn, C. *Diet, Fitness and the Offshore Worker.* Report to OSD/HSE OTH93399. Suffolk: HSE Books, 1994.

36. Cooper, J. Employee assistance programme in the offshore environment. In *Proceedings of the First SPE conference Health, Safety & Environment in Oil and Gas Exploration and Production.* The Hague, November. Richardson, Texas: Society of Petroleum Engineers. (SPE 23214), 1991.

37. Csonokay, W. & Chisholm, D. Employee and organizational assistance programme (EOAP). In *Proceedings of the First SPE conference Health, Safety & Environment in Oil and Gas Exploration and Production.* The Hague, November. Richardson, Texas: Society of Petroleum Engineers. (SPE 23215), 1991.

38. Johnson, R. & Hansen, H. Caring for the human side: Developing a critical incident debriefing response plan in a midsize international oil and gas company. In *Proceedings of the Second SPE conference Health, Safety & Environment in Oil and Gas Exploration and Production.* Jakarta, January. Richardson, Texas: Society of Petroleum Engineers. (SPE 27257), 1994.

Chapter 6

Offshore Shiftwork and Rotation Patterns

Georgina Slaven, Keith Stewart and Rhona Flin

Introduction

Twelve hour shift work schedules and long rotation patterns are a common feature of working on offshore oil and gas installations, and consequently shiftworking problems are a matter of concern for the industry. Researchers have realized for some time that shiftwork can cause a variety of problems for the individual worker including sleeping difficulties and minor health complaints. Also it has been suggested that working at night can result in an impaired capacity for job task performance. This chapter is aimed at the oil industry, but draws upon research which has been carried out in the laboratory and in a number of other industries to explain the background of shift working problems.

After a brief introduction to shiftworking practices in the oil industry a simple introduction is provided to the physiological basis for shiftworking problems. This deals with the role of the internal *body clock* in workers' adjustment to shiftwork regimes and the effects of these working schedules on the quality and duration of sleep. Health problems encountered by shiftworkers also are discussed. The third section of this chapter deals with studies of shiftworking which have been carried out in the oil industry into the effects of work patterns on sleep and health in the offshore workforce. This is followed by a selective review of the effects of time of day on individuals' capacity to perform their work tasks and the possible relationship between shift timing and workplace accidents. To conclude, some practical advice is offered highlighting the possible implications of different shift and rotation patterns for offshore workers based on the results of physiological and psychological research, mainly conducted in the North Sea.

Work Patterns in the Offshore Industry

Twenty-four hour operations are a universal feature of the offshore oil and gas industry and consequently many oil workers are called upon to perform shiftwork. Shift duration is one of the most uniform features of the industry. The majority of personnel worldwide work 12 hours on duty and 12 hours off.[1] Actual hours worked however are often greater, when job type and overtime are taken into account. Some OIMs report working between 14 and 20 hours per day during their fortnight's duty.[2] Other personnel, such as the installation medic and senior supervisors also may be on-call 24 hours a day. Start and finish times vary depending on location and the nature of the operation. Historically, drilling crews work noon to midnight, though personnel on production installations can work any number of shift systems typically from 0600 to 1800 or 0800 to 2000. Certain positions only require personnel on day shift, though most involve both day and night shifts.

A second feature of offshore work patterns, in common with industries in remote work locations, is prolonged periods away from home and family. Rotation patterns (the amount of time spent on and off the installation) vary considerably from company to company and from one country to another. A typical pattern in the United Kingdom sector of the North Sea, is 14 days on, 14 days off and more recently 21/21. In some companies, the practice is 7/7, with a small number using 14/21,[3] though this latter pattern is rapidly being phased out in favor of 14/14 in the United Kingdom. On offshore supply and stand-by boats longer rotations of 28/28 are the norm. In the United States Gulf of Mexico, 7/7 is common, though installations are typically much closer to shore than in the North Sea.

In Norway, the pattern is more complicated since the Working Environment Act specifies that no more than 36 hours per week are permissible in continuous shift work (including offshore). The Federation of Oil Workers (OFS) Tariff Agreement limits the offshore working year to 1,612 hours, working a three phase cycle of 14/14, 14/21, then 14/28. Similar legislation guaranteeing workers' rights to weekly rest periods and annual leave is enshrined in the European Social Charter, though neither the United Kingdom or Italian governments have made it law.[4] In the case of 14-day and longer work patterns, there is commonly a mid-rotation split shift when employees who work on both shifts during their time offshore change from a week on night shift to day shifts or vice versa.[5] The mid-rotation split shift is not used by all companies, some of whom prefer personnel to work all nights or all days for their entire period offshore, including some of those companies operating a 21/21 rotation.

On installations located overseas or in remote and inaccessible regions, staff tend to work longer rotations. The International Labor Organization[1] quotes examples of U.S. nationals working 28/28 on Asian locations, European expatriates in one company in Nigeria working 42/42, while Filipino staff in the same company work three months on, two months off. Whatever the work pattern, part of the offshore worker's field break is taken up by commuting to and from the heliport/airport and the flight to the installation. This can involve a few hours or up to a day for nationally located installations, or considerably longer for installations abroad.

Shift work and the Offshore Environment

The largest offshore installations may have over 300 personnel on board at any one time. Varying levels of comfort are provided by offshore accommodation depending on the size and age of an installation and the location of its permanent living quarters. These might be found either on the installation itself or on an adjacent *flotel*. Cabins usually have two to four berths with either a suite or shared toilet and washing facilities (sometimes shared with up to eight people). Newer installations and those with reduced staff levels sometimes make single cabin occupancy a possibility, though this is usually reserved for supervisory and managerial staff. Personnel tend to be considerate towards night shift workers whose cabins are often located at the ends of corridors to minimize the noise of people passing. It is common practice for cabin sharing to be based on one day and one night shift worker so that when one is working, the other can sleep undisturbed.

One of the unique features of offshore work is the close proximity between accommodation and work areas and because of this, noise and vibration are ever present despite the fact that the permanent living quarters are soundproofed. The sound of heavy utilities equipment and drilling activities contribute to the permanent hum of activity which permeates every area of the installation. It is possible that this interferes with relaxation and sleep, and could be the cause of reduced alertness and intellectual efficiency[6,7] though some evidence suggests a constant modest noise can aid sleep. In addition, a variety of other factors such as regular public address announcements and, where accommodation is on a *flotel*, movement of the installation, might cause of interference for those trying to sleep.

The Physiology of Shiftwork

Environmental disturbances are, however, not the only source of shift-working sleep problems. This next section will show that one of the primary sources of difficulties for workers who have to work at night and sleep during the day is that they are attempting to sleep at an inappropriate time for their own bodies.

The Body Clock

Human kind has evolved as a species which is mainly active during daylight hours. This pattern of living seems to have been strengthened by natural selection for a number of reasons, particularly our inability to see well at night and our lack of protection against low nighttime temperatures. Many of prehistoric man's predators were at an advantage during the hours of darkness owing to their acute nighttime vision and their warm furry coats. In evolutionary terms it was clearly advantageous for people to sleep at night and be active during the warmer, daylight hours when hunting and working could be more efficiently carried out. The reasons for sleep are still not well understood, and while generally it is accepted that one of its functions is to allow the body and mind to carry out *essential maintenance and repair* work, it also may be the case that those early humans who spent the nighttime hours asleep in a shelter were more likely to survive until morning. In view of the above it clearly would have been useful for prehistoric humans to be able to anticipate the changes which occurred in their environment over the course of the day. In very simple terms, this was achieved through what we can call *the body clock*, a biochemical mechanism located in the brain which causes cyclic changes in bodily processes. Physiologists have shown that this mechanism is still very active in modern humans.

The Origins of Shift Work

As the human mind has improved through evolution, our ability to interact with and control our environment has increased. One of the greatest breakthroughs was undoubtedly the discovery that we could create and control fire. Not only did this give us a means to stay warm and to protect ourselves from predators, but also it allowed us to begin to reclaim the hours of darkness by compensating for our inability to see well after sundown. Over the course of thousands of years artificial lighting gradually improved with the invention of technological aids such as the wax candle and the gas lamp, and these developments meant that individuals could carry on with their daytime activities after the fall of darkness. Inevitably, this led to some people working at night.

The comparatively recent development of electric lighting has meant that large scale industrial operations can carry on over the course of the 24-hour day, therefore maximizing returns on capital investment and reducing the need for uneconomic shutdown/start-up periods in continuous process and production line operations. As a result shiftwork, where different individuals take turns to perform the same function for a portion of the 24-hour day, has become commonplace in the industrialized world. Nevertheless, while we have certainly made great strides in overcoming some of our physiological shortcomings by changing the nighttime environment, there remains one factor which we have only have begun to understand and are a still a long way from taming. The body clock, which in prehistory was our ally in the struggle for survival, has for some shiftworkers become a bitter enemy. The reasons for this are discussed in greater detail below.

The Body Clock in Action: Circadian Rhythms

In physiological terms, one of the main manifestations of the internal *body clock* is what are known as *circadian rhythms*. The body's physiological processes are not constant over the course of the day, but are rhythmic and cyclical. The simplest example of this, and one of the most widely demonstrated, is the rhythm in body temperature. The body's temperature is low in the middle of the night and rises gradually over the course of the day to reach a peak in early evening after which it begins to fall again. A similar 24-hour cycle is seen in many other physiological measures, for example the secretion of melatonin, a hormone which helps us to get to sleep, rises gradually during the day and reaches a peak at night. (see Figure 6-1 for a graphic plot of these cycles.) The cyclical nature of these processes is, in part at least, controlled by our internal body clocks. Research suggests that the body clock is comprised of a number of different oscillatory mechanisms, each of which controls a set of different biological rhythms. For the purposes of this paper, however, it is sufficient to assume that all of our physiological rhythms are controlled by a unitary mechanism, the *body clock*. Circadian rhythms are remarkably resistant to sudden changes in routine and, provided a relatively regular sleep/wake cycle is maintained, normally are quite stable.

The Role of Environmental Cues

Circadian rhythms are the result of two factors: the internal body clock and time cues in the environment, both of which are essential to keep us tuned to our 24-hour world. The fact that both of these factors are necessary was demonstrated in a famous experiment in the early 1960s. Researchers asked a group of people to spend two weeks in a room with no clocks and no windows and told them to go to bed and get up whenever they felt like it. They discovered that people continued to go to bed and get up on a regular cycle despite the fact that they had no way of knowing what time it was. The most surprising finding however, was that people tended to follow a 25-hour day. This meant that they would go to bed and get up on average one hour later every day. An individual who would have gone to bed at 2300 on the first day of the study would probably have been going to bed at around 0500 after one week. This finding showed that the body must have some internal way of judging external time, a *body clock* in other words. The odd thing is that it seems to run slow!

As we have seen, most of our body rhythms have a 24-hour cycle. Something, therefore, must be adjusting them to the proper time every day. This is where environmental time cues, or *zeitgebers* (from the German for *time givers*) come into play. A great number of external factors help to keep our circadian rhythms on a 24-hour cycle. For prehistoric man the most important of these cues was probably the cycle of day and night. Today, however, we have far more signals to external time, for example clock time. We also have a very large number of social cues, such as mealtimes, the habitual timing of sleep, the behavior of other people, perhaps even the timing of the news on TV. Usually, we have a good idea of what time it is and our internal body clock is kept in phase with external time cues producing circadian rhythms.

Under normal circumstances our circadian rhythms reach their respective peaks and troughs at the same time each day. This means that they are *in phase* with each other and with the sleep/wake cycle. This helps us to go to sleep at night and wake up again in the morning. In the evening our temperature gradually drops and certain hormones may be secreted in greater volumes in preparation for sleep. During the night while we are still asleep, our temperature gradually begins to rise again several hours before we are due to wake up. In this way the body anticipates changes in our environment and prepares us in advance (see Figure 6-1).

Adjustment of the Body Clock

So far in this chapter we have seen how humankind has evolved a sophisticated system for anticipating the periodic changes which take place in our environment. Since this process was so important to the survival of our prehistoric ancestors, perhaps it is not surprising that it is very resistant to any changes which are forced upon it by a switch in routine such as occurs when a nightshift schedule is taken on. Laboratory and field studies show that over 10 days of uninterrupted night work is required before the body's circadian cycle fully adjusts to a new sleep/waking pattern. Moreover, it has been found that the body quickly reverts to the normal day/night cycle during rest days following night work. The problem of adjustment is dealt with in the following two sections.

Adjustment of the Body Clock—Jet Lag

The simplest example of a situation where the body clock is called upon to adjust to a new regime occurs when we travel by jet airliner and cross the

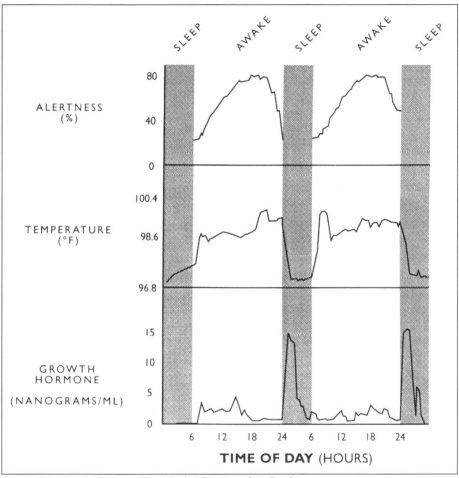

Figure 6-1 Circadian Timing of Physiological Functions Over Two Days

world's time zones. In this case we lay ourselves open to *jet lag syndrome*. For example, if a woman travels to Tokyo on business, she can easily wind her watch forward the necessary ten hours and begin to operate on Japanese time as soon as she reaches the terminal building. The watch immediately tells the correct time. Regrettably for the traveler, she cannot simply wind her body clock forward in this fashion. It takes time to adjust. In this situation, like many other long haul air travelers, she will very probably experience *jet lag*, a phenomenon which is characterized by a general feeling of fatigue and malaise, accompanied by an inability to get to sleep at night.

Jet lag is caused by a desynchronization between the internal body clock and external time. With large time zone shifts, this means that at night the body's systems are functioning as if it were daytime, and during the day they operate as if it were night. For example, when the traveler goes to bed at night, body temperature is far higher than it normally would be at that time and consequently will probably sleep only fitfully. Jet lag passes, but slowly. Research has shown that it takes a week for European travelers to the USA to adjust fully and for their circadian rhythms to be in phase with environmental time. Some offshore staff travel long distances across time zones to reach their installations and the fact that jet lag might affect their performance should be taken into account by permitting appropriate rest days where possible.

Adjustment to Shiftwork

Shiftworkers face a very similar problem to the long distance air traveler. They attempt to work at a time when their body wants to be asleep. For a shiftworker to be comfortable working at night, he or she needs to make a similar adjustment to the one the traveler has to make. Air travelers, however, have a considerable advantage over shiftworkers in that they are attempting to move their circadian rhythms onto a normal pattern of living where external factors such as daylight, clock time and social activity all support the adjustment. Nightshift workers face a situation where most of their activities occur at an abnormal time of day and consequently, as the body clock is attempting to change it gets very little support from the outside world. For example, nightshift personnel start work when it is getting dark and most people are going to bed, and finish work to go home to sleep when most people are getting up to start work. Moreover, in summer, day sleep may be difficult due to high temperatures.

Offshore shift workers undoubtedly have some advantages over their onshore counterparts in that their living and working environment is set up as a 24-hour society. Meals and recreation are designed to fit in around work schedules and provisions are made to ensure that night workers can get adequate sleep when they are not on shift. On the other hand, because of the unique nature of the offshore working environment, the shift rotation systems which workers follow are designed around practicalities such as available bed space and helicopter flights. For this reason, there is not as much flexibility in the design of shift rotation patterns as there is in the majority of onshore businesses, and consequently there is little opportunity to alter the shift system in an attempt to reduce adaptation problems for workers.

The Importance of Sleep

Shiftworkers often complain that their day sleeps between successive night shifts are disturbed. Onshore this is often put down to environmental factors, for example noise from traffic and children, bright light and temperature. It is likely, however, that the main cause of disturbed day sleep is that it occurs at an inappropriate point on the internal body clock, at a time when the body is not prepared for sleep. This is only partially made up for on days off and therefore, over a number of nightshifts, the worker will build up a sleep debt which manifests itself in fatigue. To understand how fatigue is built up, it is necessary to understand what happens when we sleep.

Researchers have recognized for some time that, when the electrical activity of the brain of a sleeping person is recorded using a device known as an electroencephalogram (EEG), several distinguishable stages of sleep can be identified. As a person falls asleep, the waves which are recorded on the EEG gradually reduce in frequency until *deep sleep* is reached. The length of time this process takes depends on the individual concerned, though for the majority of people it requires around half an hour. Four stages of sleep take place on the way to *deep sleep* of which Stage 1 is the earliest and lightest sleep and Stage 4 the last and deepest sleep. The passage of these sleep stages is characterized by a gradual lowering of the heart rate, respiration, and blood pressure of the sleeping person. After around 30 minutes of deep sleep, the process is reversed with higher frequency brain waves being recorded, and pulse and respiration rates increasing. The sleeper, however, does not wake up as this process continues. Instead, a new stage of sleep is entered where EEG recordings resemble those of the waking state. This indicates that the brain is active, however, paradoxically this is the stage of sleep during which a person is hardest to wake.

Another characteristic of this latest stage of sleep is that the eyeballs of the sleeper are seen to move back and forth behind his or her eyelids and for this reason this stage is commonly known as Rapid Eye Movement (REM) sleep, while stages 1-4 are referred to as non-REM sleep (NREM). It is this REM stage of sleep which is most often associated with dreaming. Typically, a person will have four or five REM periods a night, each of which is preceded by a period of NREM sleep. As the night goes on, the periods of REM sleep get longer while the periods of NREM sleep get shorter and are not as deep.

While some debate remains as to the precise function of each stage of sleep, it does seem likely that the REM and NREM periods of sleep serve different purposes. For example, one theory suggests that REM sleep may be related to brain repair, while the slow wave portion of sleep is important for body repair. Nevertheless, the fact remains that among normal human adults the regular pattern of sleep described above is universal and predictable, provided it remains locked onto a normal circadian cycle with sleep at night and activity during the day. No matter what the specific purpose of the different stages of sleep, it does seem important that their ordering and relative pro-portions remain constant. It is also important to maintain the length of time an individual normally sleeps, as research has shown that even one or two hours less sleep can result in increased fatigue and reduced alertness. However, there are considerable individual differences in the amount of sleep required; some people need only six hours, while others may need eight or nine.

The Effects of Shiftwork on Sleep Quality and Quantity

Despite the marked difference in their living and working environments, both onshore and offshore shiftworkers have a common concern which is the quantity and quality of sleep they can get between nightshifts. In general, night workers report a higher incidence of sleep disturbances than other shiftwork-ers. These problems concern falling asleep, disturbed sleep periods and spon-taneous early awakenings. There is evidence to suggest that when they are working nights, shiftworkers may obtain up to 25% less sleep during their main sleep period than they do when they are working during the day. For example, one study found that night shiftworkers spent an average of one hour less per day sleeping than day shift workers.[8] Another study presented surprising evi-dence which seems to suggest that when on nights, workers actually sleep more in total than they do when they are on days owing to a tendency to take long naps outside their main period of sleep.[9] These long naps are assumed to be an attempt to compensate for the relatively poor quality of sleep which work-ers get when they try to sleep during the day, since this is an inappropriate time for sleeping in terms of the phase of the internal *body clock*.

So what actually happens when we attempt to sleep during the day? The first thing to say about day sleep is that it appears to be lighter than night sleep. The earlier, high frequency, stages of NREM sleep tend to last longer than at night and there is a reduction in the important deep, slow wave, sleep of stages 3 and 4. Day sleep therefore seems to be lighter and more fragile than night sleep. As a proportion of sleep, the amount of REM does not seem to be affect-ed that much when the main sleep period is during the day, although in absolute terms there is certainly some loss. Its distribution throughout the sleep period dramatically changes as well, and rather than increasing in duration as sleep progresses, REM is seen to reduce as the time for waking approaches.

There is evidence that when the sleep schedule is returned to a normal pattern, losses of slow wave sleep are compensated for but that REM sleep can-not be caught up in the same way.[10] Thus it seems that over a long period of night shifts, a cumulative sleep debt will build up. Extensive research has found that under normal circumstances the first five hours of sleep are absolutely essential for sleep restitution.[11] It seems that as the organization of the stages of sleep is disrupted, the quality of sleep is also degraded. Thus, attempting to move onto a night working schedule causes individuals to lose sleep because of a lack of harmony between the timing of work and the body's underlying circadian clock.

Health Implications of Shiftwork

There is evidence to suggest that there are important health implications for staff who work 12-hour shifts over a prolonged period of time as is the case for the majority of offshore workers. These effects, however, are not entirely clear cut since most of the research in this area has focused on onshore, three-phase, 8-hour shift patterns, with only three, five or seven days of continuous working. Fatigue, sleep disturbance and social hardships are major short term problems which can be caused by an inability to adapt to working unusual hours.

Perhaps more worrisome, it seems quite possible that, over a period of time those individuals who suffer from coping difficulties will become prone to physical illness. Cardiovascular, psychiatric, chronic fatigue and gastrointestinal problems all have been linked, with varying degrees of certainty, to long term shiftworking. Indeed it has been said that for those failing to cope, "shift-work is probably bad for the heart, almost certainly bad for the head, and definitely bad for the gut."[12] For example, recent research at a British nuclear power plant[13] shows that shift work and particularly night work may be a risk factor associated with physiological, psychological, and social disturbance. In this particular study, night shift workers suffered the most sleep disturbance compared with day and evening shift workers, though some workers preferred the night shift. It appeared that ability to adjust to a different sleep pattern was associated with a greater tolerance to shift work.

Studies Of Shiftworking Offshore

A significant amount of research on the effects of shift work has been conducted onshore, though generalizing the effects of these studies to the unique environment which workers encounter in the offshore oil and gas industry is problematic. Some researchers have, however, chosen to focus on the effects of shiftworking offshore, and their studies have provided a valuable insight into the impact that this pattern of working can have on workers' sleep and health.

Workers' Sleep Quality and Duration in the Onshore and Offshore Sectors of the United Kingdom Oil Industry

The only comparative study of on and offshore shift work in the United Kingdom sector of the North Sea to date, focused on control room operators.[14] Drawing on a sample composed of 84 offshore and 88 onshore control room operators, the researcher found some interesting patterns in the duration and subjective quality of sleep in the two groups. Both groups reported that their sleep was of a longer duration and of a higher quality during their off shift leave periods than during either the day or the night shift periods at work. The sleep duration of the onshore group, the majority of whom worked fast rotation shifts (i.e. no more than two or three successive night shifts) was consistent with the results of most previous studies in this area with workers reporting that they obtained more sleep when on days than on nights.

For the offshore group however, all of whom were working one week of nights followed by one week of days, no difference was found between sleep duration when working on the day or night shifts. Additionally, for the offshore group, subjective sleep quality was higher on the night shift than on the day shift, the opposite pattern to that found for onshore workers who rated the quality of their day shift sleep as being higher than that attained on the night shift. The researcher concluded that "the sleep pattern of offshore workers is different from the normal pattern of day/night shift sleep hours for onshore workers, and suggests that the *round-the-clock* environment which operates offshore may facilitate adaptation to night work."[14] It is important to note, however, that a significantly larger proportion of the offshore group in this study reported sleep problems when compared with the onshore group. This might be accounted for by the inevitable noise and vibration caused by 24-hour operations.

The study also found higher levels of anxiety and lower levels of shift pattern satisfaction in the offshore population compared with onshore workers. The researcher concluded that, in some cases, shift dissatisfaction, anxiety and sleep problems may become a vicious circle such that "inability to sleep, or disturbed sleep may give rise to particular anxiety and frustration among individuals prone to impatience and irritation, and this irritation may itself serve to make sleep more difficult."[14] It seems one cannot conclude that working night shifts offshore necessarily results in sleep problems. Rather, it may be the case that neuroticism and anxiety act in conjunction with shift work to trigger these difficulties.

These findings seem to offer support for the proposition that offshore workers have some advantages over their onshore counterparts in terms of their working environment. As was discussed earlier, the offshore environment is set up as a 24-hour society. Because of this it seems to provide more *zeitgebers* (time cues) to facilitate adaptation to night work. For example auditory and social cues such as equipment noise and people moving about are similar at all times of the day. Also, the canteen provides meals for both shifts and leisure facilities are available 24 hours a day. Equally important is the fact that offshore workers are less likely than their onshore counterparts to have their sleep disturbed. Permanent living quarters are artificially lit and rarely have windows in cabins so avoiding bright light is less of a problem than onshore. Moreover, the air conditioning systems which are common in offshore accommodation blocks ensure that high or low day time temperatures do not make it difficult to sleep. In terms of social factors, it seems that offshore workers have an advantage in that they do not have to adjust to their family being on a normal daily routine or cope with the kinds of social and domestic responsibilities which can often impinge on day-time sleep.

Sleep and Psychosomatic Problems in the Norwegian Offshore Oil Industry

The apparent advantage offered by the offshore environment for adaptation to shiftwork was not reported in the findings of a study conducted in the Norwegian sector of the North Sea.[6] In 1989, Phillips Petroleum commissioned Rogaland Research Institute to investigate the extent of sleep and psychosomatic problems (i.e. problems which have both psychological (mental) and somatic (bodily) components) in offshore workers in the Ekofisk field. From a large sample of 1,730 they found that night shift workers (working midnight to midday) suffered the most sleep problems. Also those working continuous night shift reported the most psychosomatic complaints such as stomach trouble and headaches. The midnight to midday rotating shift (i.e. with a mid-rotation rollover from midday to midnight) caused the most difficulties. The individuals working this shift pattern, who experienced problems switching their circadian rhythms onto a night working schedule when first going offshore, found that, just as they were beginning to adapt, working hours changed to midday to midnight and new readjustment problems arose. The researchers concluded that neither of these shift patterns (continuous or rotating midnight to midday shifts) could be recommended from a sleep or health viewpoint.

The Effects of Shiftworking on Cardiovascular Functioning in Russian Offshore Oil Workers

An interesting study conducted in Russia examined the cardiovascular functioning (measured by heart rate, ECG indicators, arteriole blood pressure, stroke volume and cardiac output) of drilling crews on mobile drilling units in

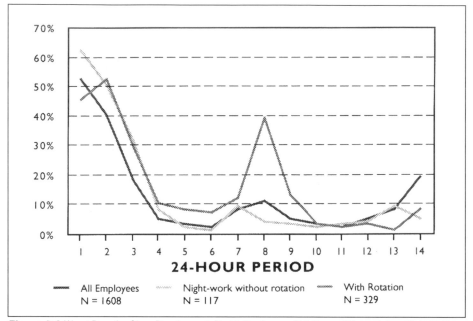

Figure 6-2 Worst Days for Sleep Requirement, By All Employees, Rotating and Non-rotating Night Shifts
Reproduced with kind permission of Phillips Petroleum Company Norway

the Caspian Sea.[15] Crews worked either 7-or 15-day schedules on day and night shifts. The study focused on the effects of rotation patterns rather than type of shift. They found substantial changes in cardiovascular functioning suggesting the onset of over strain from day 9 for those working a 15-day schedule. As a result, they recommended a maximum 7-day schedule, which reportedly received wholehearted support from the drilling crews. It is unlikely that such a recommendation would be embraced worldwide, and certainly not in the United Kingdom offshore sector, where cost-cutting initiatives such as CRINE are now favoring a move to three week schedules to reduce the number of crews required and helicopter flights.[16]

Evidence from the research reviewed highlights the difficulties of being able to attribute health problems to shift working per se. The relationship between shiftwork and health is complex. Gastrointestinal and cardiovascular problems have been linked, with varying degrees of certainty, to shiftwork. In terms of psychosomatic complaints and sleep, individual differences such as age, general health, and personality attributes can interact with shiftwork to cause detrimental effects such as poor sleep duration and quality leading to chronic fatigue.

It is also important to note that it is common practice for potential off-shore workers to undergo medical examinations before assignment offshore, and various guidelines exist regarding the minimal health and fitness criteria for offshore workers (see chapter 3). It is likely that workers who suffer health problems as a result of working shifts offshore will be screened out of offshore work. The ILO states that a report from company doctors of Elf Aquitaine Norway and Phillips Petroleum Company Norway found that only 1 out of every 20 offshore workers continued to work offshore until pension age.[1] Many of the others had left as they had lost their health certificates. It is also likely that those workers who could not adapt to working shifts or long rotations self-selected themselves out of working offshore.

Shiftwork, Job Performance and Accidents

Research findings have provided evidence that the capacity of workers for safe, productive output is impaired at night. Of course this is not always apparent since despite the reduction in performance capacity, normal work-load levels are such that they are still within that capacity. The danger lies in periods of high workload which may be necessitated by an emergency or even a tight working schedule. Two important underlying causes for this reduction in night shift performance capacity seem to exist. These are fatigue and circadian performance rhythms.

Fatigue

Over the course of a period of night shifts a sleep debt is built up by the worker which, as mentioned previously, seems to be a result of the poor quality of day sleep. The major effect of this accumulation of sleep debt is fatigue which is manifested in sleepiness, irritability, and a reduction in the ability to concentrate.

Circadian Performance Rhythms

Psychologists have realized for some time that, even when fatigue is taken into account, a large number of tasks are not performed as well at night as they are during the day. In the early hours of the morning, both body temperature and alertness are at their lowest ebb. At the same time of day resistance to falling asleep and many performance capabilities are at their lowest. Accuracy and speed of simple repetitive and vigilance tasks mirror the daily rise and fall of body temperature.

Worker performance varies not only with the time of day, but also interacts with work schedules to produce different performance levels. We seem to be better at performing the majority of tasks during the periods of our circadian cycle which are associated with wakefulness and activity. In much the same way that our body rhythms take time to adjust to a new working schedule, our performance rhythms must also adjust. As a consequence, at least for the first few days of a night shift schedule, workers are likely to be operating at a time of day when they are not capable of their optimum performance.

Neither of these relationships is entirely clear cut and it is likely that there is a substantial interaction between the two factors which means that as fatigue increases as a result of a growing sleep debt, decrements due to circadian performance rhythms will be exacerbated, though some argue that sleep debt and adjustment of circadian rhythms cancel each other out after prolonged shiftwork.

Research into the Effects of Time of Day on Performance

Night work has been associated with decrements in work performance in terms of speed and accuracy.[17] In the study of nuclear power plant workers discussed earlier, it was found that subjective alertness decreased dramatically for night shift workers.[13] A long-term study of control room operators working 12-hour shifts found performance and alertness decrements initially identified in a 7-month follow-up study had persisted following more than three years exposure to shiftwork.[18]

The rhythms of tasks involving high memory load, however, do not appear to follow the same pattern as the majority of tasks where a day time advantage is common. Complex tasks requiring a high memory load deteriorate over the waking day, with the lowest performance levels in early evening. Two studies examined the effect of time of training presentation on recall of information in night nurses.[19,20] Results showed that immediate recall of training information was superior following a 4 a.m. presentation compared to an 8:30 p.m. presentation, though this effect only held for those who had not adjusted to night work.

Similar findings emerged from a study of chemical plant process controllers (a job with a high memory load) which found that fewest errors occurred on night shift, a finding not attributable to a lower workload on the night shift.[21] Personnel worked a rapidly rotating shift pattern, with the result that they appeared not to adjust their circadian rhythm but remained diurnal (daytime adjusted). It seems that for tasks involving a high memory load, personnel might perform better on a rapidly rotating shift pattern to prevent circadian adjustment; whereas, for simple monitoring and low memory load tasks longer shift rotations which facilitate circadian adjustment enable better performance levels.

A recent review of shift work studies for the European Foundation for the Improvement of Living and Working Conditions identified eight studies which found a higher incidence of accidents on the night shift, and three of those studies also found a greater severity of accidents at night.[22] However, the authors caution that accident rates and severity very much depend on the nature of the work at night, the style of working behavior (tends to be more relaxed at night and more risky jobs can sometimes be left over until the day shift), and the lack of a night shift medic which may result in the non-reporting of minor accidents and injuries. Research conducted at the NASA Ames Research Center has also highlighted the deleterious effects of night work for aircrew.[23] Pilots were more fatigued, were subject to negative emotions and had slower reaction times during night flights. They also found that "sleep does occur on the flight deck, despite federal regulations forbidding in-flight rest."[23] On the basis of their findings a USA industry/government working group have drafted guidelines for controlled aircrew rest in-flight. Similar decrements in pilot error were also found during the extended flight operations for Desert Storm.[24]

An analysis of Norwegian drilling injuries found a significant increase in injury rates on crew change over days (i.e. changing from day to night shift or vice versa).[25] They also found significantly more injuries to the drill crew between midnight and 6 a.m. compared with 6 p.m. to midnight, concluding that "sleepiness and biological rhythms do affect the drill crew during the night period."[25] Drilling is very physically demanding work and may therefore be more susceptible to the effects of circadian rhythms and the cumulative effects of fatigue.

Also it has been suggested that the length of time a worker has been on shift might have an effect on his or her performance. Subjects in a twelve hour simulated drilling control room study did not differ significantly in reaction times and corrective action when presented with a simulated *kick* before, at the start, or at the end of the simulated shift. All of the subjects exhibited behavioral strategies designed to cope with the boredom of long shifts. The researchers suggest that these behaviors must occur offshore and could have implications for safe operating procedures.[26]

Another line of evidence for performance decrements at night comes from the fact that many of the major industrial accidents involving human error have occurred at night. For example, the Three Mile Island incident occurred at 0400, Chernobyl at 0123, Bhopal at just after midnight, and the Rhine chemical spillage in the early hours of the morning. It is likely that offshore emergency response (see chapter 8) will also be affected by the time of day, since at night there are fewer workers on duty and personnel will need to be awakened to take appropriate action. Weekly exercises should periodically reflect this type of scenario.

Designing Better Shift Systems

The impact of rotation and shift work patterns on offshore workers is difficult to determine, and the various factors which detrimentally can affect performance cannot easily be disentangled. Therefore making any recommendations concerning what are the best and worst shift and rotation systems is very difficult to achieve with any rigor. The only way to be sure of raising night time safety and performance to day time levels is to have shiftworkers' bodies totally adjusted to a night work routine. The only way to achieve this, however, is to create a *nocturnal sub-society* which not only always works at night, but also remains on a nocturnal routine on rest days. This clearly would be highly undesirable owing to the effects it would have on a worker's quality of life and in any case would be impossible to enforce. Owing to the constraints of the offshore work environment, there is little room for complex shift designs. Bed space, helicopter flights, and the continuous work process make simple shift patterns a necessity. Some factors associated with work systems in general which are likely to cause shift work coping problems include

- First shift starting times earlier than 7 a.m.[6]
- Rotating hours that change mid-trip[14,6]
- 12-hour shifts involving critical monitoring tasks[8]
- 12-hour shifts involving a heavy physical workload[8]
- 12-hour shifts with exposure to harmful agents and substances[8]

All of the above are invariably present in the offshore work environment. Suggestions for improving shift work and rotation patterns offshore were made by the various researchers whose work has formed the basis for this chapter. They include

- avoid using rotating shifts
- change shift hours to 0700-1900/1900-0700
- protect sleep conditions for night shift workers

A preventive measure suggested by United Kingdom researchers is to include measures predicting an individual's tolerance for shift work within the selection procedure for jobs involving night work.[13] Individual factors likely to cause shift work coping problems include[8,27]

- being over 50 years of age
- being a *morning type* individual

- a history of sleep disorders
- being a neurotic introvert
- a history of gastrointestinal complaints
- high blood pressure

Many of these factors are routinely checked in medical examinations for offshore work, and incorporating the others should not be problematic or onerous. In addition various measures exist to identify one's ability to cope with shift work though there is limited evidence to support their validity.[27,28,29] However, a study of offshore workers health noted that the financial and time-off incentives to work offshore may result in workers denying any ill-health effects, as "The strong incentives may force them to deny this maladaptation to themselves and others. The resultant ill health may also be denied for fear of losing their livelihood."[30]

Consideration should also be given to the differential effects of night work on various job functions. Work which involves a heavy memory load may be performed better on a rotating schedule, while simple monitoring and vigilance tasks are more suited to longer rotations which facilitate circadian adjustment.

Examples of good practice in dealing with the effects of shift work where it is an unavoidable work practice include some German companies who offer health cures to shift workers as they recognize that night work is a risk factor for health. At Daimler-Benz AG, employees working shifts have a right to retire with full benefits two years earlier than usual.[1]

While 12-hour shifts and long rotations are unavoidable offshore, educational programs may help workers to alleviate some of the problems involved in adjusting to night work. Information about sleep, diet and health may help to limit the adverse effects of night work.[8] Preliminary research on the effectiveness of such an education program covering napping strategies and eating habits for offshore wireline and testing staff showed encouraging results, though longer term measures are required to demonstrate its effectiveness.[31]

While it is unlikely that all of the above suggestions can be incorporated into work practices and employee benefit schemes, companies would be wise to reexamine their shift and rotation arrangements to determine whether they have the best possible pattern in place within the constraints of their own particular operating procedures.

Further Reading
For slightly more detailed, but highly readable accounts of the effects of circadian rhythms and shiftwork see either of these publications.

European Foundation for the Improvement of Living and Working Conditions.
Bulletin of European Studies on Time, Number 3: Guidelines for Shift Workers. Dublin:
EFILWC, 1991.

Monk, T. & Folkard, S. *Making Shiftwork Tolerable*. London: Taylor & Francis, 1992.

References
1.   International Labour Organisation *Safety and Related Issues Pertaining to Work on
     Offshore Petroleum Installations*. TMOPI. Geneva: International Labour Office,
     1993.

2.   Flin, R.H. & Slaven, G.M. *Managing Offshore Installations: A survey of OIMs*.
     Offshore Research Report. Aberdeen: The Robert Gordon University, 1991.

3.   Sutherland, V. & Cooper, C. *Stress and Accidents in the Offshore Oil and Gas Industry*.
     Houston: Gulf, 1991.

4.   Earnshaw, L. Accepting the unacceptable. *New Law Journal*, 17 July 1992: 1011-
     1012.

5.   Shrimpton, M. *Rotational Work Systems: Community and Regional Development
     Implications*. Newfoundland: Institute of Social and Economic Research, 1994.

6.   Lauridsen, O., Tronsmoen, S., Berland, J., Gitlesen, J., Ringstad, A., Pedersen, T.,
     Eriksson, L & Nome, T. *Shiftwork and Health*. Report to Phillips Petroleum
     Company Norway. Stavanger: Rogaland Research Institute, 1991.

7.   Cox, R.A.F. *Safety and Health in the Oil and Gas Extractive Industries: Proceedings of an
     International Symposium*. London: Graham and Trotman, 1983.

8.   Tepas, D. & Monk, T. H. Work schedules. In G. Salvendy (Ed) *Handbook of Human
     Factors*. New York: Wiley, 1985: 819-843.

9.   Tilley, A.J., Wilkinson, R. T., Warren, P. S. G., Watson, B. and Drud, M. The sleep
     and performance of shiftworkers. *Human Factors*, 24, 1982: 629-641.

10. Akerstedt, T. Adjustment of physiological circadian rhythms and the sleep-wake
     cycle. In S. Folkard and T. H. Monk (eds) *Hours of Work - Temporal Factors in Work
     Scheduling*. New York: John Wiley & Sons, 1985.

11. Campbell, S. Effects of sleep and circadian rhythms on performance. In
     Handbook of Human Performance, Vol. 3, 1992: 195-216.

12. Monk, T. & Folkard, S. *Making Shiftwork Tolerable*. London: Taylor & Francis, 1992.

13. Smith, L. & Folkard, S. The impact of shiftwork on personnel at a nuclear power
     plant: an exploratory survey study. *Work and Stress*, 7, 1993: 341-350.

14. Parkes, K. R. *Human Factors, Shift Work and Alertness in the Offshore Oil Industry*.
     London: HMSO, 1993.

15. Alekperov, I., Melkumyan, A.N. & Zamchalov, A.I. Some peculiarities of the physi-
     ological validity of shift work schedules for the crews of floating oil drilling plat-
     forms. *Journal of Hygiene, Epidemiology, Microbiology and Immunology, 32*, 1988: 385-
     390.

16. Institute of Petroleum *CRINE: Cost Reduction in the New Era*. London: United
     KingdomOffshore Operators Associations and the Institute of Petroleum, 1994.

17. Monk, T.H. Shiftworker performance. In *Occupational Medicine: State of the Art Reviews, 5*, 1990: 183-199.

18. Rosa, R. R. Performance, alertness and sleep after 3.5 years of 12h shifts: a follow up study. *Work and Stress, 5*, 1991: 107-116.

19. Monk, T.H. & Folkard, S. Concealed inefficiency of late-night study. *Nature, 273*, 1978: 296-297.

20. Folkard, S. & Monk, T.H. Shiftwork and performance. *Human Factors, 21*, 1979: 483-492.

21. Monk, T.H. & Embrey, D.E. A field study of circadian rhythms in actual and inter-polated task performance. In A. Reinberg, N. Vieux and P. Andlauer (eds) *Night and Shift Work: Biological and Social Aspects.* Oxford: Pergamon Press, 1981.

22. European Foundation for the Improvement of Living and Working Conditions *Bulletin of European Studies on Time: Statistics and News.* Dublin: EFILWC, 1993.

23. Rosekind, M. R., Gander, P. H., Miller, D. L. Gregory, K. B., Smith, R. M., Weldon, K. J., Co, E. L., McNally, K. L. & Lebacqz, J. V. Fatigue in operational settings: Examples from the aviation environment. *Human Factors, 36*, 1994: 327-338.

24. Neville, K. J., Bisson, R. U., French J., Boll, P. A. & Storm, W. F. (1994) Subjective fatigue of C-141 aircrews during Operation Desert Storm. *Human Factors, 36*, 1994: 339-349.

25. Lauridsen, O. & Tonnesen, T. Injuries related to the aspects of shiftworking - a comparison of different offshore shift arrangements. *Journal of Occupational Accidents, 12*, 1990: 167-176.

26. Løvås, F. L. & MacCulloch, S. *The drillers function and his tools - an integrated safety problem.* (Working paper no: SOT-A-24/87). Stavanger, Norway: Rogalandsforskning, 1987.

27. Scott, A.J. & Ladou, J. Shiftwork: effects on sleep and health with recommendations for medical surveillance and screening. *Occupational Medicine: State of the Art Reviews, 5*, 1990: 273-299.

28. Lavie, P. Chillag, N. Epstein, R. Tzischinsky, O., Givon, R., Fuchs, S. and Shahal, B. Sleep disturbances in shift-workers: a marker for maladaptation syndrome. *Work & Stress, 3*, 1989: 33-40.

29. Moore-Ede, M.C. & Richardson, G.S. Medical implications of shift-work. *Annual Review of Medicine, 36*, 1985: 607-617.

30. McPherson, G. *An Investigation into the Effects of Shiftwork in Offshore Workers.* Diploma in Occupational Health Nursing. Aberdeen: The Robert Gordon University, 1992.

31. Wertz, R., Bartz, S., Sirios, E.G. & Stampi, C. Preliminary study on alertness in wireline and testing operations. Paper in Proceedings of the Second International Conference on Safety, Health & Environment in Oil & Gas Exploration & Production, Jakarta, January. Texas: Society of Petroleum Engineers, 1994.

Chapter 7

Motivation
Jackie Burnett and Robin Tait

Introduction

It is widely believed, as Kurt Lewin (1938) and others have stated that motivation interacts with ability to predict effective performance. Thus managers have the choice of promoting employee performance through enhancing ability or motivation. Enhancing ability can be achieved through improved selection practices and well-designed training experiences, but both can be slow and costly and are not under the control of individual supervisors. An understanding of human motivation in the workplace, therefore, would seem to hold great potential as an avenue through which managers can enhance subordinates' performance.[1]

As the above quote suggests, managers have an important role to play in motivating their subordinates to perform well. The term *motivation* originates from the Latin *movere* which means to move and is commonly defined as that which "energizes, directs and sustains human behavior in the workplace."[2] Management guru Charles Handy likens motivation to the 'E' factors: energy, emotion, effort, enthusiasm and excitement in achieving desired results and expenditure (of time, money etc.).[3] Defined in these terms, motivation is a topic which tends to fascinate most managers who usually want to know "what will make my staff work the way I want, at the level I want, when I want it?"! In the offshore working environment, motivation has become a pertinent issue for managers as various initiatives such as the Cost Reduction Initiative in the New Era (CRINE) have led to an increased drive for higher levels of performance.[4]

This chapter will begin with a consideration of the three sets of factors which should be taken into account when explaining the motivation process in work settings.[5] The first relates to individual needs, the second relates to characteristics of the job and the third relates to characteristics of the work environment. These factors interact with one another as shown in Figure7-1. The chapter will then go on to consider key issues for managers when implementing employee involvement as a motivational strategy to increase productivity. It will conclude with practical guidelines on how to achieve higher levels of motivation among offshore staff.

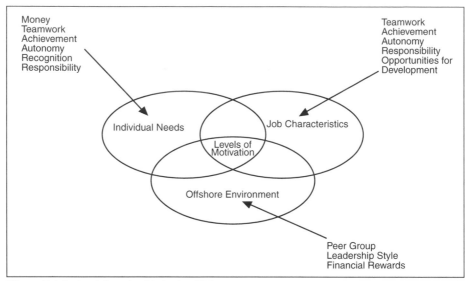

Figure 7-1 Factors Influencing Motivation Offshore

The Individual

The first step in managing the motivation process is for offshore managers to understand what motivates their individual members of staff (i.e. what needs do their staff want to satisfy at work?). Drawing upon research undertaken in the offshore oil and gas industry, this section will begin by identifying what motivates people to choose a job offshore and then go on to examine the more pertinent question of what motivates them to work hard when they get offshore.

Why Work Offshore?

So what has attracted people to offshore employment? A report by the International Labor Office suggests:

> Like other work in remote locations, jobs on offshore installations entail prolonged absences from home with the problems such a way of life involves, in addition to the difficulties intrinsic in an offshore environment. The compensating factors that have attracted people to this work have traditionally been relatively good pay and a rotation pattern providing a lot of time off.[6]

Other research studies have also emphasized extrinsic motivators. For example, Jackie Burnett examined the motives for originally choosing to work offshore among a random sample of 40 offshore workers from a production platform in the United Kingdom sector of the North Sea. The financial package, lack of employment opportunities onshore, and the relatively long periods of leave to spend with the family were the most frequently mentioned reasons for originally working offshore. In this study, only four respondents mentioned the challenge and enjoyable nature of the work offshore as a key factor. Similarly, 22 personnel specialists from operating companies, drilling contractors, diving and service companies were asked to identify the motivating factors they believed attracted prospective candidates to offshore employment. '*Time off work, onshore,*' '*financial remuneration,*' '*benefits package,*' and '*ability to live where they want,*' were their typical responses.[8]

The pull of extrinsic motivators can create a paradoxical situation for many offshore employees where the value of their jobs is not the work itself but rather release from it. As one commented, "the only problem with this job is the two weeks offshore."[9] Preferences for working offshore or onshore were assessed in a group of 84 production control room operators.[10] Only a third of respondents expressed a definite preference for offshore work, 18% were neutral, while 49% indicated that they would prefer to work onshore but were constrained by the lack of employment opportunities and pay rates.

It has been the accepted tradition among Norwegian offshore workers that the intrinsic values of the job (e.g. creativity, self-reliance, individual responsibility) have to be sacrificed in favor of external rewards such as money and leisure time at home.[11] To what extent this sacrifice is acknowledged by, and applies to, offshore workers in other oil producing areas is yet to be fully investigated.

Individuals may be attracted to a particular industry for a variety of reasons but in the longer term, they may self-select out, as only those individuals suited to the work environment remain.[12] This may be particularly applicable to an unusual work environment such as oil exploration and production. An early British offshore research study found evidence that roughnecks and roustabouts who worked offshore for mainly financial reasons (e.g. because they were unemployed) were most likely to leave due to a dislike of shift work and difficulties with home life, while those who were intrinsically attracted to the job itself tended to stay and perform well.[13]

What Motivates Workers Offshore?

What motivates employees to work hard when they get offshore? Is money still the most effective motivator? Several studies involving employees onshore show that money does get people to the workplace, but will not necessarily get them to work harder.[14] Other factors such as having an interesting and enjoyable job, a feeling of accomplishing something worthwhile, recognition for good work, advancement and promotion, participation in decision making, increased responsibility, challenge and personal growth, freedom to plan and organize work are more important motivators. To what extent are these factors as important to the offshore workforce?

In the same study by Burnett mentioned earlier, 40 offshore workers (19 were the oil operating company's own, directly employed staff and 21 were contractors from a number of specialist companies) were asked "What makes you perform better/work harder on the job?"[7] The results showed that the top three motivators were, working in a close-knit team, having challenges and problems to solve, and financial incentives (see Table 7-1). Interestingly, team work as a motivator was more frequently mentioned by operator staff while contractors tended to stress the importance of financial incentives. This finding may relate to differences in perceived job security between the two groups; however, this area requires further research.

One of the factors that may inhibit the creation of close-knit teams offshore are different work rotation patterns. Some installations have rotations where certain categories of personnel, for example, contractors work two weeks on/two weeks off, whereas most directly employed staff work two weeks on/three weeks off. In addition, offshore managers may work two weeks on/three weeks off and one week onshore in the office. This makes it more difficult for offshore supervisors and managers to motivate offshore employees by creating close knit teams as the individuals within their work teams may be changing constantly.

Table 7-1: Offshore Motivators and Demotivators

Motivators	%	Demotivators	%
Team work	33	Lack of confidence in management	30
Challenges/problems to solve	33	Fatigue	20
Financial incentives	18	Unfair treatment by operator staff	13
Feelings of achievement	18	Job insecurity	13
Support and guidance from manager	18	Nothing has a demotivating effect	8
Freedom to plan and organize work	10	Routine/boring work	8
Opportunities for advancement	8	Rate of pay	5
Complete whole piece of work	8	Problems at home	5
Recognition for achievements	5		

Source: Burnett, 1994: 14-15

Burnett's study also emphasized the important role of managers in motivating their staff to perform well. In fact, the relationship between employees and management can be a motivator or demotivator. When offshore workers were asked, "What makes you reduce your effort on the job?" — a lack of confidence in management (i.e. low commitment to staff, lack of clear direction, perceived hidden agenda and poor communication) appeared top of the list (see Table 7-1). Once again a difference emerged between operator and contractor staff. The 8% of workers who mentioned, "nothing has a demotivating effect," were all contractors, with one explicitly stating "I can't reduce my effort; I would be replaced". Similarly, a quarter of the contractors mentioned the unfair treatment they received from operator staff (e.g. delaying tactics, not listening to ideas or suggestions) as a demotivating influence. It should be mentioned that this study examined motivation across a small, heterogeneous group of offshore workers in terms of age, work experience, and job role.[7]

To summarize, in order to directly influence the motivation level of individual staff, it is important that offshore managers and supervisors identify the personal goals of their subordinates. Different people are motivated in different ways. Offshore managers and supervisors need to recognize these differences if they are to understand and influence the motivation of their staff. An individual's personality and circumstances (e.g. level of education, age, previous work history, family circumstances, cultural background) can have a significant influence on what motivates him/her in the workplace. Once the individual's needs have been identified, the manager can then respond appropriately to them. For example, an employee with a strong desire for personal development should be given opportunities to use his or her abilities to acquire new skills; whereas, an employee with strong needs for recognition will respond well to constructive feedback and praise. Also it should be noted that individual motives are likely to change over time as personal circumstances change and that a variety of different needs can be present at the same time.

The Job

The second set of factors which impact on the motivation of individuals are those concerned with intrinsic rewards, that is job characteristics such as responsibility, variety, autonomy, opportunities for growth and development, and achievement. This section will review the research findings undertaken offshore examining the degree of intrinsic rewards in offshore work.

Offshore work has traditionally been seen as lacking in intrinsic rewards due to the strict adherence to regulations and fixed procedures to ensure the integrity of the installation.[10] Indeed, as stated by one Norwegian researcher[9]: "with certain exceptions, much offshore work is experienced as dull and boring, with little scope for learning, variation or self-determination."[9] She asserted that the lack of meaningful activity together with the perceived lack of control experienced when working offshore results in a *passivity syndrome*. This refers to a collection of behaviors such as passivity (i.e. waiting for instructions before acting, not offering opinions), personal withdrawal and disinterest which has serious implications for safety and quality of work performance offshore.

Perceptions of job characteristics offshore can be gained by examining the perceptions of stressors (factors that cause stress) in research undertaken by Valerie Sutherland and Cary Cooper and Karen Sutherland during the 1980s.[15-17] The top ten sources of stress, in order of highest ratings from V. Sutherland and Cooper's study of 310 operators and contractors are shown in Table 7-2.[16] The routine nature of the job was found to be the highest stressor (for a more detailed discussion on the topic of stress see chapter 5).

Table 7-2: Top 10 Stressors Offshore

Routine nature of my job
Lack of offshore insight by onshore management
Feeling trapped into offshore work because no suitable onshore work is available
Dissatisfactions with onshore management
Helicopter landing/taking off in poor weather
Increase in the number of mechanical failures in helicopters flying to rig
Flying in poor weather
Lack of job security
Lack of union recognition
Unpleasant work conditions due to noise

Source: V. Sutherland and Cooper, 1991: 58.

Research relating to measures of job satisfaction provides further insight into the characteristics of offshore jobs. Sutherland found contractor staff were significantly less satisfied than operator staff with regard to the freedom to choose one's own method of working, responsibility given, opportunities to use abilities and the job as a whole.[17] This finding may be partly explained by the tendency of operating companies, until fairly recently, to recruit well qualified staff for key posts on their rigs and platforms. The less senior positions with less responsibility, would be filled by contractor staff.

Research undertaken in the 1990s, has portrayed a more optimistic picture of job characteristics offshore. The majority of 622 respondents in a recent study of British offshore workers reported a high degree of decision latitude (77% agreed "I can work in my own way", 72% agreed "I am able to decide on my own work pace") and a variety of work tasks (86% agreed that their work tasks are varied, only 17% agreed "my work tasks are boring").[18] These findings contradict much of the earlier work on characteristics of offshore jobs. These statistics are perhaps a reflection of the moves towards multi-skilling and employee involvement offshore (see section on employee involvement). Somewhat paradoxically, the same survey found that 54% of those surveyed felt that "the tasks I carry out have been planned in detail by others". This last finding is more in keeping with the idea of a procedurally driven work environment where there is a strong emphasis on safety (see chapter 10).

The motivating effects of what individuals do in their jobs cannot be ascertained without also taking into account what the individual brings to the work situation in terms of needs.[5] Not everyone values or will be motivated by a job rich in intrinsic rewards.

The Work Environment

The third set of factors which impact the motivation of individuals are those concerned with the characteristics of the work environment such as peer group interactions, styles of leadership, and financial rewards. Each of these factors will be reviewed below.

Peer Group

Peer group pressure is undoubtedly a strong motivational force offshore because of individuals working and living together for 24 hours a day for two or three weeks at a time. Individuals can be motivated to gain rewards that come from peers (e.g. friendship and approval) and, therefore, behave in ways which are consistent with the norms or values of the group. It may be that the intimate nature of the offshore environment means peer group pressure and group norms have a stronger influence offshore than onshore. Research shows that organizational socialization can be very pervasive as described by Michael Kirton:

> *Every organization has its own particular climate and at any given time most of its key individuals reflect the general outlook. They gradually communicate this to others in the organization and in time due to recruitment, turnover and such processes the cognitive style will reflect the general organizational ethos.*[19]

There is some anecdotal evidence that the social pressure offshore may be far greater than comparable jobs onshore. As a statement from one oil platform respondent points out: "the survival factor - a necessity to be tolerant and sociable to a degree never imaginable to our onshore contemporaries".[10] Peer pressure can be a strength in terms of social support from peers but a weakness when group norms, which require individual compliance, conflict with organizational expectations. For example, there may be peer pressure on individuals not to take on extra tasks, offer suggestions, or work outside functional areas.

Supervisor's Leadership Style

Supervisors are "those at the first level within the organizational hierarchy on an offshore platform who are responsible for the work performance of their team."[10] The offshore supervisor has a major role in structuring the work, setting performance targets, and controlling many of the desired outcomes for performing well, ranging from financial incentives to recognition. Research has highlighted that the offshore supervisor can be a source of stress. For example, in one offshore study, 33% of respondents reported high stress due to "having a difficult boss to work for."[11] Research undertaken onshore in the USA has shown that 60% to 75% of employees in any occupational group and in any organization consistently report that the most stressful aspect of their job is their immediate supervisor.[21]

Offshore supervisors have an important role to play in motivating their subordinates. For example, Burnett's offshore study asked non supervisors (n=24) to comment on strategies they would use if they were a supervisor to motivate their subordinates.[7] These responses were then compared with the supervisory group's (n=16) responses to motivation strategies which they thought worked well on their shift. The most frequently mentioned strategies in both groups were (1) the supervisor establishing an open working relationship with subordinates (i.e. being supportive and honest, listening, holding regular meetings, treating crews with respect) and (2) giving recognition for a good job/constructive feedback. The importance of giving recognition for a job well done was also emphasized in the study mentioned above, on causes of stress offshore. In this study, 48% of 194 contractors reported suffering from stress related to "no recognition for doing a good job."[15]

David Carnegie's study is the only one, to date, which has measured the leadership characteristics of British and Norwegian offshore supervisors using the Multifactor Leadership Questionnaire.[20,22] Self perceptions of 100 supervisors' leadership styles were obtained on 11 behavioral dimensions related to *transformational, transactional and laissez-faire leadership. Transformational leaders* are admired, respected and trusted, behave in ways that motivate and inspire their team, raise expectations and beliefs, stimulate new ideas, and pay particular attention to individual needs for achievement and growth by acting as a coach or mentor. *Transactional leadership* occurs when the leader rewards or disciplines the team member depending on their performance. *Laissez-faire leadership* occurs where the leader abdicates the leadership role. In the study, the supervisors surveyed felt that their style was primarily transformational, paying particular attention to each individual's needs for achievement and growth. They did not see themselves as adopting a laissez-faire approach. It should be noted that these are the supervisors' perceptions of their own style, their shifts may have held a different view! (For a more detailed discussion on offshore managers and supervisors see chapter 4).

Financial Rewards

Money is undeniably an important factor in influencing an offshore worker's level of motivation. As noted earlier, it is one of the key reasons why workers choose to work offshore. Not only does money provide the means of satisfying many material needs but it is also a symbol of achievement and recognition.

Money can be an effective motivator where financial rewards are directly associated with performance and achievement. For example, according to one theory of work motivation, three conditions are necessary for motivation:[23]

Motivation Force = Expectancy x Instrumentality x Valence

Expectancy refers to an individual's belief that the effort he/she invests will lead to a certain level of performance, *instrumentality* refers to the individual's belief that the performance level will lead to a particular outcome (e.g. reward) and *valence* refers to the value the individual places on a particular outcome. Therefore, employees will display more effort when they perceive a link between their effort, their performance, and the financial reward they receive. Walter Newsom has summarized the practical applications of this theory in the nine C's model (see Table 7-3).[24] This is an easy checklist of questions for managers to consider when trying to understand the motivation level of their individual staff. This model is useful as it shows that the problem may not just be with the individual staff member, the manager may not be communicating well enough with his or her staff.

Table 7-3: Nine C's Model of Motivation

---

1) Capability: Does the individual have the ability to perform the job well?
2) Confidence: Does the individual believe he or she can perform well?
3) Challenge: Does he or she have to work hard to perform the job well?
4) Criteria: Does he or she know the difference between good and poor performance?
5) Credibility: Does he or she believe the manager will deliver on promises?
6) Consistency: Does he or she believe that all individuals receive similar preferred outcomes for good performance and similar less preferred outcomes for poor performance?
7) Compensation: Do the outcomes associated with good performance reward the individual?
8) Cost: What does it cost an individual, in effort and outcomes forgone, to perform well?
9) Communication: Does the manager communicate with the individual? (This is necessary for the effective use of the other eight C's).

Source: Newsom, 1990: 53.

One of the most popular motivation strategies implemented offshore is gain sharing. All gain sharing programs have three factors in common: (1) they are additional compensation systems aimed at individual departments, plants or companies (2) they focus on improvements in productivity or cost reduction, and (3) they offer financial bonuses to employees for improvements in productivity.[25]

The key question is do financial incentives such as gain sharing work? Research has shown that gain sharing improves productivity in a majority of cases and often has a positive impact on employee attitudes. According to John Cotton, most proponents of gain sharing have hypothesized that improvements in productivity come about through increased employee involvement, better communication and cooperation within the organization, improved understanding of organizational objectives by employees and greater acceptance of change rather than the anticipation of financial gain.[25]

The excessive use of money as a motivator can create expectations among staff which management will find difficult to fulfill in the long term. Oil companies need to be careful when setting targets for improved productivity. Financial incentives raise expectations which if not met may, as Alfie Kohn points out, have a detrimental effect on motivation:

> . . . not receiving a reward one had expected to receive is also indistinguishable from being punished. Whether the incentive is withheld or withdrawn deliberately, or simply not received by someone who had hoped to get it, the effect is identical. And the more desirable the reward, the more demoralizing it is to miss out.[26]

This is particularly pertinent for the offshore industry due to the complicated interfacing of offshore operations and the considerable influence of external factors such as weather, geology and onshore processing capacities which may severely limit the workforces' ability to influence productivity. Therefore, despite their best efforts, offshore workers may fail to meet productivity targets. Trying to control for the range of external factors which exist in this industry can create very complicated formulae which are then used to trigger financial incentives. Not only is this an administrative burden on offshore management but individuals may not perceive a clear link between effort and performance.

According to another theory of work motivation, the unfair distribution of rewards may impact motivational levels.[27] This factor relates to the sixth C (consistency) in Newsom's model. Perceived inequity creates tension and anxiety which may well result in a reduction of effort and enthusiasm. This is a pertinent point for the treatment of contractors who traditionally have been paid a lower salary, and have less holiday or sick pay compared to operator staff.

"Job dissatisfaction could be significantly reduced if the 'them' and 'us' gap was narrowed."[17]

Therefore, there are a number of factors to consider when allocating financial rewards related to employees' perceptions, beliefs and values. Offshore managers need to be more aware of the underlying psychological process which determines the overall motivational effect of financial rewards.

Offshore managers need to pay particular attention to work environment factors such as peer pressure, supervisory style and allocation of financial rewards. Traditionally, offshore managers have relied heavily on financial incentives as the key motivator. The current climate, with increased drives for higher levels of performance coupled with financial restraints, has led the oil and gas industry to seek to harness the benefits of peer group pressure and adopt a more open and participative leadership style. These both are seen as increasingly important motivational strategies. The latter often encompasses new employee involvement schemes.

Motivation Through Employee Involvement (EI)

There has been little systematic attempt, until fairly recently, to enhance the commitment and motivation of the offshore workforce through changes to their job content and levels of responsibility.[28] However, the number of United Kingdom fields now in a declining production phase and a persistently low oil price have forced oil companies to do more with less.[29,30] Many oil and gas companies have turned to employee involvement (EI) as a way of enhancing employee productivity (see Endnote at the end of this chapter). The impetus for trying to increase EI, and hence motivation, is therefore instrumental rather than altruistic. In this section, the concept of EI will be explored, how it is thought to affect productivity, and the specific constraints on its effectiveness in the offshore environment will be examined in detail.

What is Employee Involvement and How Does it Work ?

Michael Salamon defines EI as, "measures introduced by management intended to optimize the utilization of labor and at the same time secure the employees' identification with the aims and needs of the organization."[31]

There are a range of measures which fall under the broad banner of (EI), for example, quality circles, gain sharing, job enrichment and self-directed work teams. It is clear that these are very different forms of EI. The common elements that link all EI initiatives are (1) *power,* i.e. providing people with sufficient authority to make decisions; (2) *information,* i.e. timely access to relevant information in order to help make effective decisions; (3) *knowledge and skills*, i.e. by training and developing employees, organizations can increase the expertise of staff so they can perform a greater range of tasks; and (4) *intrinsic rewards*, i.e. those which help satisfy employee's needs for achievement, provide recognition and responsibility and enhance self-worth.[32] The degree of EI that actually exists in an organization is dependent on factors such as how much power is actually devolved, how much information is shared.

Major reviews of the literature[25,33] have suggested two main ways in which EI influences productivity. The first is through a greater involvement of the workforce in decision making leading to a greater flow of and better coordination of important information. This leads to decisions being made on the basis of more complete information. The second way suggests that EI enhances productivity through meeting the higher level needs of employees such as achievement and self-esteem. This leads to improved satisfaction which in turn enhances motivation and leads to improved productivity.[33]

Among the practical examples of EI offshore are the safety representatives established on all United Kingdom offshore structures following the Cullen report.[34] Other examples include devolving responsibility for monitoring and controlling budgets down to departmental levels[30] and the training of offshore workers in a much wider range of skills and then encouraging them to adopt a wider team based perspective as opposed to single discipline working practices.[29]

Factors That May Limit the Effectiveness of Employee Involvement

While it is recognized that EI initiatives can lead to increased motivation and hence improved productivity, the context in which EI is implemented will determine its overall effect. In the offshore context, in particular, there is a range of specific factors which need to be considered if employee involvement is to be successfully implemented. Each of these factors will be examined below.

Geography

Taking geography first, offshore platforms are ultimately controlled by onshore managers. However, as well as the giving and receiving of orders, much of the support work, from logistics to catering to technical advice, has to be conducted via telephone or radio, fax or computer links. Face to face contact between offshore staff, particularly lower level offshore staff and onshore staff is limited. This is a barrier which may prevent the full benefits from EI being realized.

The geographical distance and lack of face-to-face contact are facets of offshore life which have helped develop the widely recognized *us* and *them* mentality between offshore and onshore workers. Evidence of the divide between the two groups was shown in one study where the second highest rated stressor for offshore staff was found to be the lack of offshore insight by onshore management (see Table 7-2)[16]. One reason for this maybe the MUM effect which stands for *minimize unpleasant messages*.[35] This filtering process is a well known barrier to upward communication in organizations. Offshore managers' reports to onshore management may give a distorted picture of the offshore situation emphasizing the positive aspects and downplaying negative information. The MUM effect may be exaggerated when senior management visits offshore are infrequent and where it is not possible to obtain regular direct feedback from the offshore staff by, for instance, walking the job. Hence, the hoped for benefit of greater information flow leading to decisions being made on complete information may be lost.

There is another reason why lack of face-to-face contact is important. The full range of non-verbal cues that make up so much of the content of a message are not available with most of the communication media used between on and offshore such as e-mail and fax. This makes it much more difficult to build effective working relationships, where the existence of a good rapport between onshore and offshore staff leads to much freer and more open communication. It is also much more difficult for onshore managers, with far fewer opportunities for face-to-face contact, to provide their offshore staff with the support, encouragement, and empathy necessary to create a desired motivational effect. Hence for practical and psychological reasons geography may interfere with the, hoped for, enhanced information flow that an EI initiative seeks to create.

Employment Status

The second factor is the differing employment status of the offshore workforce (i.e. the oil company's own, directly employed staff, and contractors from a number of specialist companies). Some of these contractor staff may work on the platform for many years, while others may only spend a day or a few weeks on that particular installation before being sent to another. This factor has been identified as a source of conflict and discontent, particularly for contract workers who are normally employed under less favorable working conditions.[17] Contract workers also tend to undertake the less attractive and more physically demanding parts of the job.[17] Where there is resentment and discontent it would seem logical to assume that communication will be less open and motivation levels lower than in workplaces where these problems do not exist. Indeed Burnett showed that unfair treatment by operator staff had a demotivating effect among some contractor staff.[7] Depending on whether contractors view their terms and conditions of employment as equitable may have a major bearing on the success of EI offshore. EI initiatives try to foster cooperation, taking responsibility and being proactive in the pursuit of organizational goals. Some contractor staff may feel reluctant to do this because their perceived status and level of reward is less than operator staff.

Work Rotation Patterns

The third factor is the work rotation patterns which are examined in greater detail in chapter 5. This factor operates on a number of levels and can create formidable obstacles to information flow. For example, there is obviously a need to communicate at shift changeovers which take place as a result of the 24-hour, two-shift system operation. While in this regard offshore is similar to many large scale onshore industrial plants with 12-hour shifts, there is also the question of end of trip changeovers. The bulk of offshore workers in the United Kingdom sector now work an equal time rotation (i.e. two weeks on/two weeks off, or three weeks on/three weeks off). End of trip changeovers may take place on the steps of the helicopter landing pad and only last two to three minutes. Normally notes are left concerning past problems and future tasks. However, these end of shift changeovers have been recognized as a possible source of ill-feeling and oversights because of incomplete information being transferred.[36] Simple omission through forgetfulness or, more deliberately, for ulterior motives (e.g. to avoid blame for mistakes), can affect the accuracy and amount of information flow.

In many offshore sectors it is normal to share each position between two people. This *back-to-back* system can lead to information transfer problems between the two people involved. However, in the Norwegian offshore sector the problems are exacerbated because of the different trip rotation patterns (i.e., two weeks on/three weeks off, two weeks on/and four weeks off). Under this system three or more people may share one offshore job. While employee involvement may increase information flow, this change of personnel, bringing with it a change of personalities, beliefs, and values could act as a powerful factor mitigating against the consistent use of this information to facilitate major changes.

Knowledge Differentials

The fourth important factor which may limit the effectiveness of EI offshore is differences in technical knowledge. There are two aspects to this in the offshore oil industry. For the sake of simplicity we can assume there are two key groups of people with two very different kinds of knowledge who are essential to the safe operation of an offshore installation. These are the craft trained operators/technicians and the highly qualified and specialized engineers.

Before looking at these in detail, it is important to recognize that any off-shore installation is a very large and complex interlocking set of systems covering such areas as drilling, production, utilities, and safety. Installations are designed onshore by the engineers. Once assembled, the installation is operated and maintained by the operators/technicians. There is a wide differential between the theoretical and practical knowledge of each group. Furthermore, while expert in their own area of the plant, technicians and operators will not necessarily be aware of how an innovation or alteration in their area will affect the interlocking systems of the whole platform. Suggested improvements will, in the majority of cases, need to be sanctioned by onshore engineering support staff in case of safety or other implications.

A knowledge gap between these two groups adds to the *us* and *them* mentality mentioned earlier and brings with it communication difficulties and delays while ideas and suggestions are evaluated and, if approved, implemented. Thus in terms of employee involvement there may be very little action that can actually be taken by offshore operators/technicians without reference to some higher authority onshore. How far this limits the scope for involving employees is outlined below (see section on procedure driven work practices).

The Legacy of Past Management Style

Many working in the oil and gas industry would probably agree with observers that it traditionally has been neither open nor democratic in its management practices.[37,38] This history of autocratic, hierarchical management style and practices in the industry may also affect the ways in which involvement initiatives operate offshore. As described in detail below, the concern for doing the job according to detailed procedures may conflict with a more participative management style.

Under an autocratic, hierarchical management style, communication would tend to be limited to the giving and receiving of orders and reporting back of monitored activities. A rather dated text puts the situation, at least in the early days of the offshore oil industry, rather succinctly: "Every care is taken . . . to ensure the loyalty and cooperation of the employees. If this is not forthcoming, they are dispensed with and replacements sought . . . orders are carried out, immediately, or dismissal follows."[39]

While the situation has changed greatly since the early days of the offshore industry, recent research points out that management style may act to stifle the sort of communication which might allow employee involvement to flourish:

Anecdotal data drawn from the questionnaires suggested a restrictive culture which doesn't encourage asking questions, making suggestions or clarifying misunderstandings[40] and Dissatisfaction with employee relations seemed to be the most significant problem offshore. This relates to the way the firm is managed, the attention paid to suggestions made, chances of promotion, recognition for good work and rate of pay.[16]

To summarize then, the possible advantages involvement would bring through greater, more wide ranging information flows may be lost to the organization. An authoritative, hierarchical, management style, where it still exists, may act as a powerful disincentive to employees offering ideas or sharing information. In addition, it reinforces the idea that workers should do what they are told, when they are told. By implication, it does not allow for, or encourage, additional voluntary effort beyond meeting the obvious requirements of the job, hence the potential benefits of employee involvement may never be realized.

Procedure Driven Work Practices

EI proponents often cite it as a way of releasing potential and of allowing the workforce to generate ideas and be creative. Previous research shows that there is little scope for this in normal offshore work. Offshore work is characterized by the lack of control that workers have over their work.[9] One of the principal reasons for this is that, "Both onshore and offshore oil and gas production necessitates close adherence to regulations and fixed procedures to ensure the safety of the plant."[10] This is a major problem for the oil industry as far as employee involvement is concerned. Sandra Dawson outlines the conflicting needs of adherence to procedures and empowerment (a key employee involvement initiative for many oil companies): "Routine procedures must be seen as critical and be encouraged and monitored, but people should also be developed to be alert, take initiative and to think laterally."[40]

The Scope for Employee Involvement Offshore?

So how much scope is there for EI offshore? David Clutterbuck has highlighted the paradox present in all employee involvement initiatives: "Convincing a newly empowered workforce that freedom and discipline are essential bedfellows is perhaps one of the most difficult tasks."[41] In other words, there is a danger that the philosophy behind EI initiatives, which stress initiative and creativity, may encourage dangerous practices. The idea of questioning and then experimenting, in the search for a new and better way, may be a risky seed to plant in the minds of a workforce dealing with a complex system which must be tightly controlled for safety reasons. This important point has been recognized by oil operators which have gone down the EI route: "This is not about setting people free and breeding a kind of corporate anarchy. It is about allowing employees the space to be all that they can be and harness the ideas and enthusiasm that comes from being a valued member of the team."[29]

It is important for offshore managers to recognize and take steps to overcome the factors which may limit the effectiveness of EI offshore. The general guidelines at the end of this chapter incorporate practical advice on how to maximize the benefits of EI.

Guidelines for Improving Motivation

There are several strategies offshore managers and supervisors can employ to motivate their staff more effectively.

1. Identify and understand the needs and personal goals of their staff. It is important to be aware of assumptions which may be either false or misleading. There is a common tendency for people to assume that others have the same motivations as themselves, in the absence of information to the contrary.[42] As one offshore worker stated: "It is my experience that supervisors have little or no inclination as to what motivates or demotivates me in terms of non-financial rewards."[7] Similarly, not everyone values or will be motivated by an enriched job as highlighted by Jack Singer: "To assume that all workers desire involvement opportunities is to lack sensitivity to individual needs."[43]

2. There are individual differences in motivation and offshore employees are potentially motivated by a range of factors. Money is not the only motivator. There are intrinsic rewards supervisors can directly influence which may be more effective than money in getting staff to work harder such as working in a close knit team, challenges/problems to solve, giving responsibility for results of work, giving recognition for good work and opportunities to develop skills and abilities.

3. Recognize the limitations of money as a motivator. A greater awareness of the underlying psychological processes (i.e. staff's beliefs, perceptions and expectations) can enable suitable steps to be taken to deal with the potential problems. Following Newsom's nine Cs can help here.

4. Recognize that working in a close knit team is a powerful motivator offshore. It is important that individuals are encouraged to feel part of a team and that team rewards may be as valued as individual ones. The creation of close knit teams is much more likely where work rotation patterns for supervisors and team members are the same.

5. Offshore managers and supervisors are restricted in the rewards they have at their disposal compared to onshore managers. They can hardly let a shift go home early or have a day off in lieu. Thus it is important for supervisors to give recognition to their team for a job well done in other ways, saying "thank you."

6. Recognize the demotivating effects of individuals perceiving themselves to be treated less fairly than their colleagues doing the same type of job. By seeking to harmonize terms and conditions of employment the demotivating effects will be reduced.

7. Be aware of the advantages to be gained through the mechanisms behind employee involvement and take appropriate action to ensure the contextual difficulties peculiar to working offshore do not interfere with these. For example, recognize the particular communication problems that end of shift and end of trip changeovers bring with them. Supervisors can, by formalizing these changeovers, minimize information loss and reap the benefits of improved coordination, using face to face communication where possible.

8. The *them* and *us* mentality between onshore and offshore staff and even between different groups of staff on the platform can lead to conflict and misunderstandings. Team building seminars for developing mutual understanding and trust between shifts/groups can be effective here. More frequent visits by onshore managers offshore will also help counteract the criticism that they suffer from a lack of insight into offshore work.

The essence of managing motivation offshore is to be more sensitive to the individual needs of workers and to take appropriate steps to deal with the many and various barriers to communication to which this industry is subject.

Endnote

The arguments over the terms employee involvement and employee participation are beyond the scope of this chapter. However to get a clearer idea of the differences between them it is useful to contrast Salamon's definitions. He defines involvement as follows, "measures introduced by management intended to optimize the utilization of labor and at the same time secure the employees identification with the aims and needs of the organization". Whereas participation is defined as, "philosophy or style of organizational management which recognizes both the need and right of employees, individually or collectively, to be involved with management in areas of the organization's decision making beyond that normally covered by collective bargaining."[31] Employee participation then, entails a recognition of and willingness to meet the needs of employees. This may be because of bottom up pressure for a share in decision making or the particular beliefs of the management team involved. Employee participation would often, for example, involve trade union representation acting as a separate power block arguing, and exerting pressure, for a share of power. The lack of trade union power offshore and management's traditional reluctance to share power, coupled with the fact that the driving force behind employee involvement is management, all point to employee involvement as being the appropriate term to describe initiatives in the offshore oil and gas industry.[44]

Further Reading
Sargent, A. *Turning People On: The Motivation Challenge.* London: IPM, 1990.
Robertson, I. T. Smith, M. & Cooper, D. *Motivation (2nd ed.).* London: IPM, 1992.

References
1.   Deci, E. L. Motivation research in industrial/organizational psychology. In V. H. Vroom & E. L. Deci (Eds.) *Management and Motivation,* London: Penguin, 1992.

2.   Steers, R. M. & Porter, L. W. *Motivation and Work Behaviour,* 5th Ed. New York: McGraw-Hill, 1991.

3.   Handy, C. *Understanding Organisations.* London: Penguin, 1993.

4.   Potter, N. CRINE gaining ground, *Petroleum Review,* Sept., 1994: 398-400.

5.   Porter, L. W. & Miles, R. P. Motivation and management. In J. W. McGuire (Ed.) *Contemporary Management: Issues and Viewpoints.* Englewood Cliffs, N. J.: Prentice Hall, 1974.

6.   International Labour Office *Safety and Related Issues Pertaining to Work on Offshore Petroleum Installations.* Geneva: International Labour Organisation, 1993.

7.   Burnett, J. Measuring motivation in the offshore oil industry. Paper presented at the British Academy of Management Conference, Lancaster, Sept. 12-14, 1994.

8.   Flin, R. Slaven, G. & Whyte, F. Selection for hazardous occupations: offshore oil installations. In M. Smith & V. Sutherland, (Eds.) *International Review of Professional Issues in Selection and Assessment,* Vol. 2. Chichester: Wiley, 1996.

9.   Solheim, J. Offshore commuting and family adaptation in the local community. Paper presented at the conference "Women & Offshore Oil, St. Johns, Newfoundland, September 5-7, 1985.

10. Parkes, K. R. *Human Factors, Shift Work, and Alertness in the Offshore Oil Industry.* Health and Safety Executive Offshore Technology Report (OTH 92389). London: H.M.S.O., 1993.

11. Holter, O. H. *Catering for Oil: Catering and the Reproduction of North Sea Communities.* Oslo: Work Research Institute, 1984.

12. Caplan, R. D., Cobb, S., French, J. R. P., Van Harrison, R. & Pinneau, S. R. *Job Demands and Worker Health.* N.I.O.S.H. Research Report, U.S. Government Printing Office, 1975.

13. Livy, B. & Vant, J. Formula for selecting roughnecks and roustabouts. *Personnel Management,* Feb, 1975: 22-25.

14. Hall. L. Morale boosters, *Personnel Today*, 22 Mar., 1994: 33-35.
15. Sutherland, V. & Cooper, C. L. *Man and Accidents Offshore - An Examination of the Costs of Stress Among Workers on Oil and Gas Rigs*. Colchester. Essex: Lloyds of London, 1986.
16. Sutherland, V. & Cooper, C. L. *Stress and Accidents in the Offshore Oil and Gas Industry*. Houston, Texas: Gulf Publishing Company, 1991.
17. Sutherland, K. M. Psychosocial factors: an investigation of the offshore oil industry. Unpublished PhD Thesis. The Robert Gordon University, 1994.
18. Flin, R., Mearns, K., Fleming, M. & Gordon, R. *Risk Perception and Safety in the United Kingdom Offshore Oil Industry*. Final report for the Oil Industry/Offshore Safety Division, HSE (OTH 94454). Sudbury: HSE Books, 1996.
19. Kirton, M. J. Adaptors and innovators - why new initiatives get blocked, *Long Range Planning*, 17, 2, 1984: 137-143.
20. Carnegie, D. Effective supervisors on offshore petroleum platforms. Paper presented at the Fourth Offshore Installation Management Conference, The Robert Gordon University, Aberdeen, 27 April, 1995.
21. Hogan, R., Curphy, G. J. & Hogan, J. What we know about leadership, *American Psychologist*, June, 49, 6, 1994: 493-504.
22. Bass, B. & Avolio, B. *Transformational Leadership Development: Manual for the Multifactor Leadership Questionnaire*. California: Consulting Psychologists Press, 1990.
23. Vroom, V. *Work and Motivation*. New York: Wiley, 1964.
24. Newsom, W. Motivate now, *Personnel Journal*, Feb, 1990: 51-55.
25. Cotton, J. L. *Employee Involvement*. London: Sage, 1993.
26. Kohn, A. Why incentive plans cannot work, *Harvard Business Review*, Sept-Oct, 1993: 54-63.
27. Adam, J. S. Injustice in social exchange. In L. Berkowitz (ed.), *Advances in Experimental Social Psychology*, Vol. 2, New York: Academic Press, 1965.
28. MacFarlane, C. Participation: the lost strand in offshore safety. Paper presented at the STUC-COMETT Conference in Glasgow, Mar., 1993.
29. Thomson, R. L., Howden, B., Neill, S. & Lindsay, S. Taking the BP Forties Field to 2010. Paper presented at the Offshore Europe Conference in Aberdeen, Sept., 1993.
30. Oliver, H. Empowered teams can reduce operating expense. Paper presented at the IIR conference 'Empowering Flexible Work Teams Offshore', Aberdeen, 23-24 Feb., 1994.
31. Salamon, M. *Industrial Relations*. New York: Prentice Hall, 1992.
32. Lawler, E. *High Involvement Management*. San Francisco: Jossey-Bass, 1986.
33. Miller, K. I. & Monge, P. R. Participation, satisfaction and productivity: a meta-analytic review, *Academy of Management Journal*, 29, 4, 1986: 727-753.
34. Royle, D. J. C. Workforce involvement in the United Kingdom offshore oil and gas industry. Paper presented at the Offshore Europe Conference, Aberdeen, 5-8 Sept., 1995.

35. Rosen, S. and Tesser, A. On reluctance to communicate undesirable information: The Mum effect, *Sociometry*, 33, 1970: 253 263.

36. Mykletun, R. J. (1994) Maintaining communication between different shifts to ensure continuity and prevent ill-feeling building up between shifts. Paper presented at the IIR Conference 'Empowering Flexible Work Teams Offshore', Aberdeen, 23-24 Feb, 1994.

37. Buchan, J. M. Approaches and attitudes of managers to collective bargaining in the North East of Scotland. Unpublished Ph.D. Thesis, The Robert Gordon University, Aberdeen, 1984.

38. Ramsey, J. Creating the right culture for flexible team working. Paper presented at the IIR Conference 'Empowering Flexible Work Teams Offshore', Aberdeen, 23-24 Feb., 1994.

39. Kitchen, J. *Labour Law and Offshore Oil*. London: Croom Helm, 1977.

40. Dawson, S. Managing safety offshore, paper presented at the Offshore Operations Post Piper Alpha conference, February, 1989.

41. Clutterbuck, D. The power of empowerment, *Modern Management*, Dec., 1994: 16-18.

42. Baron, H, The motivation questionnaire, *Personnel Management*, Jan, 1994: 67.

43. Singer, J. A. Participative decision making about work, an overdue look at variables which mediate its effects. *Sociology of Work and Occupations, 1, 4*, 1974: 347-371.

44. Tait, R. & Hutton, A. Is empowerment right for us? An examination of the barriers to empowerment in the offshore industry. Paper presented at the Strategic HRM Conference, Nottingham Trent University, Dec., 1994.

Emergency Response: Command and Control

Keith Stewart and Jan Skriver

Introduction

Major disasters in the offshore oil and gas industry such as *Piper Alpha,* *Alexander Kielland, Seacrest, Ocean Ranger, Glomar Java Sea* and *Bohai II* have all resulted in a high number of fatalities. Accident reports from these, as well as other disasters have helped to shape emergency response procedures through their description of the deleterious consequences of ineffective or inadequate management. This chapter focuses on the potential problems facing an off-shore manager who may be involved in offshore emergency response management. Mainly emphasis will be placed on the challenges facing the management team on an installation which is experiencing an emergency. However, many of the issues raised apply equally well to other individuals who may be involved in an emergency, for example standby vessel captains, managers of nearby installations, and onshore emergency response teams.

Offshore emergency response is a complex process which, to be suc-cessful, needs to be supported by an efficient and well coordinated manage-ment structure. Regulation 8 of the British Offshore Installations (Prevention of Fire and Explosion, and Emergency Response) Regulations 1995 requires each installation to have an Emergency Response Plan, containing sufficient information for the guidance of personnel:[1]

- on the organization and arrangements to take effect in an emer-gency, and
- on the procedures by way of emergency response to be followed in different circumstances.

Emergency response regulations are not unique to the British sector in the North Sea but are found across the world.

Fundamental to effective emergency management is the performance of the OIM the senior manager responsible for command and control and his or her team who set in motion the appropriate steps to deal with the incident which faces them (see chapter 4 for details of day-to day-duties). The resolution of an offshore emergency is, of course, equally dependent on the task performance of individuals such as the members of stretcher teams, fire teams, and helicopter crews, who have been specially trained for their own emergency response roles. This chapter will focus, however, solely on management issues and does not seek to deal directly with the technical procedures with are involved in tackling the various potential offshore emergencies.[2,3]

The first section of the chapter traces the historical and legislative background to the OIM position in the United Kingdom sector. Current perspectives on emergency response in the offshore industry following the *Piper Alpha* disaster and the ensuing legislation which followed it are then discussed. The second section presents an outline of the emergency response arrangements, in particular the command structure, which are typical on the majority of production platforms in the United Kingdom sector of the North Sea. The remainder of the chapter focuses upon the performance of the OIM and his or her team, and some of the measures which can be taken to try to ensure that their performance is not degraded in the confusion of an emergency.

Emphasis is placed on the ways in which the pressure of emergency response management can impact an individuals' capacity for efficient work and the ways in which the careful design of management systems and the emergency control center can help to reduce those effects. In this discussion the issues of stress, decision making, team working, and the work environment are specifically examined. These are by no means the only important issues in the human factors of offshore emergency response; however, they should serve to indicate the importance of such considerations in the management of offshore safety. While the material mainly is drawn from Europe, there have been offshore emergencies in all parts of the world and the psychological and management principles of command and control are universal.

Historical and Legislative Background: The Origins of the OIM Position

The Situation Prior to *Piper Alpha*

While offshore emergency response is managed on a team basis, in law however, the responsibility is invested in the OIM. To understand why the responsibility has been placed on one individual, it is necessary to trace the historical background for the creation of the OIM position in the United Kingdom sector of the North Sea.

On December 27, 1965 the *Sea Gem*, an offshore self-elevating barge being used as a drilling rig, collapsed, capsized, and sank while drilling, 43 miles east of the Yorkshire coast. Of the 32 men who were on board at the time of the incident, 13 lost their lives. Alan Sefton points out that at the time, there was no specific safety legislation relating directly to offshore activities other than that which was set out in the model clauses to licenses issued under the Petroleum Production Act 1934.[4] In September 1964 the Minister for Power indicated to licensees (which in the case of the *Sea Gem* was BP Petroleum Development Limited) that all operations should be carried out in accordance with those parts of the Institute of Petroleum's Model Code of Safe Practice which were related to the safety, health and welfare of personnel. In his report of the Public Inquiry into the demise of the *Sea Gem*, Roland Adams, QC stressed that the code included only recommendations regarding safe practice and was not issued in the form of regulations or instructions.[5] He concluded that the structure and layout of the code made it inappropriate as a piece of quasi-legislation and recommended that there should be statutory provisions in Britain for regulating the management of artificial islands and fixed structures on the outer continental shelf.

One of the recommendations in the Institute of Petroleum's code which Adams suggested required further consideration was the following: "*On board an offshore platform the individual in full charge of all operations carried out on or from the unit, and to whom all personnel are responsible in an emergency, should be clearly defined.*"[5] Adams pointed out that on *Sea Gem* there was no confusion as to who this individual should be, and that it was accepted that the toolpusher (the individual in charge of drilling operations) was in full charge of the installation. Despite the fact that the tribunal made no criticism of the conduct of *Sea Gem's* tool-pusher, Adams suggested that the rapid turnover of personnel in this position may not have been, "*conducive to a general feeling . . . that a known and trusted person was in command.*"[5] Adams therefore proposed that

> . . . *a named person and one whose powers of leadership are recognized should be in full charge of all operations carried out on or from the unit rather than the fortuitously allocated performer of a particular function related more to the technique of drilling than to the safety and well-being of the barge's whole company.*"[5]

He also recommended that on installations there should be a chain of command equivalent to that established in the merchant marine.

Following the loss of the *Sea Gem* it was recognized that, where safety was concerned, it was not sufficient to base arrangements for the operation of offshore installations on the Petroleum (Production) Act 1934. The Mineral Workings (Offshore Installations) Act 1971 was passed with a view to improving procedures for offshore exploration and production activities and, among other things, empowered the Secretary of State to make regulations for the safety, health, and welfare of persons on offshore installations.[6] It was this act which required that an OIM be appointed for each installation. Section 5(5) of the act deals with the range of the OIM's responsibility in an emergency:

> . . . *where at an offshore installation there is an emergency or apprehended emergency endangering the seaworthiness or stability of the installation or otherwise involving a risk of death or serious personal injury, the installation manager may take or require to be taken any such measures as are necessary or expedient to meet or avoid the emergency; and no regulation or condition having effect by virtue of this Act shall apply to prohibit or restrict the taking of any such measures by virtue of this sub-section.*[6]

Thus, a burden of responsibility is placed on the OIM. Nevertheless, as Sefton stresses, the Health and Safety at Work Act 1974 has applied to offshore installations since 1977, and has made it the responsibility of employers to ensure the health, safety, and welfare of their employees while at work, and to provide any necessary information, instruction, training and supervision.[4] Sefton points out that it is the responsibility of the employer to make certain that adequate systems and procedures are in place to support the OIM in his role. The responsibilities of the OIM are dealt with in *A Guide to the Offshore Installations and Pipe-line Works (Management and Administration) Regulations 1995*.[7] The legislation regarding offshore safety management and emergency response was subjected to considerable scrutiny following the *Piper Alpha* disaster in 1988, an event which proved to be a watershed in the history of offshore operations.

The *Piper Alpha* Disaster

The *Piper Alpha* oil and gas production platform, operated by Occidental Petroleum (Caledonia) Ltd. was located 110 miles northeast of Aberdeen, Scotland, in the British sector of the North Sea. At around 2200 hours on the July 6, 1988 there was an explosion on the production deck of the platform which, evidence presented at the Public Inquiry suggests, was caused by the ignition of a cloud of gas condensate leaking from a temporary flange. The resulting fire spread rapidly and was followed by a number of smaller explosions. At around 2220 hours there was a major explosion caused by the rupturing of a pipeline carrying gas to *Piper* from the nearby *Tartan* platform. Over the course of the next few hours an intense high pressure gas fire raged punctuated by a series of major explosions which served to hasten the structural collapse of the platform. Of the 226 persons who were on board the installation only 61 survived. The great majority of the survivors escaped by jumping into the sea, some from as high as 175 feet.

In the time which has elapsed since the disaster the suggestion has been made that the emergency on board *Piper* could have been managed more effectively. Sefton made the following observation:

> *The explosion on Piper Alpha that led to the disaster was not dev-astating. We shall never know, but it probably killed only a small number of men. As the resulting fire spread, most of the Piper Alpha workforce made their way to the accommodation where they expected someone would be in charge and would lead them to safety. Apparently, they were disap-pointed. It seems the whole system of command had broken down.[4]*

Lord Cullen's report into the *Piper Alpha* disaster contained a number of criticisms relating to the performance of *Piper Alpha's* OIM on the night of the disaster. Criticisms were also leveled at the OIMs of the adjacent *Claymore* and *Tartan* platforms.[8] These installations were linked to *Piper* by hydrocarbon pipelines, the rupturing of which caused massive explosions and the rapid spread of the fire on *Piper*. Cullen suggests that had the production of hydro-carbons by these platforms been stopped sooner, the situation on *Piper* might have deteriorated less rapidly. The report pools the evidence of survivors from the disaster and describes in as much detail as possible, the actions of *Piper's* OIM during the early stages of the emergency. Evidence is also presented regarding the actions of the *Claymore* and *Tartan* OIMs during the same peri-od. The following quotations illustrate their behavior of the OIMs on the fatal night.

> *The OIM had been gone 'a matter of seconds when he came run-ning back' in what appeared . . . to be a state of panic . . .The OIM made no specific attempt to call in helicopters from the Tharos or elsewhere; or to communicate with vessels around the installation; or with the shore or other installations; or with personnel on Piper.[8]*

> *The strong impression with which I was left after hearing the evi-dence as to the response of Tartan and Claymore was that the type of emer-gency with which the senior personnel of each platform was confronted was something for which they had not been prepared.[8]*

> *The failure of the OIMs to cope with the problems they faced on the night of the disaster clearly demonstrates that conventional selection and training of OIMs is no guarantee of ability to cope if the man himself is not able in the end to take critical decisions and lead those under his com-mand in a time of extreme stress.[8]*

The latter point was addressed by Flin and Slaven in a project commis-sioned by the Health and Safety Executive.[9] On the basis of their study of selec-tion and training strategies for OIMs in the United Kingdom and the

Norwegian sector of the North Sea, they concluded that prior to *Piper Alpha* there had been no formal procedures for selecting and training OIMs for emergency response and that only few had received any kind of emergency response training. Those who possessed some knowledge of how to handle an emergency had received their training elsewhere, in the armed forces or the merchant navy, before they started work in the offshore oil and gas industry. Flin and Slaven recommended that in terms of emergency command responsibilities:

- a satisfactory assessment of competence to take command in an offshore emergency should be required in the selection criteria for the OIM;
- all OIMs should receive training to enable them to take the command role in an emergency.[9]

This training should encompass realistic simulated emergencies and advice on planning for emergencies, emergency management, decision-making, and dealing with stress. Emergency command training should include regular exercises for the OIM and his or her emergency response team.

The Cullen Recommendations and Subsequent Legislation

In his report on the *Piper Alpha* disaster, Lord Cullen made over 100 recommendations regarding the safe management of offshore installations. Many of them have since been incorporated into legislation. For example The Offshore Installation (Safety Case) Regulations 1992 provide the following guidance notes relating to emergency response.

58. The organization and arrangements should include adequate provision for: (a) establishing and maintaining a command structure by competent persons throughout an emergency, including arrangements for people who become disabled;

(I) . . . Among other matters, emergency exercises should provide the OIM and the command team with practice in decision-making in emergencies, including decisions on evacuation. All OIMs and deputies should participate regularly in such exercises.[10]

The Offshore Installations (Prevention of Fire and Explosion, and Emergency Response) Regulations 1995 also deal with the management of an offshore emergency.[1] These regulations state, among other things, that those responsible for offshore installations should arrange in advance *"(a) for command by competent persons which can be maintained so far as is practicable, throughout an emergency; (b) for there to be a sufficient number of persons on the installation com-*

petent to undertake emergency duties and operate relevant equipment."

Both The Offshore Installations (Prevention of Fire and Explosion, and Emergency Response) Regulations 1995 and The Offshore Installation (Safety Case) Regulations 1992 share common themes with U.S. Occupational Safety and Health Administrations (OSHA) Process Safety Management Regulations.1,[10-12] Emphasis is on hazard and risk assessment, safety management systems, and emergency planning with particular attention being paid to command and control, evacuation of personnel, and effective training of emergency response teams. Australia, Norway and The Netherlands, similarly, are looking to introduce new safety case-based regulations.[12] These will, in line with the U.S. and United Kingdom regulations, stress that emergency response preparedness should encompass events identified in installation specific risk assessment but also be extendible to cover other incidents that may arise.

The cultural changes which have occurred in the offshore oil industry since the tragedy on the *Piper Alpha* include a significant maturation of the industry's attitude to safety. Some hard lessons have been learned. The current safety regime which is now in place in the North Sea has been largely driven by the recommendations made by Lord Cullen. Companies now must demonstrate to the industry regulator, the United Kingdom Health and Safety Executive, that they have a workable safety management system in place on each of their installations. Central to this safety management system is the position of the OIM and his or her emergency response team. Much emphasis has been placed on the need for companies to assess the competence of their OIMs for emergency management.

The majority of the post incident comment on the apparent mismanagement of the *Piper Alpha* incident has tended to focus on the roles played by the OIMs of the three installations concerned. Perhaps this is not surprising since the OIM position was created with the aim of placing the legal responsibility for installation management in the hands of that one individual. Nevertheless, while it makes a certain amount of legal sense to focus responsibility in this way, in practice emergency management responsibility should be shared across a trained team with a hierarchical command structure. On the majority of installations today such a structure exists and it is clear who should take charge should the OIM become incapacitated. The emergency response team should be available to offer advice and help spread the workload. Clearly the OIMs on all three installations involved on the night of the *Piper Alpha* disaster faced very difficult decisions. What cannot be said with certainty is how much help they received in trying to make those decisions. The experience of the aviation industry, where black box flight recorders give us an insight into the conduct of crews immediately prior to fatal accidents, suggests that the contribution of team members other than the captain can be absolutely crucial. More than one aviation disaster has been ascribed to the inability of a second in command to assert him or herself at a crucial moment.

Emergency Response Offshore

Responsibility for handling an offshore emergency rests with the installation manager, whose job requires not only day-to-day management for a wide range of functions, but also the ability to take the role of the incident commander should an emergency such as a fire, an explosion, or a blow-out arise.[9] OIMs are required to take appropriate action to deal with any such situation, however, unlike the manager of a land based petro-chemical plant, they cannot call upon the emergency services for immediate assistance. In the short term, an emergency must be dealt with by the installation's own personnel, many of whom will have undergone specialist training in areas such as fighting oil and gas fires and first aid. It seems appropriate to introduce a generic emergency response team to clarify their roles in an emergency. Emergency response organizations, however, are not standardized and differ not only between different operating companies, but also between each installation within the same company.

In an emergency, the OIM has at his or her disposal a number of emergency teams, each serving a particular purpose, that are deployed through a well defined hierarchy of command and control. At the top of the structure is the Emergency Command Center (ECC) which is commonly based in the radio room or the control room. Personnel in the ECC could comprise the OIM (in overall control), the operations supervisor (the deputy OIM), a radio operator, the safety officer, the permit controller, and a communications technician. If drilling were taking place, the drilling supervisor would also go to the ECC in an emergency. The ECC team's duties include assessment of the situation, directing emergency response and possible evacuation, ensuring effective communications and record keeping, maintaining links with onshore management and other installations, keeping installation personnel updated on the situation, and directing local support and resources. While overall responsibility lies with the OIM, decision making is distributed to other team members and other teams are involved in emergency response offshore. These include

- The emergency or incident team, directed by the on-scene commander, and responsible for fire fighting, damage control and the rescue of casualties;
- The process control team, whose duties include shutdown of operations and making the production areas safe, starting-up and sup-

porting the emergency plant, and keeping the ECC informed about the state of the plant;

- The medical team, consisting of a medic and first aiders, responsible for the treatment of casualties;
- The assembly/evacuation team, responsible for the consolidation of the installation's roster and the identification of any missing personnel, keeping the ECC informed about the assembly and evacuation status, and controlling the evacuation of personnel from the installation;
- The wireline team responsible for securing the well and making the drilling area safe;
- The drilling response team, responsible for fire fighting and damage control in the drilling areas.

In the event of an emergency the ECC will notify and request help from onshore organizations. In response to such a request any or all of the following resources can be mobilized: the Coast Guard, helicopters based both onshore and offshore, offshore medical support, and the company's onshore emergency response team. The latter will provide support and suggestions and contact the local police and hospitals as well as dealing with the media and relatives. (Figure 8-1 illustrates the complex emergency response set up.)

Perhaps the most important role of the offshore emergency team is to supply the OIM with the information required to make appropriate decisions. Thus the ECC can be viewed as an information processing system gathering such details as the state of the incident, the response of fire and medical teams, and the availability of helicopters for evacuation. Their job is to collate the huge amount of information available and to use it to build a shared understanding of the incident. This shared understanding is absolutely vital to emergency management since it allows for a coordinated response plan to be formulated and put into action. Common to all installations however is the general principle that the OIM and the command team should be remote from the incident scene, whether that be a gas release, a helicopter crash, or a man overboard. This serves an important purpose in that it allows them to maintain an understanding of the wider range of problems which face the installation without getting preoccupied by the details of the incident itself. Establishing and keeping current with the big picture is a central theme of the philosophy of emergency management across a number of domains such as aviation and the emergency services and is a major aim of offshore emergency command.

Figure 8-1 An offshore emergency response command center.

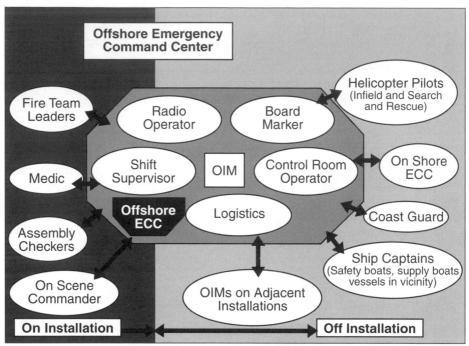

Thus, as in any emergency, much responsibility is placed on the shoulders of the incident commander.[13] As the senior manager, he is ultimately responsible for deciding on a course of action, particularly the order to evacuate the installation. Kennedy in a study of evacuation, escape and rescue from offshore installations, identified the decision to evacuate in time as one of the most crucial to be taken by the OIM, with the greatest potential for error.[14] The emergency evacuation of an offshore installation is by no means a simple operation. The majority of European installations are located over 100 miles from land and are subject to the extreme weather conditions of the North and Irish Seas. Helicopter evacuation, which in good weather would be the preferred option, can be dangerous in bad weather, and is sometimes impossible. Even where conditions favor the use of helicopters, this operation can take several hours. Evacuation to the sea by totally enclosed lifeboats is a secondary option, and can be very difficult and dangerous in cold seas where a swell of 20 to 30 feet is not uncommon. In severe winter weather it may well be the case that the best means of survival for the crew is to remain on board the installation controlling the problem until evacuation is possible, the situation becomes untenable, or the problem is resolved.

OIMs need to know how to make decisions using their team. They must delegate tasks while ensuring that all team members have the same understanding of the big picture, that is of the developing incident and of the current response plan. In addition, they need to ensure that the team works well as a unit. Studies of team performance in various fields stress that the successful completion of team tasks often depends on the synchronization of team member activities rather than the summation or aggregation of these activities.[15] The issue of team work will be discussed later in the chapter.

Stress

This section examines what may be a major psychological impediment to effective performance in an emergency, the experience of stress. Most of us have an understanding of what it means to experience stress. A driving test, a busy day at the office, asking for a bank loan; all of these are situations which we might find stressful in that our personal capacity for performance is fully stretched (see chapter 6 for a discussion of occupational stress). The broad argument presented is that stress can cause the performance of an OIM and his crew to become degraded when they are faced by a real emergency, but that the effects of stress can be minimized. Preparation in terms of the implementation of measures such as good team working practices, a clear management system, and user-centered design of the ECC itself, can help to combat the debilitating effects of acute psychological stress. The discussion will be focused upon acute stress, that is stress which is intense, has a fast onset, is new or unexpected, and is of limited duration. This is the type of stress which individuals experience when they suddenly are faced with a emergency.

Susan Folkman proposed that people experience stress in an environment where (1) their resources are taxed or exceeded, and (2) their well being is threatened. This is a useful definition for our discussion of the effects of stress on the members of an offshore ECC team. Like a military engagement, or an aviation emergency, an offshore emergency is not something which those involved likely are familiar, for the simple reason that such occurrences are very rare.

Acute stress can have a very marked effect on an individual's ability to perform in a given situation. One of the major effects of acute stress seems to be that it interferes with cognitive functioning or, put in more simple terms, it vastly reduces our ability to think clearly. Stress, it has been said takes up part of the cognitive space available to us for mental activity. Thus, there is a very real danger of managers under stress making a serious error because of a reduction in their ability to think effectively. On the face of it there seems to be a real and very dangerous irony in the fact that at the one time when an individual needs to perform to the very best of his or her ability, that individual's capacity for performance could be severely reduced.

Fight or Flight

Stress response shows similarities to our discussion in chapter 6 of the physiological support of shiftworking problems. The problem again is that while man has developed to interact with the environment, the environment which we now inhabit has changed far too rapidly over the past few thousand years for the process of evolution to keep up. The way humans react in a stressful environment can be understood if the challenges to survival which faced the earliest humans are considered. They most likely were to survive in a dangerous situation such as an encounter with a predator or a hostile competitor, if they tried to defuse the threat by force or to distance themselves from the source of the danger in as short a time as possible. Through evolution, the human body has developed a psycho-physiological system for achieving this known as the fight or flight reaction. In short, when our early ancestors perceived a situation as highly threatening, their bodies would undergo a series of rapid and subtle physiological changes, for example the release of adrenaline and the redirection of blood to the major muscles, to prepare them to either stand and fight or to make their escape as quickly as possible by running.

The fight or flight reaction is very good at preparing us to deal with situations where we need to react in a physical manner, although, one of its drawbacks seems to be that it causes a reduction in our capacity for mental performance. This was not a major problem for a caveman escaping from a tiger, and is still not a major problem for a soldier running from a live grenade. However it is a considerable problem for an individual who needs to reduce a threat by thinking clearly and devising a plan of action. The relevance of this to the offshore emergency situation now should become clear. An offshore emergency, like an aviation incident or a process problem at a nuclear power plant, is not a situation which can be dealt with by simple fight or flight. As has been said already, the successful resolution of an offshore emergency relies upon the skill of the OIM and his team in gathering information about the problem they face, devising a workable action plan, and putting it into operation in as calm and efficient a manner as possible. Acute stress restricts our ability to act in this fashion.

In his report, Cullen was critical of the management performance of the installation managers on the three platforms involved in the *Piper Alpha* incident. It seems highly likely that the reported ineffectiveness of these individuals was not simply a lack of managerial competence but was to no small degree a result of the acute stress reaction which the situation provoked. However,

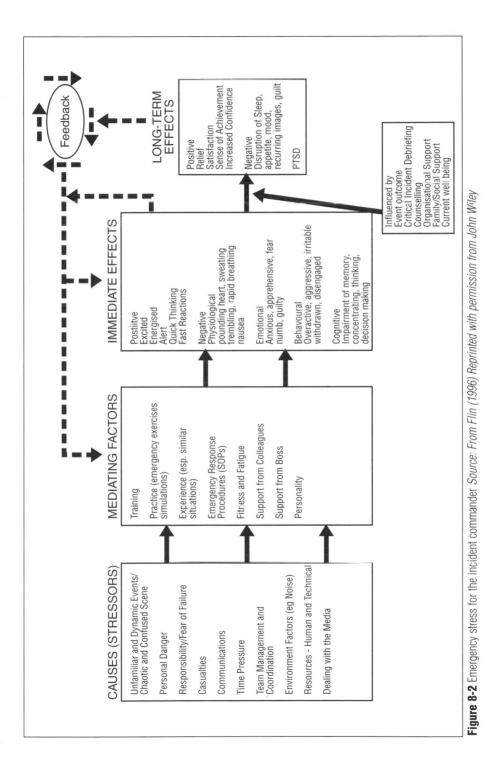

Figure 8-2 Emergency stress for the incident commander *Source: From Flin (1996) Reprinted with permission from John Wiley*

recent research has shown that exposure to stressors necessarily does not produce negative effects, particularly in personnel who have had prior exposure to such circumstances. There may be, in fact, immediate positive effects such as increased motivation, faster reactions, clearer thinking, and improved memory retrieval in response to the stimulation of a sudden challenge from the environment.[17] (Figure 8-2 illustrates the characteristic factors associated with exposure to stress.)

It was pointed out earlier that the aim of offshore emergency response efforts is to reach a point where the risks to persons have been reduced to a level equivalent to those under normal operational conditions. Also it was proposed that for such a response effort to be successful, it is essential that the OIM and his ECC team perform in an efficient, coordinated manner to gather information, build an understanding of the situation they face, and, on the basis of this, take decisions for how to deal with it. The challenge for organizations therefore is to set up a preexisting system which maximizes the utility of the physical and human resources available to an OIM in an emergency and accounts for the possibility of barriers such as stress. In the remainder of this chapter, the main management issues which need to be considered in preparing a platform and its crew for facing potential crises are addressed. The issues which will be emphasized are, broadly, decision making, teamwork, team organization, and information management.

Decision Making

Decision making in offshore installation emergencies, although identified by Cullen as one of the main contributors to the *Piper Alpha* disaster, only just has begun to receive some attention.[18] The interest has coincided with the emergence of a new field known as Naturalistic Decision Making. The research approach is holistic with emphasis on actual decisions taken by experienced decision makers within real life contexts. One model which has received widespread support is the Recognition Primed Decision model (RPD) which describes how experts reach and implement decisions in dynamic settings.[19] It suggests that experts do not use a traditional analytical approach involving option generation and concurrent evaluation, but instead the emphasis is on situation assessment and a serial evaluation of options. The key features of the RPD model are

1.   First option is usually workable
2.   Serial generation/evaluation of options
3.   Satisfying
4.   Evaluation through mental simulation
5.   Focus on elaborating and improving options

6.   Focus on situation assessment

7.   Decision maker primed to act

Jan Skriver et. al. conducted a study of experienced OIMs using a simulated table top exercise.[18] They found that the OIMs rely on their abilities to recognize and appropriately classify situations. If a situation is recognized as similar or identical to a previous situation encountered, a plausible course of action is immediately identified without a need to weigh up pros and cons. If the situation is not identified instantly, more information is sought to help in establishing a mental model of the situation. When sufficient information has been obtained the situation is reassessed and a suitable course of action is generated. This was the case for around 90% of the decisions made. Training implications derived from this study include

- limited value in training decision strategies and developing support systems based on rational choice strategy
- situation awareness is more important than deliberating about alternative courses of action
- training should focus on critical cue identification, pattern matching and building up experience through exercises and debriefings.

Team Working

As mentioned previously, the OIM is heavily dependent on his ECC team. His ability to make appropriate decisions is dependent upon the information he receives from these individuals. One way of thinking about the offshore ECC is that it is like the brain of the installation during an emergency. It is the one place where the whole of the big picture can be monitored and decisions for overall strategy in dealing with the emergency can be made. The OIM must rely upon the individuals under his command to make decisions in their own specialist areas. This type of situation has been described in two ways either as distributed decision making or the decentralization of command.[20,21]

While overall decision making power rests with the OIM, responsibility for courses of action is passed down the chain of command to individuals involved in specific parts of the collective task. A corollary to this is that it is an example of management by exception, a phrase which is common in the armed forces. What this means is that the OIM allows others to make decisions provided he or she is happy with the decisions taken. As soon as he or she disagrees with an individual's choice of action he will step in and impose his own will. The reason for this style of decision management should be clear. Distribution of decision making power shares the workload across the organization. This allows the OIM to take on a role where he can monitor the overall development of a situation without being drawn into an individual problem to the exclusion of others.

Before looking at the way the team has to work as a collective unit it is worth noting that no team can be effective if the individuals who make up that team are not competent in carrying out their own roles. The issues involved in the training of offshore personnel are dealt with in chapter 2 and consequently are not elaborated on in any detail here. Nevertheless, it is worth noting that, before team level training begins, it is necessary for team members to have acquired a certain level of competence in their assigned team roles.[22] That is to say, before they work on their teamwork competencies, they must have a certain level of taskwork competence.[23]

Robert McIntyre and Eduardo Salas noted that in their studies of U.S. Naval team training, instructors reported that often it is left to the initiative of the team members themselves to amass those individual competencies, sometimes through formal training, sometimes through personal experience.[20] Because of this, it was noted that some teams get through team training and assessment on the basis of the efforts of a few individuals. This is true of team training in any domain, not just the oil industry, and clearly has very significant implications for performance in a real emergency. It is also imperative to note that it is very important for team members to understand other individuals' tasks as well as their own, particularly the tasks of colleagues with whom they must work closely. This allows them to anticipate one another's needs and to engage in the monitoring, feedback, and backup behaviors, discussed below, which are the main characteristics of effective teamwork.

Effective offshore emergency response is based around the operation of a well coordinated emergency management team. While little research has been carried out into the operation of offshore teams, the skills required at a teamwork level are similar to those required by teams in other potential emergency management roles such as military and fire ground teams.[24] For that reason guidelines for effective team behaviors can be provided from the principles which have been derived in other domains. At the forefront of research in this area are a group of psychologists led by Dr. Eduardo Salas of the U.S. Naval Air Warfare Center Training Systems Division in Florida. Behaviors which Salas and his colleagues have identified as being typical of high performing emergency management teams in any domain are listed below.

Monitoring: Members of effective teams monitor the performance of their fellow team members to ensure that they are following procedures correctly and acting in a timely fashion during an incident. This does not imply that team members should spy on one another. Rather, there must be a psychological contract of trust whereby each individual accepts that performance monitoring is central to optimal team output.

Feedback: This is the process of telling a team-mate when his or her performance is either effective or ineffective and consequently is a follow-up behavior from monitoring. There are many potential impediments to the free flow of feedback information of which rank and experience are obvious examples. Therefore, part of the unwritten teamwork contract must be that all team members are prepared to give and receive feedback. High performing teams exhibit a climate where feedback is freely given. McIntyre and Salas suggest that a critical factor in the development of this environment is that the team leader shows that he or she is open to criticism where it is warranted.

Closed Loop Communication: In an offshore emergency, it is critical that information is passed between individuals in an accurate and efficient manner. McIntyre and Salas describe a certain type of communication, *closed loop communication,* as the basis for information management and organization in the command center environment where likely there are to be many senders and receivers of information and clearly there is a risk of confusion and loss of information. There are three steps in closed loop communication. First, the sender initiates the message by speaking to someone, either face to face or over a phone or radio link. Second, the receiver accepts the message and provides feedback to show that the message has been received. Finally, to avoid any confusion, the sender double checks to make sure that the intended message was received. McIntyre and Salas point out that this form of communication actually is part of the U.S. military's formal procedures for communication. The advantages of using this pattern of information exchange in the hectic, noisy environment of an offshore command center are obvious.

Backup: McIntyre and Salas emphasize that at the very heart of teamwork is the willingness for team members to help one another in their various tasks when an individual appears to be overloaded. For this reason it is of prime importance that members understand and are competent in the tasks facing colleagues with whom they directly interact. Thus, knowing one's job really means knowing not only one's own role but those of several other individuals.

Values: For the above behaviors to prove successful, it is important that team members hold certain attitudes. First, it is of the utmost importance that group members think of themselves first and foremost as part of a team and realize that success depends on their effective interaction with other members of the team. Next, is the requirement that team members must recognize the interdependence of the team. This means that each individual must see that for the team to be successful they must rely upon and trust their colleagues to carry out their own parts of the overall team task. This interdependence is seen as a virtue in a team and not as a weakness.

Leadership: Team leadership refers to the actions of the individual with the highest rank. In the case of the offshore ECC this is the OIM. McIntyre and Salas, however, stress that team leadership can also imply the actions of senior members of a team and the example they set. They further point out that where leaders openly engage in teamwork behaviors for example monitoring others, giving and receiving feedback, and closed loop communication, other team members are more likely to do the same. Where the example set by the leader is poor, it is likely that the team performance will also be poor. Consequently, one of the most important roles of the team leader is to act as a role model.

McIntyre and Salas have identified a leadership type which interferes with team effectiveness. They call this the *tough leadership* style as characterized by a tendency to micro manage, an autocratic management approach to team members, and a high degree of over confidence regarding the technical aspects of the task. This style seems very similar in its characteristics to what airline pilots identify as the *wrong stuff.*[21] The response of the aviation industry to problems with cockpit teamworking was to institute a training regime which concentrated on human factors skills such as communication, assertiveness, and stress management. This new training has been dubbed *crew resource management* (CRM) and is now a standard and required part of airlines' continuing training programs for crews (see chapter 12). CRM has been adapted for use in a number of industries and is now being introduced into the offshore oil industry, where communication, stress management and assertiveness training can significantly enhance team performance.[22]

The ECC Environment

In an environment such as an aircraft cockpit, the majority of the information which is essential to the crew in an emergency is presented by the onboard instruments and computers. These are laid out in a way which is familiar to the crew and, in modern aircraft at least, are designed for ease of understanding. The design of the modern cockpit is increasingly user-centered, that is it takes the needs and abilities of the human operator into consideration and consequently supports the construction of an understanding of the situation in the cockpit crew's minds.

The situation which faces an offshore installation's ECC crew in a emergency is somewhat different. Far less information is presented to them automatically than to the cockpit crew. Beyond information regarding the status of the process (which in a serious incident would probably be shut down and blown down) the ECC crew can only rely on automatic fire and gas detector displays and operation manuals in building their understanding of an incident. Because of this lack of automatically presented information, a large part of the ECC crew's task is to get details about the incident and to collate them into a meaningful whole. To do this they rely heavily on the use of white boards for writing down incident information and schematic plot plans for presenting a graphic representation of the incident. Getting hard copy of incident information in this way is absolutely essential.

One of the ways of combating the effects of stress on mental processes is to use external aids to thinking and memory. The white boards and plot plans serve this purpose, in effect they allow the emergency center personnel to externalize two critical cognitive functions, memory and the organization of the information within memory. The white boards in the ECC are used for storing and keeping current with essential information such as availability of helicopters, number of casualties, and number of persons at each meeting point. The boards are central to the emergency control center's design and consequently are prepared to impose organization on the large amount of information which is received in an emergency. For example, the board marked helicopters would list likely craft availability, their location and capacity. The boards therefore supplement the crew's memories in two ways. First, they cue the individuals to request information which they might forget to ask for in a stressful situation and in so doing perform a function similar to a check list. Second, they reduce the amount of information which team members have to carry in their heads which can be beneficial because their capacity for storing and organizing information may be impaired by stress and high workload. The boards therefore can aid the ECC crew in their storage of information. Information not only is stored in written form however.

The use of graphic plot plans is widespread in the offshore oil industry and is an extremely powerful way of presenting an overall picture of a developing incident. Take for example an oil fire in a specific module. The individual responsible for the plan would first select the appropriate graphic, put it on the wall where everyone could see it, and would then draw on it the wind direction and the direction and coverage of the smoke. He or she would then use prepared magnetic markers to indicate the position of essential personnel such as the fire teams and the installation medic and his stretcher parties. One of the main advantages of the use of this type of plan is that it allows isolated pieces of information to be seen in the context of the overall emergency. For example, the crew may not appreciate the fact that an oil fire in a certain module will seriously hamper helicopter landings until they see on the plot plan that with the wind blowing across the platform the helideck is shrouded in smoke. The graphic plan therefore places individual pieces of information in the context of the whole platform. Thus, the use of white boards and plot plans supports the storage and organization of information which might be impaired in individuals operating under extreme pressure.

Conclusions

This chapter has provided a brief introduction to some of the human factors issues surrounding emergency response management. Its central theme has been the assertion that, in an emergency, the performance of the installation manager and his team in the coordination of emergency response efforts is vital to the success of the overall operation.

There is no ideal way to deal with emergencies but many pitfalls can be avoided if the emergency response team is prepared for all eventualities, think through what can possibly happen, how the problem can be solved, and how to manage the resources available. Regular and varied exercises and drills, based on realistic scenarios, as well as simulator based training enhance emergency preparedness. Practice may not make perfect but the experience it provides increases the likelihood of effective command and control.

In the event of an emergency, it is important not to rush the response before the situation is assessed properly. OIMs should make sure that they

- Understand the problem before taking action
- Assess the risk and time factors
- Set up contingency plans
- Manage workload to allow time for decision making
- Create a shared problem model by communicating with all team members
- Delegate responsibility as and when appropriate

Oil companies realize the importance of emergency response training.[25] In the light of this increased knowledge and awareness, the European oil and gas industry is tackling the issue of emergency response preparedness in a number of ways, for example:

- Screening of personnel for offshore suitability
- Design of simple decision aids to enhance the effectiveness of decision making.
- Provision of training courses on command and control
- Improve training facilities for emergency response, incident handling, fire fighting, and abandonment of installation

Prevention of accidents is imperative but if things should go wrong, it is important to be prepared. A clearly defined command structure, clarified roles and responsibilities and well trained emergency teams, together enhance the effectiveness of emergency response.

References

1. Health and Safety Executive *A Guide to the Offshore Installations (Prevention Of Fire And Explosion, and Emergency Response) Regulations.* Suffolk: HSE Books, 1995.

2. Mullen, S. *Emergency Planning Guide for Utilities.* Tulsa, OK: PennWell, 1994.

3. Paterson, A.T. *Offshore Fire Safety.* Tulsa, OK: PennWell, 1993.

4. Sefton, A. Introduction to the First Offshore Installation Management Conference: Emergency Command Responsibilities. The Robert Gordon University, Aberdeen, April, 1992.

5. Adams, J. R. *Inquiry into the Causes of the Accident to the Drilling Rig Sea Gem.* The Ministry of Power, London: HMSO, CM3409, 1967.

6. Dept. Of Energy *The Mineral Workings* (Offshore Installations) Act 1971. London: HMSO, 1971.

7. HSE A *Guide to the Offshore Installations and Pipe-line Works (Management and Administration)* Regulations 1995. Suffolk: HSE Books, 1995.

8. Cullen, The Hon. Lord *The Public Inquiry into the Piper Alpha Disaster.* Vols. I & II. London: HMSO. CM1310, 1990.

9. Flin, R. & Slaven, G. *The Selection and Training of Offshore Installation Managers for Crisis Management.* Report to the Offshore Safety Division OTH 92374. Suffolk: HSE Books, 1994.

10. HSE *A Guide to the Offshore Installations (Safety Case) Regulations* (1992). London: HMSO, 1992.

11. U.S. Department of Labor *The Process Safety Management of Highly Hazardous Chemicals.* Washington D.C.: Occupational Safety and Health Administration, 29 CFR Part 1910.119, 1992.

12. Jones, D. & Donegani, A. Some Recent Global Trends in the Regulatory Control of Major Hazards in the Oil and Gas Exploration and Production Industries. *Proceedings of the Second SPE International Conference on Health, Safety & Environment,* Jakarta, 25-27 January, 1994.

13. Flin, R.H. *Sitting in the Hot Seat: Leaders and their Teams Manage Emergencies.* Chicester, United Kingdom: John Wiley, 1996.

14. Kennedy, B. A *Human Factor Analysis of Evacuation, Escape And Rescue from Offshore Installations.* Offshore Technology Report–OTO 93004. London: HSE, 1993.

15. Fleishman, E. A., & Zaccaro, S. J. Toward a taxonomy of team performance functions. In R. W. Swezey & E. Salas (Eds.), *Teams: Their Training and Performance.* Norwood, NJ: Ablex, 1992.

16. Folkman, S. Personal control and stress and coping processes: a theoretical analysis. *Journal of Personality and Social Psychology, 46,* 1984: 839-852.

17. Backer, P. & Orasanu, J. *Stress, Stressors, and Performance in Military Operations: A Review.* Report for the U.S. Army Institute, Contract DAAL03-86-D-001, 1992.

18. Skriver, J., Stewart, K.G., Slaven, G., & Flin, R., Emergency Decision Making. Paper presented at the British Psychological Society's London Conference, London, December 19-20, 1995.

19. Klein, G.A. Recognition-primed decisions. *Advances in Man-Machine Systems Research, 5,* 1989: 47-92.

20. Rasmussen, J., Brehmer, B., & Leplat, J. *Distributed Decision Making: Cognitive Models of Cooperative Work.* Chichester: Wiley, 1991.
21. Gray, A. M. *Warfighting*, FMFM 1. Washington: U.S. Marine Corps, 1989.
22. McIntyre, R. M., & Salas, E. Measuring and managing for team performance: emerging principles from complex environments. In R. Guzzo & E. Salas (Eds.), *Team Effectiveness and Decision Making in Organisations.* San Francisco: Jossey Bass, 1995: 149-203.
23. Chidester, T. R., Kanki, B. G., Foushee, H. C., Dickinson, C. L., & Bowles, S. V. *Personality Factors in Flight Operations: Volume I. Leader Characteristics and Crew Performance in a Full-Mission Air Transport Simulator* (NASA Technical Memorandum No. 102259), 1990.
24. Flin, R. Crew resource management for teams in the offshore oil industry. *Journal of European Industrial Training, 19,*1995: 23-27.
25. Grinde, T.A. Emergency Resource Management Training. *Proceedings of The Second International SPE Conference on Health, Safety and Environment in Oil and Gas Exploration and Production.* Jakarta, Indonesia, January 25-27, 1994.

Chapter 9

Contribution of Human Factors and Human Error to Accidents

Rachael Gordon

Introduction

This chapter considers the role of human error and human factors as causes in accidents and incidents in the offshore oil and gas industry. The chapter begins with an overview of accidents and injuries in the offshore oil and gas industry, followed by an appraisal of accident and incident reporting systems. Finally, the role of human error in causing accidents is considered, as are the steps that can be taken to intervene and alleviate these errors.

Accident and Injury Statistics

The annual frequency of serious accidents which occur in the offshore oil and gas industry is not large, thus limiting opportunities to learn from the trends of such events. Incidents which result in fatalities, serious injuries, or property damage are usually investigated in great depth since the injured party, the regulatory organizations and insurance companies are interested in determining liability. (Near-miss incidents, in which the sequence of events could have caused an accident, had it not been interrupted, are rarely investigated to the same degree). The aims of accident reporting not only are to comply with legal requirements, but also are to prevent recurrence, provide statistics to allow analysis of accident rates and trends in safety performance, and to provide a mechanism of ensuring that actions are taken to improve safety.[1]

The Costs of Accidents

The costs of large scale offshore disasters, such as those resulting from major fires, explosions, or structural collapse are highly visible and emphasize the need for research to reduce the consequences or frequency of such events. The *Piper Alpha* disaster, for example, not only involved the loss of 167 lives, but also was estimated to have cost over £2 billion (3 billion dollars), which included £746 million (more than 1 billion) in direct insurance payouts.[2] The costs of smaller scale accidents, which do not result in the loss of lives, damage to the plant, or interrupted processes, are less easy to detect, as they may be hidden in sick pay, increased insurance premium, or maintenance budgets.[2]

However, it seems to be a widely held view that small accidents also warrant investigation since they occur more frequently than serious accidents and they also involve financial loss to companies.

Definitions

An *incident* refers to all safety related events including accidents and near-misses which may or may not result in injury or damage. The definition of an *accident* is an undesirable event resulting in injury or damage, and a *near-miss* is a situation where the sequence of events could have caused an accident had it not been interrupted.[3] The Offshore Safety Division of the Health and Safety Executive (OSD, HSE) in the United Kingdom requires all accidents and dangerous occurrences on all types of installations operating on the United Kingdom Continental Shelf to be reported using the non-mandatory form OIR/9A. There are four reporting categories for offshore incidents: 1) fatalities, 2) serious injuries, 3) injuries resulting in at least three days off work (Lost Time Accident: LTA) and 4) dangerous occurrences.

Worldwide Accident Statistics

The Oil Industry International Exploration & Production Forum compiles accident statistics from 34 member companies, covering onshore and offshore oil operations in over 60 countries.[4] Since the database was set up in 1989, the Lost Time Injury Frequency (number of lost time injuries + fatalities/million man hours worked) has decreased from 5.7 in 1989 compared to 3.4 in 1994, and the Fatal Accident Rate (fatalities per hundred million man hours) has decreased from 10.4 in 1993 to 6.7 in 1994. The majority of the improvement in the LTIF is due to contractor operations where the LTIF has decreased from 8.1 in 1989 to 3.6 in 1994. The major improvements in LTIFs have been in South America (33% improvement), Europe (17%) and Canada (14%). The number of days lost due to injuries was reported to be 73,635 days, equivalent to a work force of 334 man years.

In 1994, there were 58 fatalities, 37 less than in 1993. (The only other year to have less than 60 fatalities was 1988 when there were 55 recorded fatalities.) Of the 58 fatalities recorded, 38 were contractor personnel and 20 were company personnel. The main causes of fatal accidents were motor vehicle (16), struck by an object (11), explosions (8), falls (5), caught between objects (5), drowning (3), aviation (3) and electrocution (2). The majority of fatalities occurred during production (33), drilling operations (13) and five occurred during exploration operations. There was a large reduction in Fatal Accident Rates in production operations from 72 in 1993 to 33 in 1994.[4]

The most dramatic decreases in LTIF rates from 1990 to 1994 were by offshore contractors (9.6 in 1990 to 3.6 in 1994) and offshore company staff (5.3 in 1990 to 3.8 in 1994). The LTIF rates of onshore personnel, by comparison, were less dramatic and for the onshore company staff, their LTIF rates increased slightly from 1990 to 1994 (see Table 9-1).[4]

Table 9-1 Worldwide Lost Time Injury Frequencies by Type of Employee

YEAR	1990	1991	1992	1993	1994
Onshore company	1.9	2.6	3.1	2.7	2.2
Offshore company	5.3	4.0	4.3	4.5	3.8
Onshore contractor	5.3	4.8	4.3	4.3	4.5
Offshore contractor	9.6	8.8	6.9	5.6	3.6
All regions	4.7	4.5	4.3	3.9	3.4

Source: E & P Forum (1995) E & P Forum Accident Statistics. (from Table 3)
Reproduced by permission of the E & P Forum, 1994.

UKCS Accident Statistics

The following section is a summary of the OSD, HSE Offshore Accident Statistics Report recording data from 1980-1995.[5] Table 9-2 illustrates the changes in the estimated workforce frequencies of accidents and incidents during the previous 15 years. Lost Time Injuries were only recorded as injuries resulting in over three days off work after 1990. The report shows that the frequency of fatalities, serious injuries and Lost Time Injuries have decreased over this period, whereas there has been an general increase in the number of dangerous occurrences have decreased (from 633 in 1993-4 to 594 in 1994-5). Note that the estimated workforce frequency has also decreased over this period from 34,200 in 1993-4 to 27,200 in 1994-5.

The International Labor Organization has listed some of the international accident databases currently in use.[6] VERITEC (Veritas Offshore Technology and Services A/S) has been compiling offshore accident data since 1975 and the data have been housed with the Worldwide Offshore Accident Database (WOAD) since 1983. WOAD offers a more detailed account of the accidents than the E & P Forum Database although the data for injuries and fatalities have been limited to absolute figures. The accident trends indicate that although fixed installations are more numerous than mobile ones, generally more accidents have occurred on mobile rigs since 1975, in particular on jackup rigs.

Table 9-2 Estimated United Kingdom Offshore Oil Industry Workforce, Number of Fatalities, Serious Injuries, Lost Time Accidents and Dangerous Occurrences from 1980-1995.

Year	Estimated Workforce	Fatalities	Serious Injuries	Lost Time Injuries	Dangerous Occurrences
1980-89 ave/year*	27,300	7.3 (24)**	68.2	-	187.2
1989/90	30,700	3	76	-	303
1990/91	36,500	13	84	744	386
1991/92	33,200	13#	73	571	373
1992/93	29,500	5	79	511	525
1993/94	34,200	1	52	412	633
1994/95	27,200	1	41	270	594

 * figures averaged over 10 year period
** figures in brackets includes *Piper Alpha*
 # includes *Cormorant Alpha* helicopter accident
Source: HSE Offshore Accident and Incident Statistical Report. (from Table 7) Reproduced by permission of the HSE, OSD, 1995.

The above accident reports give us an idea of the relative number of serious accidents that occur each year, as well as the degree to which these accidents are declining in number since 1989 when the two recording systems were established. The greatest changes in the last five years in accident rates seem to be by the contracting companies. The fatality rate had remained the same for the past five years, and only in 1994 did it fall to any great extent. In order to plot trends in accident data from all over the world, it is important that similar reporting schemes are used so any differences found between companies or countries can be put down to cultural differences rather than differences in accident reporting policies and forms. The next section discusses form design.

Accident and Incident Reporting

Methods for Collecting Accident/Incident Reports

By investigating accident reporting methods used in other industries, it is possible to learn from not only what they have found, but also the methods by which they reached their results. For the past few decades, the civil aviation industry has spent much time and money on investigations into aircraft accidents. The aviation industry uses subjective information from crew members as a major source for their investigation into accidents and incidents as well as hard data from voice and black box recordings. The aviation industry has found that a balance between the two methods, a structured interview guide with a checklist, is an efficient way of investigating accidents (see Table 9-3 for an example of a checklist).[7] Often this is used in the offshore oil industry as well.

Table 9-3 An Example of a Human Factors Checklist for Accident Reporting Forms on Offshore Installations.

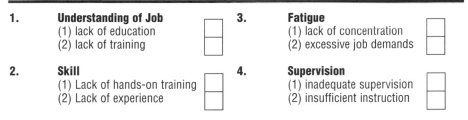

1.	**Understanding of Job** (1) lack of education (2) lack of training	☐	**3.**	**Fatigue** (1) lack of concentration (2) excessive job demands	☐
2.	**Skill** (1) Lack of hands-on training (2) Lack of experience	☐	**4.**	**Supervision** (1) inadequate supervision (2) insufficient instruction	☐

Accident Reporting Forms

Accident reporting forms can take the following formats:

1) *Open text*, where responses asked for in an open question format make it difficult to standardize reports and to compare between various entries, but it does not constrain responses and can give more detailed data.

2) *Multiple choice*, where a series of options are provided to each question, although it allows for swift analysis, not all incidents can be described this way. Multiple choice questions are often used for the following topics:

- *incident description*—category, severity, type
- *activities leading to the incident*—location, operations, work undertaken, protective equipment
- *immediate causes*—action that caused incident, conditions present causing accident
- *root causes*—personal factors, job factors, procedure-related, permit-related
- *safety management issues*—systems that failed, recommendations to avoid recurrence

3) *Keywords* help standardize free text while allowing some flexibility. They provide a list of keywords from which the person can choose the relevant option(s) and write them in the provided space. However, it is important that these keywords are understood by all those who are required to use them and that they are easy to use so that completing a form is not made unduly difficult or time consuming.

The majority of offshore oil and gas industry accident reporting forms have questions which require written answers (open questions) and they often have sections with multiple-choice questions where the injury and cause of accident can be described from a checklist with a set of specified options.

An accident reporting form will tend to contain most of the following basic items:[1]

- Type of incident: injury, disease, property damage, material loss, process disruption, poisonous or flammable substance leaks, fire or explosion, dangerous occurrences, environmental harm, near-misses, hazards.
- Personal details of people involved, including supervisor at the time
- Date, time and location of occurrence
- Work being carried out, experience of persons involved
- Equipment being used, including safety equipment and devices
- Equipment failures
- Protective clothing being worn
- Other people working in the area
- Permits being issued, procedures being used
- Contributory factors, e.g. environmental conditions, any hazards present

Reporting forms which have more details may include some of the following human factors causes of accidents: details of job training, level of job instruction, level of fatigue, concentration, job demands, time pressure, inadequate supervision, or inadequate planning of the job. It must be noted that this is only a sample of possible human factor causes of accidents, and when implementing human factors categories into an accident reporting form, those who will be using the form should have training in how to use this section of the form and the categories used need to reflect patterns of previous human factor causes of accidents.

Incident Investigation

In an ideal world, all incidents and accidents that occur would be thoroughly investigated to determine all root causes of the accidents. For the most part, incidents and accidents are investigated to some extent. Initially, the incident is usually described by a worker directly involved in the event. In the case of an injury, the investigation would usually involve the injured person visiting the medic to receive treatment. A brief report would be written by the supervisor in charge at the time including the injured person's description of the accident, and finally comments are normally added by the supervisor, the safety officer and the Offshore Installation Manager. Copies of the accident report would be given to the onshore Safety Department, the immediate supervisor, the OIM, the legislative authority (depending on severity) and where there is an injury, a copy is kept in the Medical Center.

For serious accidents, investigations are usually based on technical accident causation and human error models. Those involved in the incident are interviewed and an analysis of what occurred is recorded. For minor accidents, the investigators are the supervisors and safety officers and they usually have some training, although there is not always the time and resources for in-depth training with regard to, for example, human factors causes of accidents. For a serious incident, teams will fly to the installation from the onshore office as will government accident inspectors. It has been argued that incident investigations usually result in the emphasis being placed on specific incidents rather than on general patterns and on technical rather than human factors.[1]

Near-Miss Reporting

A *near-miss* is a situation where the sequence of events could have caused an accident had it not been interrupted. *Near-miss* reporting relies on the responsible person reporting the event so that the causes leading up to the event can be identified and communicated to personnel across the installation. The incentives for personnel to report these are few and it is necessary to create an environment in which personnel will be more likely to report near-miss incidents, no matter how insignificant they may seem. To create such a blame-free culture environment, it should be made clear to personnel that they will not be punished or vindicated when they report such an event, rather they are to be encouraged to. However, the details surrounding the event should be presented to all personnel on the installation to make them aware of the causes and possible consequences. This technique is used in aviation confidential near-miss systems in the United Kingdom and U.S. and by a number of offshore oil companies.

It is the aim of all oil companies to have the lowest possible accident rate, with ideally no accidents occurring. However, a low accident frequency rate does not necessarily mean that the installation will be safe in the future. Designing broader incident reporting systems, which also include near misses and minor accidents, would allow a better understanding of how to prevent future accidents.[8] Near-miss reporting can provide information about common events and provide data for safety studies about types and rates of failure.

In order to define what events should be reported, it is necessary to know the system's potential to cause injury and damage. In addition, a knowledge of the hazards that are present, how they are controlled and how control can be lost is important for the reporting of near misses. An assessment of the types of accidents which could have occurred, and the incidents which had the potential to cause injury or damage should also be recorded. For the majority of oil companies near-miss reporting does exist, although the extent to which companies use the information as educational preventative measures is dependent on the resources that are available.

One of the legal requirements for accident reporting on the United Kingdom Continental Shelf is to report *dangerous occurrences*, i.e. incidents which do not result in injury or property damage, but are significant in terms of the potential seriousness of the incident, such as a load falling from a crane which did not result in damage to the plant or injury to a person. In order to determine the level of investigation required for an incident and the likelihood of it reoccurring, there are several *Incident Potential* systems currently used to evaluate the actual risk associated with incidents. One method involves the incident being broken down through a series of questions concerning the potential for loss, and severity, giving each incident a *potential* score and combining the scores to calculate a hazard rating. Another approach, called the Incident Potential Matrix, uses a scale which measures the severity of the incident on one axis and the number of people and the amount of risk to property on the other; the intersection of the two measures would indicate the actual incident's potential seriousness.[1]

In a marine seismic operation in Europe and Africa, the Incident Potential Matrix (IPM) was introduced as part of the reporting system on the vessels to stimulate the reporting of near accidents/hazardous situations.[9] The aim was to use the IPM as a tool to identify the most dangerous situations in operations, thus enlightening the crew on the necessity of accident and near-miss reporting. Investigation showed that the frequency of near-misses that were reported increased and the database of these incidents gave valuable information about the most dangerous situations that crew members were exposed to.

Exchange and Use of Accident Data

In order to increase the offshore accident information base six companies combined their accident data into a database called *Synergy*.[10] In 1992, three Norwegian oil companies (Norsk Hydro, Saga Petroleum and Statoil) together with three offshore contractors (Aker, Braathens Helikopter and Smedvig) developed the first version of the system and data are now collected by the Rogaland Research Institute in Stavanger, where the companies send their accident reports via electronic mail. There is an increasing emphasis on the immediate as well as basic causes of accidents which include the human factors. Each company receives an updated version of the database quarterly and the system has been extended to be used in English as well.

The operating company, Shell's answer to Synergy is: GUARD (Group Unified Accident Reporting Database) which uses feedback from accidents that have occurred, and includes the use of immediate and underlying causes (which is described in the section on Error Reduction Strategies)and areas of weakness.[11] Accident information is entered into a computer to which details on the corrective actions are also included. The main emphasis of this system is on the identification of basic causes which include personal, organizational and job factors; definitions of the causes of accidents are provided with the system. In addition, the system should be kept simple and flexible so that operating companies can meet their individual needs. This system can provide an accurate historical base of accident information and which could serve as a data base for safety studies and can help promote consistent safety recording and reporting and increase the reporting of non-injury related accidents and unsafe acts throughout Shell worldwide.

The above section has outlined the various methods used to collect data, in particular the accident reporting form, its form and content. The investigation process of incidents and the use of near-miss reporting are detailed with a brief description of databases which have been developed to combine accident data from different companies around the world. In the following section, the human contribution to accidents will be discussed in detail including methods used to measure the human involvement in industrial accidents/incidents.

The Role of Human Factors in Accident Causation

In the past, industrial accidents were reported mainly in terms of technological malfunctions whereas the human element in accident causation tended to be ignored. Since the frequency of technological failures has diminished, the role of human error has become much more apparent. Accidents such as the *Piper Alpha* disaster illustrate that the performance of a highly complex sociotechnical system is dependent upon the complex interaction of technical as well as human, social, organizational, managerial and environmental factors. Also these factors can be important co-contributors in a chain of catastrophic events. The psychology-related domain of human factors has the potential to deal with many of the problems raised by high reliability organizations, such as the physiological bases of human action, cognitive function, group working, organizational conditions of work, strain and stress and risk communication.

Human factors as a subject addresses issues regarding safety and accidents at the *individual, group* and *organizational* levels. At the *individual* level (i.e. optimization of the human-machine interface), the indicators, signals, controls, alarm systems and visual display units are evaluated. Health risks (such as work overload) and the contribution of human error to the probability of accidents are also of concern. At the *group* level, the relationships between members of a work group, and between individuals and their supervisors, have the potential to influence the safety of an installation, as does the design of the workplace. Third, at the *organizational level*, various factors may contribute to an increase in incidents and accidents, including cost-cutting programs and the level of communication between offshore and onshore management. Other factors at the organizational level may contribute to a decrease in the frequency of accidents, such as incident reporting systems and the causal analysis of accidents, both of which need consistent classification schemes for the adequate categorization of incidents and their causes, as well as feedback to the work force.[13]

Causes of Accidents

From accident analyses, statistics reveal that human factors seem to dominate the risks in complex installations.[15] Even equipment failures usually can be traced to human failure. The majority of systems accidents can be traced back to *fallible decisions* made by designers and high-level managers. The adverse consequences of these decisions could be alleviated if line management was competent to make these decisions. However, if line-management is limited by resources, put under undue time pressure, has inappropriate perceptions of the hazards, is ignorant of the hazards or has motivational difficulties, it is unlikely that they will identify these problems. In this case, *line-management deficiencies* could result in a management failure (such as deficient training) revealing itself as a human error (such as performing a task incorrectly). However, if the management failure had been rectified, the task might have been carried out correctly.

The *psychological precursors for unsafe acts* are dependent on the task under completion, the environmental influences, and whether or not there are hazards present. These *psychological precursors* are latent conditions which can play a significant role in encouraging and shaping a large set of unsafe acts. An unsafe act only can be defined in relation to the presence of particular hazards and therefore acts such as not wearing ear protectors or a hard hat, are only unsafe when they occur in a potentially hazardous situation (i.e. in a noisy environment, or when objects are likely to fall from above).

At the lowest level of *safety defenses*, Personal Protective Equipment (PPE) for the work force and guards for preventing direct contact with dangerous materials can help prevent injury, while at the other extreme, there are control room operators and automatic safety devices. The various levels of defense only can be breached by many causal factors occurring simultaneously, some of which will be latent failures while others will be triggering events. The practical application of this theory is described later in this chapter.

Human Factors Accident Causation Categories

Rainer Miller, Max Freitag and Bernhard Wilpert compiled a classification scheme of human factors causes of accidents based on different theories from different psychological domains used for analyzing accidents in nuclear power plants.[20] The scheme comprises eight categories:

1) *general aspects*: time, state of system, operational phases, locus, affected parts, characteristics of the component and actors,

2) *organizational aspects*: interorganizational cooperation, safety culture,

3) *personal aspects*: characteristics of acting person and group characteristics,

4) *process factors*: content and characteristics of task, level of task, procedures for task, information about task, tools and safety devices,

5) *aspects of the failure*: the trigger, the failure type, violations of rules and procedures,

6) *aspects of causes*: conditioning factors, communication, erroneous decision-making and level of information processing,

7) *aspects of feedback*: feedback characteristics, error consequence, error discovery,

8) *external impacts*: lightning, flood.

A database was established by the Commission of the European Communities in 1984 for collecting information on worldwide major industrial accidents, called "Major Accident Reporting System" (MARS). From 1984 to 1994 the most common causes of accidents were found to be component failures and pipework failures, and the second most common were operator errors. The underlying causes of accidents were detailed as: 1) *managerial/ organizational omissions*, which included insufficient procedures, related to design inadequacies, insufficient operator training and lack of a safety culture, 2) *design inadequacy*, which included analysis of the inadequacy of the process, codes/practices provided for limited protection only and 3) *short cuts.*[21]

The U.S. Office of Marine Safety, Security and Environmental Protection and the Office of Navigation Safety and Waterway Services have recently developed a strategy to prevent casualties resulting from human error.[22] They categorized human errors into five groups: 1) *management* (e.g. faulty standards and inadequate communications) 2) *operator status* (e.g. inattention, carelessness, fatigue), 3) *working environment* (e.g. poor equipment design), 4) *knowledge* (e.g. inadequate general technical knowledge) and 5) *decision making* (e.g. poor judgment, inadequate information). The largest problems were found to be fatigue, crew coordination, and inadequate technical knowledge. Researchers believed that the reason for the persistence of marine casualties were the lack of root-cause investigations, lack of identifying and analyzing high risk operations, and lack of identifying, developing and implementing measures to prevent human errors.

This section has outlined the various levels of human error from fallible decisions made by management, line-management deficiencies to the psychological precursors of unsafe acts. In addition, categories of human factors accident causation which have been used in other industries, such as the nuclear, chemical and U.S. marine industries, are described indicating that similar factors have been addressed across the industries.

Human Error

Theories of Human Error

Rasmussen's Skill-Rule-Knowledge Framework. Jens Rasmussen's model was devised to track errors made by supervisors in onshore industrial installations, especially in hazardous process plants during emergencies. The model was derived from the verbal protocols of technicians involved in *trouble-shooting* and three levels of performance were found to correspond to the technicians' level of familiarity with the environment and task. The three levels of performance derived from this study are now used within the systems reliability community as the market standard.[14] The three levels of performance are: 1) skill-based, 2) rule-based and 3) knowledge-based. At the *skill-based* level, performance is governed by patterns of preprogrammed instructions and errors occur when monitoring of the task fails. *Rule-based* performance applies stored rules (such as *if-then* rules) to form solutions to problems. Errors at this level usually occur when situations are misclassified leading to the use of wrong rules or not using the correct procedures. *Knowledge-based* performance is used in novel situations, where actions are planned on the spot by using stored knowledge and conscious analytic processes. Errors arise when the resources are limited, or there is incorrect or incomplete knowledge. As expertise in an area increases, control of performance moves from knowledge-based towards skill-based levels.

By classifying human errors at the worksite by these definitions, it is possible to focus on the actual problem, whether it be a monitoring failure, using the wrong rules, or applying incorrect or incomplete knowledge. By understanding the basis of the accident/error, it is possible to target the problem area. James Reason expanded on this theory of accident causation which is detailed in the following section.[15] This theory has been used as a Human Reliability Assessment technique which is described later in this chapter.

Reason's Generic Error Modelling System (GEMS). GEMS is a framework used to locate the origins of basic human error types, devised by Reason & Mycelia.[16] Rasmussen's three performance levels were used by Reason as the basis for the following categories of human errors: 1) skill-based slips and lapses, 2) rule-based mistakes and 3) knowledge-based mistakes.[15] *Slips* are actions which are carried out incorrectly; *lapses* are errors which have resulted by the omission of an action and *mistakes* are the result of the failure of intended actions to achieve their desired consequences.

At the *skill-based* level, tasks are performed without conscious control (after an intention has been stated) and routine and nonproblematic activities are dealt with in familiar situations during this level of performance. Distraction or preoccupation with another task can lead to slips and lapses where monitoring of the task fails. *Rule-based* and *knowledge-based* performance are only brought into play after an individual has become conscious of a problem. For an error to occur at this level, attention would not necessarily have to stray far from the problem. Problem solving failures may occur when the incorrect rule is applied (*rule-based*) or the person is unfamiliar with the problem (*knowledge-based*). In addition to slips, lapses and mistakes, violations are also unsafe acts which Reason describes as deliberate deviations from procedures deemed necessary to maintain the safe operation of a potentially hazardous system.[15]

Human Error Categories

The types of errors that personnel in industrial settings make, have been summarized by Kontogiannis and Embrey (cited by Brazier & Black).

- *Action errors:* where either no action is taken, the wrong action is taken or the correct action is taken but on the wrong object.
- *Checking errors:* the checks are omitted, the wrong checks are made or the correct check is made on the wrong object.
- *Retrieval errors:* when information that is required is not available, or the wrong information is received.
- *Transmission errors:* when information has to be passed on to someone else, either no information is sent, the wrong information is sent, or it is sent to the wrong place.
- *Diagnostic errors:* when an abnormal event arises, the actual situation is misinterpreted.

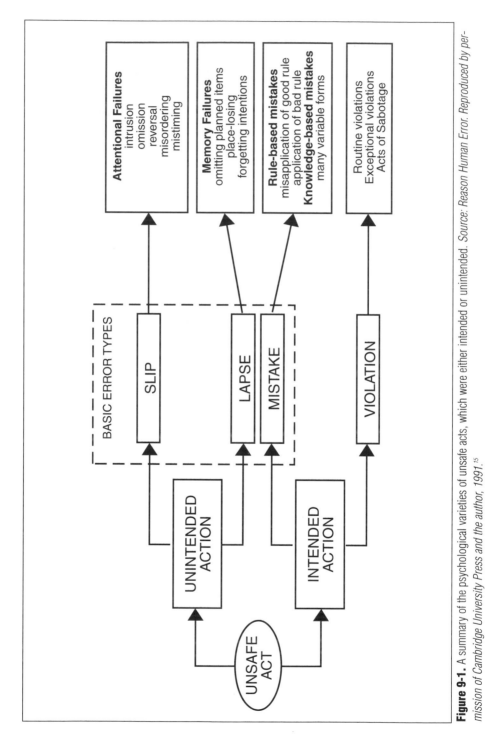

Figure 9-1. A summary of the psychological varieties of unsafe acts, which were either intended or unintended. *Source: Reason Human Error. Reproduced by permission of Cambridge University Press and the author, 1991.*[15]

- *Decision errors:* when the circumstances have been considered but the wrong decision is made.

From research into human errors in the nuclear industry, Rasmussen categorized 200 significant events into the following human error categories: omission of functionally isolated acts, latent conditions not considered, other omissions, side effects not considered, alertness low, mistakes among alternatives, strong expectation, manual variability, lack of precision, spatial orientation weak, absent-mindedness and familiar association.[17] These results indicate that the majority of errors made in the nuclear industry are omissions and errors which had been made previously but had not been detected.

International Nuclear Power Operations distinguished between 180 significant events in the nuclear industry in terms of their root causes, from which 387 root causes were identified.[18] The human performance problems were broken down into the following categories: deficient procedures or documentation, 43%; lack of knowledge or training, 18%; failure to follow procedures, 16%; deficient planning or scheduling, 10%; miscommunication, 6%; deficient supervision, 3%; policy problems, 2%; other, 2%. At least 92% of the causes of accidents were man-made, only a small proportion of the root causes were actually initiated by front-line personnel (i.e. failure to follow procedures) and most originated in either maintenance-related activities or in poor decisions taken within the organizational and managerial domains.

In a North American study, errors during normal conditions at a pipeline system control room, such as failing to open a valve when preparing a pipeline, were identified as slips or lapses.[19] Slips and lapses only occur when either a *distraction* or *preoccupation* is present. Other slips include *inappropriately timed checks*, which are likely to occur immediately following a period of absence from the task, caused by interruptions and *omission* errors. Omission errors are most likely to occur when, 1) there is a large number of steps in the sequence, 2) when the information is complex, 3) when the procedural steps are not in an obvious order, 4) when instructions are given verbally (and there are more than five simple steps), 5) when instructions are given in written form and isolated steps are given at the end of the sequence and 6) in a highly-automated, well-practiced task and there are unexpected interruptions.

Abnormal conditions have been found to play an important role in accidents in complex technological systems where there can be interference by more familiar situations. One of the problems when dealing with errors in unfamiliar situations is the low probability of the occurrence of such situations. When an abnormal situation arises, the operator has to generate procedures by functional evaluation and causal reasoning, based on knowledge of the system properties. This suggests that more than one operator be involved in the problem solving during an abnormal, rare event.

Latent Errors

When considering human errors in systems disasters, two kinds of errors can be involved: *Active errors* (slips, lapses, mistakes and violations) which have been described above (see Figure 9-1) and whose effects are generally almost immediate and *latent errors*, whose adverse consequences may lie dormant within the system for a long time, only become evident when they combine with other factors to breach the systems defenses. *Active errors* are most likely to be caused by front-line operators (e.g. control-room crews, production operators), whereas *latent errors* are more likely to be caused by those who are removed from the direct control interface (e.g. designers, high-level decision makers, managers, construction workers and maintenance personnel). In most cases, safety programs are aimed at the operators, at reducing active failures in order to reduce specific causes which are unlikely to occur in the same combination.

In one of their studies in the nuclear industry, Miller *et. al.* found that in 20% of the incidents, outside (contracting or subcontracting) companies were involved, and for the majority of these cases there was a time lag between the error and the consequence.[20] This indicates that the main contribution from the outside firms did not result in immediate incidents, rather they resulted in incidents which occurred later (i.e. latent errors). Wrong and missing procedures contributed to incidents in 22% of all cases. In the other half of the cases there was a time lag of more than 15 minutes and up to eight hours between the error being made and the consequence, where most errors were maintenance, again indicating that latent errors play a major part.

Error Reduction Strategies

Improving Incident Reporting and Feedback Systems

Various accident researchers have identified changes to improve accident reporting systems in order to prevent accidents and incidents occurring in the future. The necessary steps to prevent the occurrence of future accidents described from a traditional engineering point of view, would be to 1) make immediate technical recommendations, 2) investigate ways of avoiding hazards, and 3) investigate ways of improving the management system.[23] From a psychologist's point of view, Reason describes the causes of accidents in terms of active and latent failures, which points the finger at the decision makers, line management, individuals, and system defenses.[15]

Others believe that by creating a human factors database on incidents and accidents, more accidents and incidents could be prevented.[1,15,24] This would include identifying latent errors, events that trigger accidents, human errors and error inducing conditions present before and after the event. In addition to an accident database, task inventories could be performed to describe work groups' objectives and operating procedures, the hazards and the potential of the work group to cause an accident, and the possible outcomes of incidents. In addition, the operator's performance could be regularly reassessed, by studying operator's habits during routine activity. Brazier states that it is important that this type of the safety program is open to all employees and must be perceived as quite separate from any element of blame; moreover, it should be realized that this kind of change may not happen rapidly.[1]

Reason believed that in order to have adequate safety control, a feedback system is required (see Figure 9-2) as is the ability to respond rapidly and effectively to the actual and anticipated changes in safety.[15] Figure 9-2 indicates the various feedback loops which can be used to manage safety and which constitute the Safety Information System (SIS).

Loop 1, *reporting of accidents and incidents*, constitutes the minimum requirement for SIS. However, success in reducing the number of accidents means that there are very few accidents which can be used for analysis, in order to prevent further accidents. Furthermore, the accidents which are reported are generally at the tip of the iceberg. Each accident has unique characteristics and if the goal is to remove the chance of other dissimilar accidents from occurring in the future, feedback from this *retrospective* reporting system is of limited use. However, this method encourages the awareness of types of accidents that can occur. Loop 2 involves the *auditing of unsafe acts*, by sampling the frequency and nature of unsafe acts. Analysis of unsafe acts can enable managers to assess weak spots and failures before an accident occurs. Examining the types of unsafe acts which are prevalent can indicate which underlying problems are leading to unsafe acts being performed more than others.

The *psychological precursors* of unsafe acts (Loop 3) are more difficult to assess directly as they tend to be variable. At Loop 4, information in terms of general latent failures (or line-management deficiencies) can be audited before an incident ever need occur. Auditing at this level has been demonstrated on North Sea gas platforms and in an Australian desert drilling operation by Reason and colleagues.[25,26]

Anticipation and Prevention of Accidents

A program called TRIPOD was developed to highlight the importance of underlying (latent) factors in the causation of accidents.[26] Underlying latent

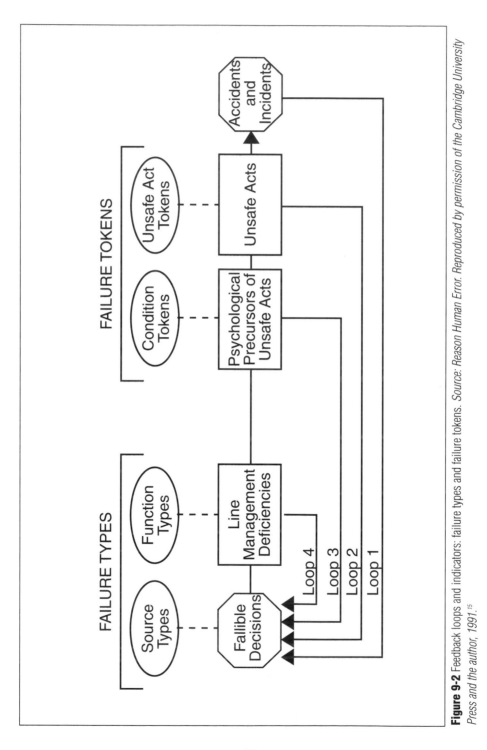

Figure 9-2 Feedback loops and indicators: failure types and failure tokens. *Source: Reason Human Error. Reproduced by permission of the Cambridge University Press and the author, 1991.[15]*

failures are central to the idea of how accidents happen and are referred to as General Failure Types, which include *hardware, design, maintenance, procedures, error enforcing conditions, housekeeping, incompatible goals, organization, communication, training and defenses.* These General Failure Types often lead to specific unsafe acts and triggering events. In order to assess the state of an organization or activity in terms of it's underlying latent problems, an instrument was developed, called a Failure State Profile, to measure the extent of the underlying problems on the basis of a sample of General Failure Types.

Specialist personnel on the desert rig (e.g. tool-pusher, drill supervisor) rated their rig on each of the General Failure Types. From these data, a checklist was developed which was sent out to six rigs. The results indicated that *training* appeared to be the main problem and *defenses* and *hardware* appeared to be the least important of the General Failure Types. There were differences between the beliefs of drilling supervisors and tool pushers with regard to the problematic General Failure Types, where the tool pushers tended to believe that *incompatible goals* and *error enforcing* conditions were the main problems after *training;* whereas, the drilling supervisors thought that *organization* and *operating procedures* were the main problems after *training.* Rig staff (tool pushers and drill supervisors) thought that *communication* on the rig was good, whereas office staff thought it was poor. The TRIPOD approach consists of a general understanding for safety and how accidents happen as well as an instrument to enable companies to identify their real underlying safety problems and latent failures.

Other oil companies have developed tools which identify the Performance Influencing Factors and aim to reduce the potential for human error.[27] Exxon has tested such a tool in Canada, France, USA, Australia, and the United Kingdom and has found that it provides insights into how to implement management systems. There are four stages in this analysis: 1) *Screening Components:* Out of 37 items, users are asked to identify which are of primary and secondary interest to the safety of the installation. 2) *Data Gathering:* A questionnaire which refers to the operations being analyzed asks users to section the PIFs into high, medium and low priority with regard to installation safety. 3) *Interpretation of Components:* describes a method to analyze the scores of the individual factors. It involves a discussion on the scores given to each factor in order to identify opportunities to improve the usability of specific systems and practices. 4) *Solution Component:* provides reference to specific methods, such as task analysis that will reduce the vulnerability to error for the identified areas of opportunity. This process requires training for a cross-section of selected personnel and the necessary software to guide personnel to general solutions and is more likely to be effective with a human factors specialist present. This method was found to help with the development and upgrade of procedures and it provided an insight into establishing a procedures-based culture.

Human Reliability Assessment Techniques for Reducing Human Error

Over the past thirty years, Human Reliability Assessment (HRA) has been developed originally for the nuclear and chemical industries and is largely concerned with the elements which promote human error in high risk systems. The purpose of HRA is to assess the likelihood and consequences of such errors and then to propose and implement measures to reduce the impact or frequency of the human error.[28] HRA developed rapidly after the highly documented *Three Mile Island* incident in the U.S., in which a nuclear accident occurred where human error was revealed to have been a significant contributing factor to the cause and development of the accident. In order to reduce the likelihood of human error, HRA uses human error probabilities (Probabilistic Risk Analysis, PRA) and detailed theoretical modeling of the human operator. PRA defines the expected frequencies of accidents and determines the state of the plant in regard to defined risk criteria.

Human Error Identification (HEI) techniques question what can go wrong. If the error is not identified, then it's contribution to risk cannot be assessed. It is important that HEI techniques are auditable so that errors can be classified in the following ways: 1) *External Error Mode* (EEM) (i.e. errors of omission, commission or extraneous errors) and 2) *Performance Influencing Factors* (PIF) are those factors which increase or decrease the likelihood of human error, focusing on management as responsible for safety. PIFs fit into six categories:

1) corporate factors (e.g. management, financial pressure, safety audits)
2) process factors (e.g. technology, workplace hazards)
3) machine interface factors (e.g. controls, displays)
4) environmental factors (e.g. work patterns, physical conditions)
5) equipment factors (e.g. PPE, tools, plant)
6) individual factors (e.g. experience, knowledge, personality and health).

Operational PIFs include: training, degree of time pressure, availability of procedures, design of work place, quality of information available which all have a direct effect on probability of errors occurring. *Management PIFs* include: policies for training for procedures which have indirect effects on the likelihood of error and a direct effect via organizational culture. There are a number of techniques within HEI, some of which are detailed below.

Technique for Human Error Rate Prediction (THERP)

THERP is a widely used technique for both it's quantification approach and for error identification. It is possible for THERP to identify a high proportion of the potential human errors that occur as long as the assessor has a good understanding of the task. This method identifies the possible external error modes (EEM) at each step defined with task analysis, and for each task, THERP considers whether it is possible that the task could fail. THERP also takes into account the range of PIFs which give rise to human error.

The disadvantages of THERP are that it lacks rigorous structure and there is a possibility of considerable variation in assessment, identification of errors, and error recovery from different assessors. THERP can fail in considering explicitly *why* and *where* errors occur. The advantages of THERP is that it is simple to use and it is fairly comprehensive in error identification.

Human Error HAZOP (Human Error Hazard and Operability Study)

Human Error HAZOP is a modification of the traditional HAZOP study, where the analyst's judgment is a useful resource in error identification due to their experience and involvement in safety analysis[29] Error identification for the human reliability practitioner may prove to be more difficult than for the hardware reliability analyst who knows the system in detail. Therefore it is necessary to take a multi-disciplinary approach when conducting Human Error HAZOP. The advantage of HAZOP is that it occurs at an early design stage, therefore errors are identified early and can be rectified with minimal cost. However, HAZOP is resource intensive; it is only as good as the group working on it and it is not always effective at resolving human error problems if a human factors specialist is not present.[29] HAZOP is a fairly comprehensive system, although its focus is not on the identification of causes of errors.

The Skill, Rule, Knowledge (SRK)-Based Behavior Approach

The SRK approach assumes that behavior is hierarchical, where the simplest level of behavior is skill-based, and occurs in situations which require highly practiced and essentially *automatic* behavior, with only minimal conscious control. The second level of behavior is rule-based, and occurs when a situation deviates from the normal, but is controllable by the person involved, consciously applying rules. These rules are either stored within the person's memory which can be readily accessed, for example, in the form of an emergency operating manual. The third and highest level of behavior is knowledge-based behavior, where the person involved lacks any useful rules which can be applied, and has to diagnose the situation through problem-solving skills and system knowledge. As can be seen from these explanations, SRK is behavior/ cognitive orientated, where SRK suggests that different types of error can occur within these different levels of behavior/ cognitive processes.[29]

The SRK approach questions what could go wrong in terms of external error modes, what the *internal human malfunction* could be (for example, detection failure), and what the *underlying mechanism of human malfunction* could be.[29] The most useful aspect of the SRK model is a flowchart, used to derive the psychological mechanisms of malfunctions. The disadvantage of SRK is that it can produce data *after* the event has happened, but has difficulty *predicting* incidents due to the combinations of external error modes and internal human malfunction, respectively.

System for Predictive Error Analysis and Reduction (SPEAR)

David E. Embrey stated that the main contributor to risk is human error at the management/operational level in the organisation, since many human errors result from conditions created by management policies.[30] The System for Predictive Error Analysis and Reduction (SPEAR) is a framework originally developed to provide users in the chemical industry with a consistent and logical structure to which they could apply specific techniques by human factor specialists, such as task analysis and predictive error analysis. The objectives of SPEAR are to:

- assess the risk potential of operational tasks in the system
- prioritize these tasks in increasing risk potential
- apply techniques to predict specific types of errors that are likely to occur
- evaluate the consequences of these errors
- specify measures to reduce error probability for severe consequences

SPEAR consists of four phases:

I. *Screening process.* The purpose of the screening process is to identify the human interactions with the process system which have significant potential of risk if errors occur. This involves (a) the development of an operator's task inventory, (b) the identification of a sub-set of critical tasks with risk potential and (c) prioritizing critical tasks on the basis of severity of consequence. This is an effective method for identifying tasks which constitute significant risk to a plant.

II. *Detailed error analysis.* The second phase involves detailed *error analysis* to evaluate errors which could arise in the sub-set of tasks identified in the first phase. The stages of this phase consist of four stages. 1) *Hierarchical Task Analysis* (HTA) is a method for describing the structure of tasks and the order in which the steps are performed. The information for this stage is usually based on existing procedures supplemented by interviews with operators and other relevant personnel. For this analysis (a) the overall objective of the task is defined, (b) the task is then defined in more detail, in terms of functions or sub-tasks, (c) each sub-task is broken down into individual task steps and (d) plans are developed at each stage which specify how each item is to be executed in order to achieve the objective. The HTA technique allows the analyst to choose the level of detail required for the analysis and provides a complete, structured and detailed description of what the operator actually does during the sub-tasks.

2) *Predictive Human Error Analysis* (PHEA) is a systematic process for identifying possible errors which could occur in a task. There are two stages: (a) Planned Analysis, which is concerned with those errors which could occur as a consequence of the preconditions of the task as a whole which are not being met (preconditioned planned analysis) or as a consequence of the branching condition within the plan not being carried out correctly (embedded plan analysis), and (b) an Analysis of Task Steps is carried out by applying classification of error types to each step in the analysis.

3) *Consequence Analysis* is a process where active and latent errors are considered with regard to two types of consequence ratings: (a) severity of consequence and (b) likelihood of the error occurring and leading to a consequence with regard to personnel, plant, process, or the environment. The ratings should be seen as representing the opinions of the HRA analyst and need to be validated by further discussions with plant operators and engineers, who have detailed knowledge to consider the full implications of the identified errors.

4) *Development of Error Reduction Strategies.* The HTA method has provided a basis for further error and consequent error analysis as well as providing specifications for training content, procedure redesign, information for job redesign, a comparison of work methods across shifts and provides a basis for communication analysis.

III. *Error Management Control Analysis*, the third phase, is used to ascertain (1) which Performance Influencing Factors (PIF) in the task have the greatest influence on the likelihood that the errors and consequences identified earlier will actually occur; and (2) the PIFs are considered in more detail with regard to the strategies which can be applied at the level of the individual errors. Although no numerical results are obtained through SPEAR, it is a comprehensive auditing method which provides analysis to generate specific recommendations to reduce the incidence of human errors within critical operations.

IV. *Risk Reduction and Cost Benefit Analysis.* During this phase, other risk reduction techniques are evaluated with regard to the greatest amount of reduction in risk for the least expenditure. From here, the most cost effective interventions are implemented and later, the effectiveness of the error reduction strategies are evaluated from data collection systems (e.g. incident reports).

Conclusion

This chapter has provided a brief introduction to some of the human factor issues surrounding safety and accidents in the offshore oil industry. The main focus has been on the role of human error and human factors as causes of accidents and incidents, covering both the theoretical basis of human errors as well as the practical implications of these theories.

The chapter began by briefly outlining the state of the offshore oil industry in terms of the incident and accident rates, giving indications of improvements which have occurred over the past few years, in particular by contract and drilling staff. Worldwide oil industry statistics indicated that the number of fatalities, serious injures and LTI rates have decreased.

In order to have a complete accident reporting system and thus a better understanding of the types of incidents that could occur in the future, it is important that more companies adopt the following:

- accident reporting forms with a human factors causation checklist
- administrators of the reporting form are instructed on how to use it correctly
- the results data are pooled across industry
- personnel are encouraged to report near-miss incidents

Ideally, near-miss incidents would be more thoroughly investigated and information which is fed back to personnel is complete, so that they are aware of possible hazards.

Some of the theories of how and why accidents occur have been discussed, in particular with general categories of human errors that exist and how these theories relate to industry. Many of these theories have been taken a step further and are used as practical methods to reduce human error. Factors which may have an influence on performance should be included in the accident investigation process, such as

- *organizational factors* (e.g. safety culture, management, financial pressure, safety audits)
- *machine interface factors* (e.g. controls, displays)

- *job factors* (e.g. work patterns, physical conditions)
- *personal factors* (e.g. experience, knowledge, personality and health)
- *aspects of failure* (e.g. the trigger, the failure type, violations of rules and procedures)
- *aspects of causes* (e.g. conditioning factors, communication. erroneous decision making and level of information processing)

In addition, human error types have been categorized in various ways by different researchers. At the most basic level, human errors can be classified as either *active* (whose effects are almost immediate) or *latent* (whose adverse consequences may lie dormant for a long time). Active errors are more readily identifiable than latent errors and include the following categories:

- *Slips*: attentional failures (intrusion, omission, reversal, misordering, mistiming)
- *Lapses*: memory failures (omitting planned items, place-losing, forgetting intentions)
- *Mistakes*: rule-based mistakes (misapplication of a good rule, application of a bad rule) and knowledge-based mistakes
- *Violations*: (routine violations, exceptional violations, acts of sabotage)

These categories can be used within the accident reporting process to describe the basic cause of the accident. Latent errors, which are more difficult to identify include the following categories:

- hardware
- incompatible goals
- design
- organization
- maintenance
- communication
- procedures
- training
- error enforcing conditions
- defenses
- housekeeping

It would be advantageous for companies to identify and locate the latent failures on their installation in order to assess the state of their installation in terms of its underlying latent problems. These latent errors also can be considered during the incident investigation process, so that the basic, underlying causes, which are not necessarily apparent to those involved in the incident, are investigated and changes can be made where needed for future accident reduction.

Finally, a number of different error reduction strategies have been described and examined in applied settings. There are various methods by which human errors can be reduced, from feedback of accident reports to more in-depth analysis of human error using Human Error Identification techniques. The following error reduction strategies are discussed:

- Accident report feedback (trends of accident types)
- Auditing unsafe acts (to assess weak spots and failures before accident occurs)
- Auditing of latent failures (see TRIPOD, GUARD examples)
- Human Error Identification (includes Performance Influencing Factors)
- THERP (is simple to use; includes PIFs; assessor must have good understanding of task; lacks rigorous structure; possible for considerable variation from different assessors; is limited in finding cause of errors)
- Human Error HAZOP (expert's judgment critical; multi-disciplinary approach; errors identified at an early design stage can be rectified with minimal cost; resource intensive; not always effective if human factors expert is not present; is limited in finding cause of errors)
- SRK Approach (behavior/cognitive oriented; classification system; not able to predict probable incidents)
- SPEAR (no numerical results; PIFs are considered; can generate specific recommendations to reduce human error)

Some of these approaches are being used by oil companies as additions to the Quantitative Risk Assessment for their *Safety Cases* to assess what errors humans are likely to cause and what the consequences are likely to be. A better understanding of the causes of errors and accidents on offshore installations is now a primary objective for the improvement of offshore safety.

References

1. Brazier, A.J. and Black, J.M. The development of accident and near miss incident risk evaluation criteria. Department of Chemical Engineering, University of Edinburgh, Scotland. Working Paper, 1995.
2. Health and Safety Executive. *The Costs of Accidents at Work*. HS(G)96 London: HMSO, 1993.
3. Brazier, A.J. A summary of incident reporting in the process industry. *Journal of Loss Prevention in the Process Industry, 7, 3*, 1994: 243-248.

4. The Oil Industry International Exploration and Production Forum. *E & P Forum Accident Statistics.* London: E.&P Forum,1995.

5. Health and Safety Executive, Offshore Safety Division *Offshore Accident and Incident Statistics Report.* OTO 95 953. London: HSE, OSD, 1995.

6. International Labour Organisation. Safety and related issues pertaining to work on offshore petroleum installations. TMOPI/1993, Geneva: ILO, 1993.

7. Feggetter, A.J. A method for investigating human factor aspects of aircraft accidents and incidents. *Ergonomics, 25, 11,* 1982: 1065-1075.

8. Schaaf, T.W. van der; Lucas, D. and Hale, A. (Eds). *Near Miss Reporting as a Safety Tool.* Oxford: Butterworth, 1991.

9. Karlsson, T.V. & Jahre, B.M. Application of the Incident Potential Matrix technique to marine seismic operations. In Proceedings of the Second International SPE Conference on Health, Safety and Environment, Jakarta, Indonesia, January, 1994.

10. Ringstad, A.J. and Grundt, H.J. The Synergi project. A paper presented at the European Safety and Reliability Data Association (ESReDa) Seminar on Maintenance and Databases, 1994

11. Koene, W.T.C.J., Willink, T. and Waterfall, K.W. Group Unified Accident Reporting Database (GUARD). In Proceedings of the Second International SPE Conference on Health, Safety and Environment, Jakarta, Indonesia, January, 1994.

12. Paté-Cornell, M.E. *A post-mortem analysis of the Piper Alpha accident: Technical and organisational factors.* Research Report to the Joint Industry Project: Management of Human Error in Operations of Marine Systems. University of California, Berkeley, 1992.

13. Wilpert, B. Psychology in high hazard systems - Contributions to safety and reliability. Invited Keynote Address given at the IV European Congress of Psychology, Athens, July, 1995.

14. Rasmussen, J. and Jensen, A. Mental procedures in real-life tasks: A case study of electronic trouble-shooting. *Ergonomics, 17,* 1974: 293-307.

15. Reason, J. *Human Error.* Cambridge: Cambridge University Press, 1991.

16. Reason, J. and Mycielska, K. *Absent-minded? The Psychology of Mental Lapses and Everyday Errors.* Englewood Cliffs, N.J.: Prentice-Hall, 1982.

17. Rasmussen, J. What can be learned from human error reports? In: K.D.Duncan, M. Gruneberg and D. Wallis (Eds) *Changes in Working Life.* Wiley, London, 1980.

18. International Nuclear Power Operations *An Analysis of Root Causes in 1983 Significant Event Reports.* INPO 85-027. Atlanta, Ga: Institute of Nuclear Power Operations, 1985.

19. Meshkati, N. An integrative micro- and macroergonomic framework for the reduction of human error potential: a case study of an oil and gas pipeline system's control room. In Proceedings of the Second International SPE Conference on Health, Safety and Environment, Jakarta, Indonesia, January, 1994.

20. Miller, R., Freitag, M. & Wilpert, B. Development and test of a classification scheme for human factors in incident reports. Paper presented at the IAEA Technical Committee Meeting on Organisational Factors Influencing Human Performance in Nuclear Power Plants, Ittingen, Switzerland, July, 1995.

21. Drogaris, G.K. Major accidents in oil and gas industries. In *Proceedings of the First International SPE Conference on Health, Safety and Environment*, The Hague, The Netherlands, November, 1991.

22. U.S. Department of Transportation, Quality Action Team Report. Prevention Through People, 1995.

23. Kletz, T.A. On the need to publish more case histories. *Plant/Operations Progress, 7, 3*, 1998: 145-147.

24. Lourens, P.F. Error Analysis and applications in transportation systems. *Accident Analysis and Prevention, 21*, 1989: 419-426.

25. Hudson, P.T.W., Groeneweg, J., Reason, J.T., Wagenaar, W.A., van de Meeren, R.J.W. & Visser, J.P. Application of TRIPOD to measure latent errors in North Sea gas platforms: Validity of Failure State Profiles. In Proceedings from the First International Conference on Health, Safety and Environment, The Hague, The Netherlands, November, 1991.

26. Hudson, P.T.W., Wagenaar, W.A., Reason, J.T., Groeneweg, J., van de Meeren, R.J.W. and Visser, J.P. Enhancing safety in drilling: Implementing TRIPOD in a desert drilling operation. In Proceedings of the First International Conference on Health, Safety and Environment, The Hague, The Netherlands, November, 1991.

27. Pennycook, W.A. & Danz-Reece, M.E. Practical examples of human error analysis in operations. In Proceedings of the Second International SPE Conference on Health, Safety and Environment, Jakarta, Indonesia, January, 1994.

28. Kirwan, B. Human reliability assessment. In: *Evaluation of Human Work: A Practical Ergonomics Methodology*. London: Taylor & Francis Ltd., 1990.

29. Kirwan, B. Human error identification in human reliability assessment - Part 1: Overview of Approaches. *Applied Ergonomics, 23(5)*, 1992: 299-318.

30. Embrey, D.E. and Green, M. Application of the System for Predictive Error Analysis and Reduction (SPEAR): A case study. *Proceedings of the Third European Seminar on Human Factors in Offshore Safety, Their Importance in Safety Case Implementation*, Aberdeen, September, 1994.

Chapter 10

Risk Perception
and Attitudes to Safety
Kathryn Mearns and Mark Fleming

Introduction

This chapter examines risk and safety in the offshore oil industry from a human factors perspective. As such it will discuss risk perception (feelings of safety) and attitudes to safety among the offshore work force and how these affect accident involvement. Furthermore, it will consider what individual and organizational factors influence risk perception and attitudes to safety in this unique and specialized work group. Finally, the chapter will comment on the potential implications of the reviewed research on safety management by international offshore operators. The chapter will highlight United Kingdom and Norwegian studies in particular, since no other countries appear to have addressed these issues with regard to petroleum exploration and production. However, research into human factors in offshore safety has utilized other approaches and various interventions have been made to improve safety performance. Two of these studies will be reviewed briefly.

Human factors in U.S. offshore safety

In North America, the problem of human safety on offshore installations has largely been addressed from a different perspective than that considered in this chapter. In 1979, Barbara Mueller and her colleagues carried out a 44-month incidence density study on 1,023 male workers employed on mobile drilling units in the Gulf of Mexico.[1] They measured personal and work history factors and found that age, rate of job changes, and rate of rig transfers had independent effects on injury rates. They concluded that other factors being equal, younger workers were more susceptible to injury than older workers, irrespective of the quality of supervision and training. In conclusion, the authors suggested that carefully targeted modifications of work procedures and the work environment would be the best way to reduce injuries to all workers, regardless of age and experience.

It is interesting to note, however, that at the conclusion of their paper they cite a National Research Council study of offshore safety which suggests that worker attitude is the most important factor in workplace accidents. This *safety consciousness* entails "sensitivity to hazardous situations, a high level of watchfulness, allowing for a margin of error, and a conservative acceptable level of risk."[1] These attributes are believed to increase with job experience/training and result in a greater knowledge of safe working procedures. However, Mueller and her coworkers suggest that the results of their study indicate that this *safety consciousness* may be a general attribute of maturation which becomes apparent at about 30 years of age. This is an interesting proposal although it is not borne by more recent studies of occupational safety.[2-4] Furthermore, this study does not identify any of the individual or organizational factors which lead to unsafe work practices or unsafe behavior and therefore does not make any suggestions for safety interventions.

A more recent study has utilized a behavior modification or performance maximization paradigm to improve U.S. safety in offshore oilfield diving.[5] The behavior modification approach starts by encouraging the employees themselves to specify critical unsafe behaviors and their safe counterparts. This behavioral checklist then is used to measure safety performance and the number and severity of lost-time accidents. Next, employees are trained in specific safety rules, usually by getting them to observe a *model* performing the task unsafely then safely (this is usually done by videotape or photograph). Finally, periodic unannounced observations are made of the employees while they work. In this study, supervisors on the dive support vessels were especially trained to conduct these periodic spot-checks. The researchers also established behavioral performance goals (100% safe working) and provided motivational feedback (i.e. knowledge of results) in relation to these goals. A key element of this intervention program is that the employees themselves were heavily involved in implementing it and therefore had ownership of the program.

As in many of these behavior modification studies, the results were impressive with lost-time, restricted activity and nondisabling injuries all declining significantly over the 22- month period of the study. Furthermore, in terms of cost/benefit analysis it was estimated that the company saved $283,510 in the first year (the program itself cost $40,000 to develop and implement). The average cost per lost-time injury also decreased significantly from $31,175/injury to $19,000/injury suggesting that the severity as well as the frequency of injury decreased.

It should be noted, however, that behavioral change tends to be short-lived if no attempt is made to change people's underlying perceptions, beliefs, and attitudes, although some psychologists believe that attitude change can arise from behavioral change mainly because people do not like to see their behavior as being at odds with what they feel and believe.[6] Thus any behavioral modification program should also involve measuring the target population's attitudes and beliefs before and after intervention. Such studies should also be followed up to discover whether the behavior changes noted have been short-lived or have become a permanent part of the target population's behavioral repertoire. Only in this way can one be certain that safety has become integral to the functioning of the population under study. But what are offshore workers' attitudes, perceptions, and beliefs about risk and safety, and what factors influence them? The remainder of the chapter discusses these topics in more detail.

Offshore Risk

Oil industry engineers will be familiar with the methods of quantitative risk assessment (QRA) used to estimate the likelihood of a catastrophic event occurring or components failing. Accidents statistics provide another measure of *objective risk*. There is, however, another side to risk assessment, namely the *qualitative* or *subjective* risk assessments carried out by those who are actually exposed to the risk. A person's own estimate of risk may be very different from that based on objective measurement; however, this subjective perception of risk will probably be more meaningful to the person concerned and will be used to determine whether the level of risk involved in an activity is acceptable or not (in terms of potential losses and benefits). It is acknowledged that offshore workers are a self-selected group, who in order to function adequately in the offshore environment must accept to a certain degree the hazards inherent in this type of occupation. These have been eloquently summarized as follows:

> The threats to the life and well-being of workers on [the] installa-tions may take many forms and come from multiple sources. The princi-pal ones are threats to the structural integrity of the installation, e.g. the tearing loose of a floating unit from its mooring or the capsizing of a mobile unit, fire and explosions, the blowout of a well, accidents associ-ated with drilling operations, falls and dangers associated with diving. These combine in a unique fashion dangers characteristic of much indus-trial work in general with others specific to oil and gas operations and with those associated with the marine environment.[7]

Offshore workers may be very aware of these dangers but if safety officers and safety managers are to communicate adequately about risk and manage safety on offshore installations, they need to understand how the workforce think and feel about offshore safety. Furthermore, they need to know how these feelings and attitudes can affect accident involvement.

Risk Perception

Risk perception can be described as the study of people's beliefs, attitudes, judgments and feelings towards hazards and the risks associated with them. In this context *hazard* is taken to mean "threats to people and the things they value", although it should be pointed out that there are many different definitions of the word *hazard* and indeed the word *risk*. The term *perceived risk* is actually a misnomer, since people do not perceive risks per se but evaluate the characteristics of hazards in terms of their possible consequences, usually in terms of potential losses or injuries. These hazard characteristics mean different things to different people in different contexts. As a result, risk perception research not only involves the investigation of personality factors and individual emotion, motivation, and thought processes but also social and cultural values and how they affect the judgment of hazards. Although risk perception research has mainly been concerned with how the general public perceives risks, such as environmental hazards, health and road safety, a number of studies have investigated risk perception at the workplace.[8] One premise for this type of study is that *wrong* assessments or perceptions of risk could cause accidents. If employees are not aware of the hazards or underestimate the risks associated with those hazards, they may engage in behavior that could lead to them and/or their colleagues getting hurt. Furthermore, if people have a certain type of attitude to risk/safety, for example, that accidents are not within their control, they may be more likely to be involved in accidents than people who believe that they can prevent accidents through their own actions or by influencing other peoples' actions. The human factors causes of accidents have been discussed in detail in an earlier chapter (see chapter 9). But the question of human factors and human error also needs to be raised from a management perspective. Why do employees who know about the risks still engage in unsafe behavior which can lead to accidents?

Who Causes Accidents?

When an accident occurs it is generally believed that somewhere, somehow, someone made a wrong decision or carried out a deliberate action (i.e. took a risk) which resulted in a negative outcome. This is all very well in hindsight, but were the risks identified *after* the accident, accepted after a conscious analysis of the situation before the accident? The Dutch psychologist Wilhelm Wagenaar has argued that behaviors leading to accidents can occur at three levels: operational, tactical and strategic.[9] The question of whether faulty risk assessments are the cause of accidents perhaps can be answered if we consider these different levels and the decision making processes associated with them.

Wagenaar argues that the workers at the operational level are rarely making adequate risk considerations in their execution of routine, skilled, automatic behavior. At the tactical level, the role of middle management is to apply rules which are largely dictated by circumstances so specific assessments of risk may not necessarily take place each time a rule is applied. At the strategic level, there are often many risk considerations, trade-offs between safety and costs and sometimes even a deliberate acceptance of calculated risks.

Wagenaar goes on to argue that although risk-taking can be the *cause* of many accidents, those involved at the sharp end of the system are rarely in a position to evaluate the risks they are taking. Since they are carrying out most of their activities at an automatic, pre-attentive level, there is simply no capacity for a conscious consideration of risk. In other words these people are *running risks* not *taking them*. More conscious *risk evaluation* occurs at the blunt end of the system, where the planners, designers, and managers are and it is these people, Wagenaar argues, who should be the target of risk communication campaigns. This is an interesting argument but it begs the question as to what types of risk communication campaign these people should be exposed to.

The British sociologist Robert Moore has suggested that hazards and risks are often identified and controlled most effectively by those involved in the work tasks by a process of constant monitoring or *risk evaluation from below*.[10] In order for operational-level safety intelligence to be effective, workers need to be involved in the process of risk assessment. Risk communication therefore should be a two-way process with information moving from one organizational level to another and it should also attempt to encompass *the wider institutional and cultural contexts* in which risk messages occur, (i.e. the safety climate or culture of the organization in question). It is acknowledged that many offshore operating companies already involve their work force in such procedures, e.g. United Kingdom Health and Safety Executive.[11]

It must be stressed again, however, that understanding risk perception and peoples' attitudes to risk and safety is crucial if there is to be a two-way exchange of information between management and employees regarding the identification, elimination, and control of hazards at the work place. A suggested framework for understanding how offshore workers understand and relate to risk and safety is presented in Figure 10-1. First, the worker has to be aware of the hazard, both in sensory terms and in terms of an awareness of the situation that the individual is in when the hazard is perceived.[12,13] Second, one has to tap into the individual's knowledge of the risks inherent in any hazard which will be dependent on a number of different factors including frequency of previous events and consequences, experience in dealing with the hazard, and training in coping with the hazard. This type of information could be

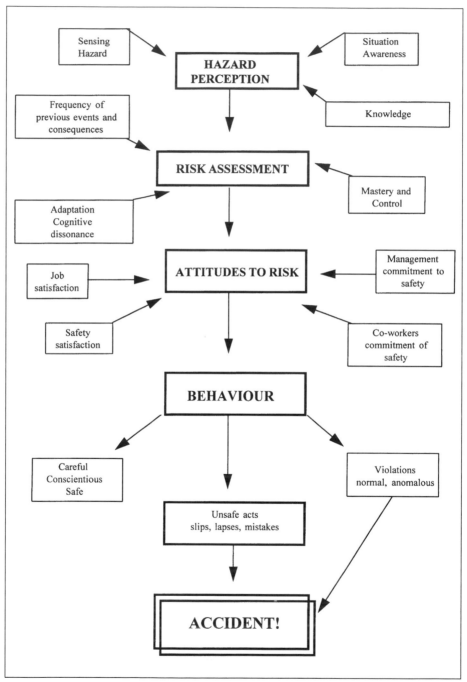

Figure 10-1 A Model of Human and Organizational Factors in Offshore Safety

acquired by using knowledge elicitation techniques such as Critical Decision Making (CDM) and incident review methods (see chapter 8).

Risk knowledge will also feed into the attitude the individual holds in relation to the risk, which, in turn, may be influenced by factors such as commitment of management and coworkers to safety, job satisfaction, and safety satisfaction. At this stage of the work it is important to target different levels in the organization and generate their specific attitudes to risk and safety through group discussions. Finally, one has to consider behavior and how the measures taken above relate to that behavior, whether it is safe or unsafe.

Attitudes to risk and safety

Whether or not workers are willing to take risks at the workplace will be partly determined by their attitudes to risk and safety. An attitude is a relatively enduring tendency to behave in particular ways towards aspects of our environment, and is therefore a relatively stable predisposition. Attitudes are believed to support beliefs, opinions, and behavior and whereas the latter are susceptible to change, underlying attitudes are more resistant to change. The safety culture of an organization can be defined as a *collective* commitment to safety which is *more* than just the sum of the individual members' own beliefs, attitudes, perceptions and behavior. Definitions of the term *safety culture* abound, however perhaps the most succinct definition has been given by the Confederation of British Industry (CBI) as "the way we do things around here."[14] "How things are done around here" will largely be determined by management's' attitudes and actions. These will be communicated to the workers and will determine, at least in part, how they behave at the work site. However, workers' behavior will also be partly determined by the attitudes of their coworkers and their own personal attitudes to risk and safety. Distinguishing between different types of attitudes and seeing how these attitudes determine employee behavior in the face of risk remains a major challenge for social scientists working in the field of occupational safety today.

This chapter so far has outlined what is meant by risk perception and attitudes to safety and has also touched on the theme of *safety culture* as a measure of the *state of safety* within an organization. The remainder of the chapter will concentrate on studies of risk perception and safety in the United Kingdom and Norwegian offshore oil industry and how these factors affect accident involvement among offshore employees.

Risk Perception and Attitudes to Safety in the Offshore Oil Industry

Feelings of safety on the Statfjord A platform

One of the first studies of risk perception and safety in the offshore oil industry was conducted by Julius Marek and his colleagues in the early 1980s.[15] In this study (which was part of a larger study on health and safety on the Norwegian Statfjord A platform), 238 offshore employees from four different occupational groups (operator staff, drillers, caterers and flotel crew), were asked to evaluate 20 risk sources on a five-point scale ranging from *very safe* to *very unsafe*. The results showed that, in general, 61% of all respondents considered their work situation to be safe, while 10% considered it unsafe, and 28% felt neither safe nor unsafe. There were substantial differences between the four groups of employees, both regarding evaluations of overall safety and more detailed assessments of the 20 specific risk sources. For example, catering personnel felt unsafe about 17 sources of risk, whereas flotel and operator groups felt unsafe about five. There were also notable differences between groups regarding which sources of risk were judged unsafe and how these judgments contributed towards feelings about safety. The four occupational groups surveyed were found to live and work in their own *worlds of risk* which were constructed according to the individual's knowledge of the technology, processes, and operations on a North Sea platform; present work conditions and tasks; organizational and administrative practices, and prior professional background. In a later article, using some of the same data set, Marek, *et. al.* discussed the importance of socio-organizational factors and safety measures with regard to controlling specific sources of risk and general safety.[16] When it came to controlling specific risks and maintaining safety on the platform, experience and skills apparently were the most important variables. Existing safety measures were perceived as being oriented towards controlling major hazards and preventing destruction of the installation, rather than controlling occupational hazards involved in cargo handling, control of falling objects, and weather conditions.

Risk Perception and Accident Involvement on United Kingdom and Norwegian Installations

Five years later, Dr. Torbjorn Rundmo of Trondheim University examined perceived risk and safety in a sample of 915 workers (92% response rate) on eight installations located on the Norwegian Continental Shelf.[17] The aim of this study was to take a number of psychological measures of the Norwegian offshore work force using a self-report questionnaire. These included feelings of safety (risk perception); attitudes to safety; perceptions of the working environment and the job situation; self-reported accidents; and a number of demographic variables, for example, age, occupation, experience offshore. The study also examined the relationship between risk perception, accidents and near misses, and whether this was affected by occupational group, or other factors such as job situation, working conditions, attitudes to safety or satisfaction with safety measures.

The results showed that with regard to major hazards (e.g. fire, explosion, blow out) 50% of the sample reported feeling safe (i.e. safe or extremely safe) on average across items. This ranged from 75% feeling safe with respect to sabotage to 46% feeling safe with respect to explosion. Similarly on average across items, 61% of respondents felt safe with regard to ordinary work injuries (although only 43% felt safe with regard to slippery surfaces and 45% with falling objects). In terms of emergency response measures, 72% felt safe on average across items (ranging from 79% for medical services and 59% for evacuation).

As in the Marek *et. al.* study, significant differences were found between occupational groups regarding feelings of safety with maintenance and construction personnel feeling the least *safe* overall. Drilling personnel felt least safe regarding occupational accidents, especially falling and slipping while administrative and production staff felt the most safe regarding major hazards, occupational accidents, and work task hazards. In addition, more people felt safe on installations that had been in operation for four to eight years than on platforms that were in start-up or older platforms. Finally, only 57% of personnel reported feeling safe regarding helicopter transport.

With regard to accident reporting, approximately 25% of those who responded to the questionnaire had experienced an injury and 40% of these had experienced more than one injury. Of a total of 355 injuries, 40% occurred during planned interventions and 30% in handling tasks. Lifting operations, especially manual lifting, as well as repair work and maintenance led to the most injuries. The majority of accidents (54%) involved the injured person being sent home from the platform, 12% entailing absence from work were treated on the platform, and the remaining 34% were minor accidents not resulting in absence from the next shift. The frequency of accidents was somewhat higher on platforms that were in start-up and on older platforms, than on platforms that had been in operation for four to eight years.

The factors affecting risk perception (feelings of safety) and accidents were identified by using statistical modeling techniques. The analysis showed that perceived risk and perceptions of the job situation (e.g. how well workers felt they were informed about work tasks and the degree to which they could determine their own work pace) were related to previous accident involvement. Further analyses indicated that perceptions of the physical job environment and satisfaction with safety and emergency response measures affected perceptions of risk and the job situation. The study showed that the newest and oldest installations came out worst in the employees' assessments of the work environment and safety conditions. The drillers, construction and maintenance personnel, and technical-mechanical personnel reported higher physical work strain and injuries than other personnel.

Rundmo goes on to discuss these findings and suggests that personnel most frequently perceive risk in connection with disasters and major accidents because they focus on the *consequences* of an injury rather than the probability of it occurring. Furthermore, the sources leading to disasters and major accidents are not as easy to control as hazards which are linked to the work tasks that employees carry out on the platform. The maintenance and construction personnel and the technical/mechanical personnel not only perceived high risk in relation to major accident sources, but also in relation to post-accident measures. Rundmo notes that these groups tend to have the best knowledge of these systems but their responses suggest that they feel the systems may have some shortcomings.

Evaluations of risk were directly connected with perceptions of working conditions and the status of accident preventive work and Rundmo suggests that physical and organizational conditions at work should be improved if perceptions of risk are to be changed. Management commitment and involvement were found to have the greatest effect on the satisfaction/dissatisfaction of the personnel, closely followed by management and supervisor support and attitudes towards accident prevention.

Finally, Rundmo suggests that the best way to reduce dissatisfaction with safety and contingency measures may be to directly improve work and safety instructions, safety training and safety devices, as well as improving management and supervisor commitment and involvement.

Rundmo carried out a follow-up study in 1994 which ran concurrently with a study of risk perception and safety on six production platforms on the United Kingdom Continental Shelf.[18,19] The Norwegian personnel's feelings of safety had increased over the four-year period. In 1990, 54% felt safe with regard to catastrophes and major accidents, compared to 66% in 1994. Furthermore, in 1990, 72% of personnel felt safe with regard to post-accident measures compared to 80% in 1994. The least change was seen in relation to occupational accidents, where 61% felt safe in 1990 and 64% felt safe in 1994.

The results of the United Kingdom study showed that, overall, 62% of respondents felt *safe* regarding major hazards with structural failure causing least concern (75% felt *safe*) and explosion and a vessel hitting the platform causing the most (56% felt *safe* on both items).[19] Regarding occupational accidents, 67% felt *safe* overall, but this ranged from 88% feeling *safe* from falling to a lower level to only 38% feeling *safe* from slipping. Overall, 80% of personnel felt *safe* executing their work tasks but working with radioactive material, flying in a helicopter, and completing a task started by others caused most concern (42%, 51% and 54% felt *safe*, respectively).

Note that the remaining percentage of respondents did not necessarily feel unsafe on these measures of risk perception. The majority fell into the category *neither safe nor unsafe* with less than 10% actually feeling unsafe in the majority of cases. As in the Norwegian study, a number of factors were found to influence these feelings of safety. These included physical working environment, whether or not the individual had experienced an accident; satisfaction with the job and safety measures; and attitudes of management and employees to safety.

Statistical analyses and modeling of the data indicated that the *organizational factors* such as management commitment to safety, job satisfaction, attitudes to safety versus production and the job situation had the greatest direct effect on workers' perception of risk and their satisfaction with safety measures. These two measures appeared to be a reasonably accurate reflection of the state of safety on the platform. Furthermore, the *individual factors* which had a direct effect (albeit small) on previous accident involvement included safety attitudes, risk perception, and satisfaction with safety.

These results gave a general overview of the perceived state of safety on a sample of six offshore oil and gas production platforms, and identified the following core areas as being worthy of further investigation.

- *Knowledge*—how individuals perceive hazards, how they perceive the control of those hazards, how individuals share and communicate information about hazards
- *Situation awareness*—perception of the work environment which influences how decisions are made and defines patterns of interactions at work
- *Organizational culture*—safety attitudes, safety culture, commitment of managers and fellow workers to safety

The objective of a new study currently underway is to measure and investigate these factors and determine their role in offshore safety.[20]

Attitudes to Safety in Offshore Workers

The aforementioned studies concentrated mainly on perceptions of risk and safety in the offshore work force; however, employee attitudes to safety are an integral part of the safety culture of any organization. Attitudes to safety were also measured in these studies and some interesting differences were apparent between Norwegian and United Kingdom workers.

Responses to the attitude statements were divided into three groups labeled:

1. *Operational vs. Safety goals,* statements about perceived pressure to put production before safety;
2. *Fatalism,* statements which suggested that accidents could not be prevented, that they are beyond a person's control;
3. *Accident Causation,* statements about accident causation and prevention.

The percentage of personnel who *agreed, neither agreed nor disagreed* and *disagreed* with each statement was recorded. With reference to *Operational versus safety goals,* it is interesting to note that about half the respondents agreed with statements such as: "There is sometimes pressure to put production before safety", "Pointing out breaches of safety instructions can easily be seen as unnecessary hassle," and "Rules and instructions relating to safety sometimes make it difficult to keep up with the production targets". Regarding *Fatalism,* the majority of respondents tended to disagree with the statements: "Accidents just happen, there is little one can do to avoid them" and "I never think about the risks now that I am used to the work".

Finally, very few respondents agreed with statements which implied that the causes of accidents were beyond their control. There were differences between sectors with regard to respondents' attitudes toward operational versus safety goals, with more United Kingdom respondents than Norwegian respondents indicating that they felt there was sometimes pressure to put operational goals before safety goals. In addition, Norwegian respondents tended to have more fatalistic attitudes toward safety than United Kingdom respondents. There were no differences between sectors with regard to respondents' attitudes to accident causes.

Another study targeting an American company operating on the United Kingdom Continental Shelf, used a self-administered questionnaire on 1080 employees (both offshore and onshore) in an attempt to measure safety culture.[21] The authors report that a measure of the safety culture could not be reliably demonstrated, but they identified six key factors which underpinned employee attitudes to safety. These were 1) overt management commitment 2) personal need for safety 3) personal appreciation of risk 4) attributions of blame 5) conflict and control and 6) supportive environment. Regarding conflict and control, the authors report that those with managerial and supervisory responsibility appeared less reluctant to take risks and compromise safety than those without such responsibilities. Furthermore, managers and supervisors seemed more convinced that a *no blame* culture existed within the company and perceived production goals as compatible with safety goals. Finally, no differences in attitudes to risk could be identified between accident and non-accident employees.

The results of these studies highlight a few issues which need to be addressed in risk communication campaigns for the offshore work force, but they have most relevance for safety management on offshore installations.

Communicating About Risks

Research on risk communication has highlighted the weak linkage between knowledge, attitudes, and behavior.[22] Attitude-behavior inconsistencies have been actively studied for many years with one general conclusion being that people consider themselves more consistent in their own behavior than outside observers see them.[23] The complexity of this type of research has taxed workers in other domains, e.g. consumer behavior, however, it is extremely relevant for safety management.[24] If we can understand and manage the knowledge-attitude-behavior association, we are well on the way to planned interventions which will make for safer working environments.

But what of knowledge, attitudes, and behavior and the findings of the above studies? It is apparent that the offshore personnel who answered the questionnaires generally had a good knowledge of the major hazards involved in working on an offshore platform and this knowledge was closely linked to the *perception of risk associated with these hazards*. Since these knowledge/perception relationships appear to be reasonably accurate for most workers, there seems little sense in attempting to change them. Perception of risk associated with occupational hazards such as slipping and falling also seemed reasonably accurate when compared to official accident statistics; personnel also felt relatively safe when carrying out their work tasks. However, in the United Kingdom study two items from the questions on work task hazards stand-out as being worthy of attention. These were the lack of feelings of safety with regard to completing a task started by others (54% felt safe) and working with radioactive material (42% felt safe in the United Kingdom study).

Regarding the completion of a task started by others, risk communication can be effective by working on the social ties that exist between people on an offshore installation, perhaps by setting the consequences of accident involvement within a social framework (e.g. "That an accident happened to Tom last week and if there isn't a change in working practices, it could happen to Dick and Harry tomorrow"). Risk communication campaigns should not only emphasize risk in relation to one's own work but should also highlight the problems of other tasks and how these can affect the individual or group concerned. Some companies already use risk communication techniques to encourage different work groups to *empathize* with the problems faced by others and *recognize* the potential for accidents occurring if interfacing tasks are not managed properly. Also at shift and crew handovers, risks need to be fully communicated from one team to the next.

Regarding lack of feelings of safety when handling radioactive material, it is important to note that this hazard cannot be seen, touched, smelled or heard (i.e. it is not salient) and only 42% of those involved in working with radioactive material felt safe from it. Workers handling the type of radioactive material which is found on offshore installations are probably most at risk from ingesting or inhaling radioactive dust rather than being at risk from radioactivity *per se*. Wearing the appropriate protective clothing should almost eliminate that risk. Any communication should highlight this fact and emphasize that the risks involved in general exposure to the low-level radioactive scale encountered on many installations are of a low magnitude, although these risks should still be taken seriously.

In conclusion, there is little evidence to suggest that offshore risk and safety campaigns are unsuccessful. For a hazardous industry in a very remote location the accident record for the United Kingdom and Norwegian offshore oil industries is fairly good in comparison with other industries (see chapter 9) but there are no grounds for complacency. The United Kingdom and Norwegian studies show that about 37% of the personnel surveyed had experienced one or more accidents in their time offshore. The reasons for employee accident involvement are many-fold and are not all related to human factors; however, the foregoing studies point to various individual and organizational factors which can affect safety on offshore installations and which need attention from safety managers.

Managing Human Factors in Offshore Safety

In this section the chapter of the implications of the findings from the United Kingdom offshore study are discussed with particular reference to situation awareness, supervision, and organizational factors.

Situation Awareness

Situation awareness is a performance-related psychological concept which has recently gained significant currency in both commercial and military aviation.[13] Accurate risk perception is an essential component of situation awareness. In any potentially hazardous environment, such as an offshore production platform or drilling rig, an ongoing awareness of one's situation, especially when involved in work tasks, must involve an assessment of current and future risk. Routine workplace decision making is founded on an analysis of the current situation and its risk potential. The findings from the United Kingdom study of risk perception and safety indicated that offshore employees appeared to be aware of the potential hazards on their platforms, and that their perceptions were in accord with the *objective* data available (i.e. QRA and accident statistics).[19]

Interestingly, the open questions from the Offshore Risk Perception Questionnaire indicated that the concept of situation awareness might be usefully applied offshore as the respondents' views on what caused accidents and how they might be prevented appeared to reinforce this concept. The most commonly cited cause of accidents was *lack of care and attention* mentioned by over a third of respondents. This raises the issue of competing motivations but also could be interpreted as an inadequate situation assessment. Good situational awareness requires effort in terms of concentration, vigilance, and attention to detail; these then produce a critical sensitivity to cues in the environment signaling a change of state (and altered risk consequences).

In response to another open question regarding advice that should be given to a new start, the most frequent responses were "always ask advice", "pay attention", "think before acting", "be aware of hazards and others round the job". In general, novices will have poorer situation awareness than experienced workers, but the problem with novices is that they do not realize they have inadequate knowledge. They do not always know what to "pay attention" to. Their initial training needs to instill rapidly fundamental situation awareness skills for their work domain and for installation life in general.

The Offshore Supervisor

The results of the studies on risk perception and safety in offshore workers suggest that we need to develop a better understanding of the role of the first-line supervisor in developing situation awareness, risk perception, and safe working practices in his or her shift. This individual plays a key role in the management of safety and in the maintenance of an installation culture which endorses safe working at all times (see chapter 4). The United Kingdom study indicated that supervisors can have slightly different perceptions of risk and feelings of safety but further work needs to be carried out with this safety-critical position to determine how supervisors make judgments of risk and how they communicate these judgments to their team.

Organizational Factors

It has been argued that United Kingdom and Norwegian offshore workers' self-reported risk perception appears to be reasonably accurate, at least in terms of feelings of safety in relation to the relative major risks. If this is the case, then it could be argued that factors which affect workers' risk perception could also be some of the factors that affect behavior. The statistical modeling revealed that six factors had a direct effect on workers' feelings of safety. Apart from the effect of working environment on risk perception, it is argued that four of the remaining five factors (job situation, job satisfaction, management commitment, and safety attitudes) can be regarded as indicators of an organization's safety culture. The fifth factor, safety satisfaction, is not a direct measure, but was found to be directly influenced by organizational factors. From these findings we could postulate that an organization's general attitude to safety may be indirectly affecting the actual risk to which its employees are being exposed. Therefore many United Kingdom researchers in this field believe that a good way to improve workers' safety is to change the organization's safety culture as this in turn affects the behavior of the most senior manager to the most junior roustabout.

Similarly, the factors which influence safety satisfaction may also affect the actual state of safety on the platform. Again, statistical modeling of the data revealed five factors which had a direct effect on safety satisfaction; (1) management commitment to safety, (2) attitudes to production versus safety, (3) attitudes to accident causation, (4) fatalistic attitudes and (5) perceived social support. The two predictors that had by far the greatest effect on ratings of safety were perceived management commitment to safety and the perception that production sometimes came before safety. Therefore the factors that appear to be important indicators of an effective safety culture are

1. A high level of communication and consultation between staff and management.
2. A work force that are satisfied with their jobs.
3. Management and workers who are interested in and committed to safety.
4. Management and workers are convinced that safety is of as important as production.

Conclusion

An underlying reason for many studies of risk perception in industrial settings has been the assumption that *wrong* assessments of risk by the work force can create problems with safety.[25] The results from the foregoing studies suggest that United Kingdom and Norwegian offshore workers have reasonably accurate perceptions of risk, certainly in relation to major hazards, and that rather than change their assessments of risk, interventions should be aimed at changing the physical and organizational working conditions which employees feel dissatisfied about. The research also indicates that attitudes toward safety are important, particularly with respect to how workers' perceive production versus safety issues. Perceived management involvement and commitment to safety is also important. These factors influence, to a greater degree, the individual's choice of behavior. Personnel do not necessarily take chances because they choose to, but because they perceive that conditions make it necessary to do so.

References

1. Mueller, B.A., Mohr, D.L., Rice, J.C. & Clemmer, D.I. Factors affecting individual injury experience among petroleum drilling workers. *Journal of Occupational Medicine, 29,* 1987: 126-131.

2. Lee, T.R., Macdonald, S.M. & Coote, J.A. Perceptions of risk and attitudes to safety at a nuclear reprocessing plant. Paper presented at Society for Risk Assessment (Europe) Fourth Conference: Rome, October, 1993.

3. Donald, I. & Canter, D. Employee attitudes and safety in the chemical industry. *Journal of Loss Prevention in Process Industries, 7,* 1994: 203-208.

4. Mearns, K., Flin, R., Rundmo, T., Fleming, M. & Gordon, R. *A Comparative Study of Risk Perception and Safety in United Kingdom and Norwegian Offshore Personnel.* Report prepared for the Norwegian Petroleum Directorate and the Offshore Safety Division of the United Kingdom Health and Safety Executive, 1996.

5. Reber, R.A. & Wallin, J.A. Utilizing performance management to improve offshore oilfield diving safety. *The International Journal of Organizational Analysis, 2,* 1994: 88-98.

6. Kleinke, C.L. Two models for conceptualizing the attitude-behaviour relationship. *Human Relations, 37,* 1994: 33-350.

7. International Labour Organization. *Safety and Related Issues Pertaining to Work on Offshore Petroleum Installations.* Geneva: International Labour Office, 1993.

8. Mearns, K. and Flin, R. Risk perception in hazardous industries. *The Psychologist.,* (in press).

9. Wagenaar, W.A. Risk taking and accident causation. In J.F. Yates (Ed.), *Risk Taking Behaviour.* Chichester: John Wiley & Sons, 1992.

10. Moore, R. *The Price of Safety: The Market, Workers Rights and the Law.* London: Institute of Employment Rights, 1991.

11. HSC. *Play Your Part: How Offshore Workers Can Help Improve Health and Safety.* London: HSE Books, 1994.

12. Bernhardt, U., Hoyos, C.G. & Hauke, G. Psychological safety diagnosis. *Journal of Occupational Accidents, 6,* 1984: 61-70.

13. Sarter, N. & Woods, D. Situation awareness: A critical but ill-defined phenomenon. *International Journal of Aviation Psychology, 1, 4* 1991: 5-57.

14. CBI. *Developing a Safety Culture - Business for Safety.* London Confederation of British Industry, 1990.

15. Marek, J., Tangenes, B. & Hellesøy, O.H. Experience of risk and safety. In O.H. Hellesøy (Ed.) *Work Environment Statfjord Field. Work Environment, Health and Safety on a North Sea Oil Platform.* Oslo: Universitetsforlaget, 1985.

16. Marek, J., Iversen, E. & Hellesøy, O.H. Risk, organization and safety on an oil platform. In W.T. Singleton & J. Hovden (Eds.), *Risk and Decisions.* Chichester: John Wiley & Sons, 1987.

17. Rundmo, T. Risk perception and safety on offshore petroleum platforms - Part I: Perception of risk and Part II: Perceived risk, job stress and accidents on offshore installations. *Safety Science, 15,* 1992: 39-68.

18. Rundmo, T. Assessment of the risk of accidents among offshore personnel. Report prepared for the Norwegian Petroleum Directorate. Allforsk. Centre for Society Research: Dragvoll; Norway (In Norwegian), 1994.

19. Flin, R., Mearns, K., Fleming, M. & Gordon, R. *Risk Perception and Safety in United Kingdom Offshore Workers.* Report for the Oil Industry/Offshore Safety Division, HSE (OTH 94454). Suffolk: HSE Books (in press).

20. Mearns, K., Flin, R. Fleming, M. & Gordon, R. Assessing Human and Organizational Factors in the Offshore Oil Industry. (Working Paper). The Robert Gordon University, Aberdeen, 1995.

21. Alexander, M. The concept of safety culture within a United Kingdom offshore organization. Paper presented at the conference on 'Understanding Risk Perception'. Aberdeen: Offshore Management Centre, The Robert Gordon University, February, 1995.

22. Handmer, J. & Penning-Rowsell, E. *Hazards and the Communication of Risk.* Aldershot: Gower Technical, 1990.

23. Ajzen, I. & Fishbein, M. Attitude-behaviour relations: A theoretical analysis and review of empirical research. *Psychological Bulletin, 84,* 1977: 888-918.

24. Chisnall, P.M. *Marketing: A Behavioural Analysis.* Second Edition. London: McGraw-Hill, 1985.

25. Mearns, K. & Flin, R. Risk perception and attitudes to safety by personnel in the offshore oil and gas industry: a review. *Journal of Loss Prevention in the Process Industry, 8,* 1995: 229-305.

Chapter 11

Industrial Relations on Offshore Installations
Douglas Gourlay

Introduction

Human Resource Management in the North Sea

It would be impossible in a chapter as short as this to include information on industrial relations when they affect offshore workforces as diverse in location and culture as the Far East, the Caribbean Sea, the Gulf of Mexico and the North Sea. This chapter therefore will focus upon human factors and human resource management in the North Sea oil and gas industry. Human resource management in that industry inevitably has been influenced by the prevailing management culture of the multi-national oil companies although with surprisingly different outcomes for Norway and the United Kingdom despite their sharing the same continental shelf. Anyone who seeks to understand the human factors of employment in the oil industry of the North Sea must appreciate from the outset that while both Norway and the United Kingdom had the industry brought to them by multi-national companies, all sharing a common philosophy concerning the management of *their* industry, the pattern of industrial relations is vastly different in each. Oil managers transferring from a British installation to one based in Norwegian waters will have to adopt a very different approach to their understanding of human factors on a Norwegian installation.

In the absence of indigenous expertise, the oil companies were responsible for most of the initial exploration and drilling in the North Sea and once fields were designated as commercially viable for exploitation, they had the technical knowledge and venture capital to build and operate many of the platforms. As employers, they brought with them the same approach to the human factors of their operations that had served them well in other parts of the world. Their philosophy of management reflected their need to contend with a physical environment more hostile than they ever had to face and consequently human factors received significantly less attention than technological concerns. The style of management was paternal at best, but over the first decade of the industry in the North Sea it would be more accurately described as uncompromising. Once the frenetic activity of the early years had given way to the more predictable but still economically challenging business of producing oil, time was found to look in greater detail at human factors.

By this time, however, Norway and the United Kingdom had sharply contrasting systems of human resource management within their offshore oil industries, the reasons for which will be explained later in this chapter. In Norwegian waters human resource management now does not differ in essentials from the prevailing pattern on mainland Norway. All the major oil companies, for instance, have found it politically convenient to join the Norwegian Employers Federation (Nœringslivets Hovedorganisasjon) and the Norwegian Oil Industry Association (Oljeindustriens Landsforening) and to work in harmony with them. By contrast, human resource management on the British continental shelf exhibits features more akin to American than to British establishments and is thus atypical of the national system, where, for example, trade unions still play a significant role.

Industrial Relations

Industrial relations may be described as the rules which govern employment.[1] These rules are of two kinds. Substantive rules govern such matters as the length of the working week, pay and holiday entitlement while procedural rules concern the manner in which the substantive rules are drawn up and how they can be interpreted and amended. These rules are decided and administered in four ways. First there is *statutory regulation* where the government intervenes in the relationship between employer and employee, almost always in order to protect the individual from injury or from causing injury to someone else. Government bodies are established to ensure compliance with the regulations and, where appropriate, to prosecute offenders; examples of this are the Norwegian Petroleum Directorate in Norway and the Health and Safety Executive in the United Kingdom. Then there is *employer regulation* when organizations determine both the substantive and the procedural rules with little or no consultation with their employees. In its extreme form this is autocracy which is unlikely to be found outside small firms. The third way is a mild form of employer regulation known as *sophisticated paternalism* which is common offshore on the United Kingdom continental shelf. Here organizations seek to provide conditions of employment which satisfy their employees to the extent that they are not interested in joining trade unions and asking them to negotiate on their behalf. Finally there is *collective bargaining*, the process whereby trade unions negotiate with the employers terms and conditions on behalf of their members. It is by far the commonest form of reaching agreement between employer and employees. It is sometimes referred to as joint regulation in contrast to the unilateral regulation where managers make decisions on their own terms. It should be mentioned here that collective bargains, contrary to the practice in the U.S. and other industrialized nations, are not normally enforceable under British law.[a] Collective bargaining may be described loosely as the standard pattern of job regulation within the British and Norwegian systems of industrial relations.

Industrial Relations on the United Kingdom Continental Shelf

However, collective bargaining as understood in the United Kingdom does not take place offshore. Collective bargaining is possible only if management accepts trade unions as legitimate representatives of employees, usually on the basis that the majority of the employees are members of the trade union(s) concerned. From the earliest days of the industry on the United Kingdom continental shelf, the oil companies have resisted all demands by the trade unions to be accorded the negotiating rights which are necessary for collective bargaining to be carried out. They have defended this stance on the grounds that the unions have never secured sufficient membership among offshore employees to justify a right to represent them. In 1976 the trade unions, with government assistance, did enter into an agreement with the employers to assist with recruitment offshore but this *Memorandum of Understanding on Trade Union Access to Offshore Installation*[b] has been of little assistance to them. Even when trade union officers do go offshore, the whole ambiance of an installation isolated perhaps one hundred miles out at sea militates against an atmosphere which is conducive to the recruitment of members.[2] The position today is that the major trade unions now accept, though they do not admit it publicly, that offshore oil industry employees do not, on the whole, want their services. It is possible that this may change, but currently the employers continue to reject trade union demands to negotiate on behalf of offshore employees on the sound argument that union membership is small.

It is not correct to infer from the foregoing comment that industrial relations offshore lack structure and stability. If it were so, it is unlikely that the fairly placid state of industrial relations on both the United Kingdom and the Norwegian sectors of the continental shelf would have continued for two decades apart from occasional flurries such as the strike of United Kingdom catering workers in 1979, some slight turmoil caused by the Norwegian union OFS in the early 1980s and the industrial action taken in 1989 and 1990 in British waters, none of which had any lasting effect.

The Structure of Industrial Relations Offshore

As stated immediately above, industrial relations on the North Sea oil and gas industry are stable and this is accounted for by the relationships between the different organizations, both management and trade union. Since differing philosophical approaches to human factors of employment characterize the conduct of United Kingdom and Norwegian industrial relations, separate sections are needed to describe their structure in each nation. This section, accordingly, is concerned solely with organizations within the British structure, some of which are discussed below.

The Individual Employers

In common with large organizations in North America, the oil companies in the North Sea have approached trade unions as a constraint to be dealt with at the level of operating decisions.[3] As a former chief executive of a multinational oil company commented "the oil companies took a collective decision, not in any way formalized, not to encourage trade unions". Far from ignoring industrial relations on that account or leaving them to be conducted on an ad hoc basis by operational managers, the companies have recruited well qualified and experienced staff to devise and implement policies which are in line with company objectives. It would be unjust to say that the employers are simply anti-trade union because, as will be shown later in this chapter, there is a forum in the United Kingdom where trade unions and management meet regularly. In Norwegian waters it is impossible to operate without involvement of trade union representatives.

On the other hand, it is impossible to come to any conclusion other than that the oil companies have sought to be in the forefront of enlightened employee-management relations to the extent that employment with them offers attractive conditions which few other organizations can match. It would be nonsense to criticize any firm which offered the best conditions of employment that were possible under the circumstances, but it must be accepted that in doing so the oil companies see as a bonus the consequent difficulty posed to any trade union which wants to recruit members. If membership of a trade union is believed to bring no advantage, what point, apart from the ideological one that a worker ought to belong to a trade union, is there in taking out membership?

The relationships between employers and their employees offshore are summed up in the term joint consultation. While four different models of consultation have been identified, its most common form (and that adopted by the oil companies) occurs when it is used "as an alternative to collective bargaining and to prevent its establishment. Here management is essentially unitarist, but much more sophisticated than the traditional anti-union owner-manager. Thus it seeks to promote harmony and the willing acceptance of management decisions."[4] This is the sophisticated paternalist approach to industrial relations which was mentioned earlier and since it must be making a major contribution to the placidity of industrial relations, its virtual adoption as standard practice is understandable.

Joint consultation implies direct communication between managers and employees. There are obvious mutual advantages in this, and in a variety of industries and establishments onshore there has been a resurgence of joint consultation. This has upset some trade unions where collective bargaining has long been established since they feel that they are being ignored. Instead of issues being taken up by the shop steward to the union for comment or for managers to communicate with their employees through the trade union, managers are speaking directly to their employees. Offshore, where collective bargaining scarcely exists, the oil companies encourage such direct communication. Oil producing companies promote this form of employee relationship so that they may hear points of view on a whole range of topics relevant to employment on their installations. Such exchanges of opinion develop trust and understanding between people at all levels who, we must remember, are living and working on a metal construction in the hostile environment of the sea.[5,6] They know, moreover, that each one of them may at any time be dependent on the other in an emergency from which there are far fewer avenues of escape than onshore.

Following the tragedy of the *Piper-Alpha* platform in 1988, accident prevention was given an even higher profile than before on offshore installations. The regulations introduced on the United Kingdom continental shelf in the immediate aftermath of the tragedy and following the Cullen Report drew particular attention to the importance of employee representation on the safety committees.[7] It has now become a requirement that each installation has a safety committee which includes employee representation at all levels. Safety committees must meet at least every three months.[c] To the chagrin of the trade unions, the government did not make it mandatory for them to appoint representatives on these safety committees. In this the government was only being consistent with the philosophy which supported the Health and Safety at Work Act of 1974. The idea is that persuasion of employers to act responsibly and reasonably on accident prevention is preferable to compulsion. This reliance on self-regulation coincides with the managerial approach of the oil companies who have adhered to their joint consultation policy and have not invited trade union representation onto these committees although Lord Cullen did say, "that the appointment of offshore safety representatives by trade unions could be of some benefit in making the work of safety representatives and safety committees effective."[7] Having avoided a legal requirement to accept trade union representation after the greatest offshore disaster in the history of their industry, it is unlikely that the United Kingdom based oil companies are any closer to accepting collective bargaining than they ever were.

The United Kingdom Offshore Operators' Association

In stark contrast to the trade unions, the offshore employers had a representative body in place within a year of the granting of the United Kingdom's first round of licenses in 1964. The United Kingdom North Sea Operators' Committee was an informal association of license holders which provided for its members a forum for discussion on any matter affecting their industry offshore. It is highly unlikely that the members did not discuss from time to time what would be their policy on employment were reserves of oil to be discovered in commercially acceptable quantities offshore. When this happened it was not difficult to convert the existing Committee into a larger and more formal body by incorporating it as the United Kingdom Offshore Operators' Association (UKOOA) with a constitution and a permanent staff. Currently there are more than thirty companies in membership and the Association is administered by a Council of 34 (who meet monthly) with 15 permanent and five ad-hoc committees.

Fundamental to any analysis of industrial relations in the North Sea oil industry is an understanding of the interrelationship of UKOOA and IUOOC (Inter-Union Offshore Oil Committee). The relationship is purely consultative, almost an extension of the industry's joint consultative approach. IUOOC has consistently misunderstood UKOOA's *modus operandi*, probably because it would prefer UKOOA to have precisely those powers which are denied to it by its constitution.

One of the more important permanent committees of UKOOA is the Employment Practices Committee with seven terms of reference, of which only the first has relevance here:

> To provide a forum where member companies can exchange opinions and, where necessary, formulate an industry viewpoint in the field of employment practices including training, employee and industrial relations.[27]

It is a body purely for internal discussion on employment issues upon which it might form a viewpoint but not a policy. This is spelled out with greater clarity in the terms of reference of one of its five subcommittees, the Liaison Panel, the function of which is,

> *To act as a channel of communications for UKOOA on matters concerning employee relations which can be discussed in general terms on an exchange of views basis with Government, the Inter-Union Offshore Oil Committee and any other appropriate body approved by the Council.*[d]

The status of the Liaison Panel has been one of continual frustration for the unions. Whereas the IUOOC has some authority to commit its members to particular policies, the Liaison panel does not, and to any IUOOC request it can only reply that the request will be communicated to the companies or company concerned. The Liaison Panel is best defined as a body which acts as the collective voice of the oil companies on industrial relations but has neither executive control over, nor responsibility, for any member company's own industrial relations decisions. In short, no UKOOA member is inhibited by any agreement or recommendation reached between UKOOA and IUOOC from making whatsoever arrangements it likes concerning the management of its employees.

The consequence of this has been that the quarterly meetings of the IUOOC and the Liaison Panel are little more than opportunities to exchange opinions on matters of mutual interest. Nevertheless, this somewhat limited outcome is not without its advantages. Individual trade union officers and managers often establish some rapport which allows useful exchange of opinion and information. An issue which may be affecting employees on one installation can be drawn to the attention of the manager by a trade union officer on a personal basis that has been built up through their regular attendance at meetings of the IUOOC and the Liaison Panel of UKOOA.

The Inter-Union Offshore Oil Committee

During 1973 it had become obvious to the trade unions in North East Scotland that the oil companies were not interested in establishing the sort of contact with them that would lead to recognition for bargaining purposes on behalf of their employees. The trade unions with an interest in recruiting and representing offshore workers accordingly decided to form an organization which would seek to persuade the oil companies to recognize them for bargaining purposes and consequently to negotiate with them appropriate terms and conditions of employment. Originally comprising ten unions, there are now eight with the Transport and General Workers Union, the Amalgamated Engineering and Electrical Union and the Manufacturing, Science and Finance Union among the more prominent members. IUOOC set off on the wrong foot by demanding rather than requesting a meeting with representatives of the oil companies and threatening industrial action if they did not comply. The companies ignored the invitation and the attempt to carry out industrial action failed dismally.

The trade unions on the IUOOC have never lost sight of the principal objective enshrined in the first paragraph of the *Charter for the Unionization of Employees engaged in the Offshore Oil Industry* which they drew up in 1975. This states, "all companies engaged in the Offshore Oil Industry . . . recognize the right of . . . unions to recruit, represent and negotiate terms and conditions of employment for all employees falling within their spheres of membership." While some companies have conceded representational rights, for example the right of union officers to attend disciplinary hearings involving their members, negotiating rights remain at best a distant prospect.

Despite the unfortunate early efforts of the IUOOC at communication with the employers, both IUOOC and UKOOA realized that more was to be gained in discussion than by confrontation. By 1976 the Liaison Panel of UKOOA had begun to meet the IUOOC on a regular three monthly basis and these meetings have continued until today. These meetings are not without their value but they are far from the negotiating sessions which IUOOC would like them to be. Officers of IUOOC unions do go offshore escorted by a member of the company's industrial relations staff and do interview prospective members but the results, from the IUOOC point of view, have been disappointing in the extreme.

The Offshore Industry Liaison Committee

Any publication about industrial relations in the United Kingdom oil industry must include a brief comment on the Offshore Industry Liaison Committee (OILC). It originated in 1989 in the aftermath of the *Piper Alpha* disaster when a group of members of various IUOOC unions set up an Oil Information Center in Aberdeen with the intention of assisting their unions in the pursuit of recognition for collective bargaining. The following year the OILC became heavily involved in industrial action offshore and eventually found that it was viewed with hostility by the employers and with some suspicion by the trade unions. OILC accordingly established itself as a separate organization but was refused membership in the Scottish Trades Union Congress (and therefore the TUC). It is now a registered trade union unaffiliated to the TUC. Although membership revolves around 2,000, this small trade union is recognized as a full player on the industrial relations scene of North East Scotland and has developed a very strong alliance with the Norwegian union OFS. This is another union not affiliated with its country's main trade union confederation (LO) but it was established almost twenty years ago and has a membership of about 6,000 offshore workers.

The Offshore Contractors' Association

Known until 1995 as the Offshore Contractors' Council (founded 1984), the Offshore Contractors' Association (OCA) is the principal organization for employers in the offshore contracting business and has over 50 member companies, all of whom are involved in mechanical, electrical, construction, and maintenance work in the United Kingdom oil and gas industry. Since OCA has a combined United Kingdom offshore and onshore workforce of over 30,000 employees with a presence on virtually all platforms operating in the United Kingdom continental shelf, it is obvious that this presence has an effect upon industrial relations.

It is estimated that today on the United Kingdom continental shelf only about 20% of offshore workers are directly employed by the operators, i.e. the oil companies such as Shell, BP, Enterprise Oil. The rest are employees of contractors who provide the operators with construction and maintenance personnel. The direct employees of the operators enjoy, on the whole, better pay and conditions of service than contractors' employees. With the growing interest over the last few years in *partnering* these discrepancies are being removed, not least in the interests of harmony on the installations where the two different classes of employee have to work and live together.[8] A distinction is currently being made between *core* employees of contractors, who may have virtually permanent jobs on particular installations (e.g. maintenance electricians) and *peripheral* or *short term* employees who are aboard the installation for periods that can be as short as one week (e.g. welders sent offshore to carry out a repair). In some cases the proportion of contracted personnel on an installation is so high that Sandy Clark, Chairman of OCA commented "How far are we from the day our member companies become responsible for operating the platform on behalf of the oil company?"[e] Iain Bell, Secretary of OCA, said that it was good news for his organization that the multi-nationals were concentrating more and more on producing and selling oil and gas and leaving the rest to contractors. "It means more work for his members, who will in future be responsible for designing, building, operating and eventually disposing of rigs for the multi-nationals."[f]

Within months of Clark's comment, Sun Oil had contracted out its Balmoral field to Brown and Root and almost all the operations on the Hutton, Lyell, and Murchison fields had been handed over to Atlantic Power and Gas by Oryx United Kingdom Energy, only a year after it took over these three fields from Conoco. In almost all fields, the oil producing companies traditionally used contractors to look after specific parts of the operation such as production chemicals and working the downhole pumps. Thus over a period of about 15 years, the offshore contractors have expanded their contribution to the industry from the original one of building rigs and platforms, commissioning them at sea and carrying out maintenance and repair to the point where they can operate the entire offshore operation on behalf of the oil companies.

The Offshore Construction Agreement

The question of collective bargaining now becomes important because it is only from the contractors that the trade unions have secured any significant recognition in the offshore oil and gas industry. The construction industry has always been heavily unionized. The move to the fabrication of drilling rigs and platforms for new clients in the offshore industry did not alter this in any way and conditions of employment continued to be regulated through collective bargaining. The immense capital outlay which precedes the extraction of oil made it important for the operators to have the work carried out as quickly as possible. Since the manual workers engaged in this task were still employees of the construction firms and, in addition, were often the same individuals, it would have been foolish even to contemplate the abandonment of collective bargaining. Accordingly, the operating companies realized that it was in their interests to permit some form of trade union involvement on their offshore establishments. With their tacit consent the Oil and Chemical Plant Constructors' Association (later merged into the Offshore Contractors' Council) negotiated the Offshore Construction Agreement (or *Hook-Up* Agreement as it became more commonly known). The first Hook-Up agreement was signed in 1976 by five trade unions and the Association but not by any operator. It covered the entire range of conditions of employment normally associated with collective bargaining for onshore workers (e.g. pay, holidays, hours of work, disciplinary procedures). The operators, who had, officially at least, no part in the agreement were nevertheless insistent that it would cease to apply *in toto* as soon as first oil was produced or at some date which they would stipulate. All subsequent work on installations was to be classified as maintenance for which there was no trade union agreement with the employers (apart from an agreement affecting electricians who were few in number.) The Offshore Construction Agreement was renegotiated at regular intervals until 1990 when the signatory unions withdrew from the agreement.

This was part of combined union policy to extract a Post Construction Agreement from the operators which would include recognition of the trade unions for bargaining purposes. Fewer and fewer employees were now engaged on *hook-up* because, quite apart from the fact that the many fields in the North Sea were now on stream, the nature of the work was changing. Technological advance now allowed the fabrication onshore of integrated modules. Most *hook-ups* and testing are now done on land and the modules are taken by barge out to their locations *with their lights on* in the jargon of the industry. Their positioning has been made possible by the huge floating cranes which have become available over the last decade. To this must be added the increasing emphasis on subsea completions tied back to existing installations or a floating production system, both of which require far fewer people in the offshore construction phase.

In summary, the majority of contractor personnel aboard installations were, by 1990, carrying out what in general terms might be called maintenance and were employed by companies who had to bid for work in competition with rival firms. The trade unions were persuaded that by refusing to sign a rene-gotiated Offshore Construction Agreement, pressure could be brought on the operators through the contractors to negotiate a comprehensive Post Construction Agreement, which would cover all employees and include recog-nition of trade unions as the bargaining agents of these employees. This would meet a long term objective of the trade unions for, as they pointed out, it was not unusual for workers originally engaged on *hook-up* terms to stay on the job after *first oil* and to suffer a considerable reduction in pay, together with the loss of the protection previously conferred by the union/company agreement. The policy did not succeed and within 18 months a new Offshore Construction Agreement was reached under the previous terms. As one senior trade union officer acknowledged, the last agreement has been generous as far as pay is concerned taking into account the small amount of *hook-up* work and the price of oil.

At present the trade unions are as far from obtaining a Post Construction Agreement as they ever were and in any case modern technolo-gy may mean that the very term is running out of date. The bulk of the employ-ees offshore, as stated earlier, are employed by contractors and apart from the fast diminishing number who still enjoy Offshore Construction Agreement terms and the catering workers who are a special case, very few of them have their terms and conditions regulated through the process of collective bar-gaining.

The Catering Offshore Traders' Association

Almost from the beginning of the North Sea oil and gas industry, catering has been contracted out by the operators to specialists in this field. Members of the Association, usually referred to as COTA, obtain contracts through competitive tendering. Following some unrest among employees in 1979 over conditions of pay and service, the oil operators actively encouraged an agreement on minimum rates of pay between the main union involved, the Transport and General Workers' Union, and the caterers. There has been little industrial strife since that time in the offshore catering industry although the work is characterized by low pay and high labor turnover in comparison with other offshore employment.

Summary

This diffusion of the offshore workforce among oil companies and contractors (some of whom are very small outfits) makes it even more difficult for trade unions to play the role to which they aspire. Furthermore, offshore workers are not only composed of different categories of employees; they are themselves very different in occupation and the OILC concluded as late as 1991 that there are as many as 10 trade unions seeking to represent them. The OILC claims this allows the operators and contractors to assert that union recognition implies multi-union recognition and so justifies their resistance to attempts to obtain collective bargaining rights. OILC interprets the employer view as follows: "It is argued that multi-unionism will produce industrial anarchy in the industry which because of its hazardous nature, cannot afford to have any challenge to managerial authority from trade unions."[9] In addition, the question arises about responsibility for industrial relations offshore: is the policy of the operator paramount or can the contractor devise and carry out a policy that may be different from that of the operator? The operators are perfectly clear where they see responsibility to lie because the UKOOA Council recommended to its members in 1978 that "The right of an OIM / manager to order anyone off company premises remains paramount."[8] It is a further indication of the virtual total absence offshore of any trade union presence that appeals against removal of a contractor's employee from an installation are the responsibility of the contractor and not of a trade union.

Accident Prevention

Interest in accident prevention has been a natural concern of all trade unions since their inception and the origins of many trade unions lay in the determination of groups of workers to seek safer working conditions.

Associated with this has been reliance upon trade unions to obtain financial compensation for their members when there is a possibility that injury was a result of a failure of the employers to observe required safety standards and practice. When one considers accident prevention in the North Sea oil and gas industry, the topic must be approached from two very different perspectives. The first is that employers have had ever increasing legal requirements to observe in the provision of safe working environments, especially following accidents when there have been many casualties with attendant loss of life such as the *Alexander Kielland* and *Piper Alpha* tragedies. The other perspective is the successful efforts of the Norwegian unions to become involved in the mechanisms established to provide safe working environments on Norwegian installations and, in contrast, the total failure of British trade unions to be accorded any formal role at all on installations on the United Kingdom continental shelf.

Accident Prevention on the
United Kingdom Continental Shelf: Trade Union Exclusion

The question of safety is paramount in the offshore industry and has already been discussed in Chapters 9 and 10. Some of the most spectacular and horrific accidents in any industry have been the three offshore disasters which occurred in the 1980s: *Alexander Kielland* (1980, Norwegian waters, 123 fatalities), *Ocean Ranger* (1982, Canadian waters, 84 fatalities) and *Piper Alpha* (1988, British waters, 167 fatalities). The consequences of these and other accidents (such as the Chinook accident off Shetland in 1986, when the rotor blade of a helicopter sheared and 45 men plunged to their death) are reflected in the measures which have been taken at the highest level to reduce the risk of working in a hostile environment. In addition, one must recall that the offshore oil industry is the only industry where almost all the employees must be transported to their place of work either by air or by boat. Other chapters in this book will address the perceptions of risk seen from the perspectives of employer and employee and the legislative requirements pertaining to the employment of persons offshore. This chapter is concerned with industrial relations and will therefore consider accident prevention (a much more positive term than safety) solely in the manner in which it impinges upon industrial relations.

Accident prevention in the offshore oil and gas industry has been approached in a different way from accident prevention onshore. There are obvious differences in the working environments, but these alone do not account for the pattern that has developed over the thirty-year history of the industry in the North Sea. In 1965 the decapodal platform, *Sea Gem*, collapsed off the Humber estuary with the loss of 13 lives and a public inquiry followed. Among the recommendations contained in the subsequent report were two which have had a direct bearing upon industrial relations. The first was "the fact that "the Sea Gem was lost in the character of a sinking ship suggests strongly that there ought to be a Master or unquestioned authority on these rigs."[10] Thus the nature of the power that came to be vested in oil installation managers has its origins in what some writers see as a mistaken similarity between a fixed installation offshore and a vessel, whereas the analogy with an isolated land-based construction might have been more appropriate. The other recommendation which concerns industrial relations is that the report advised consideration should be given to the kind of legislation that was needed for offshore installations.

Several working parties were set up to advise on this and the result was the Mineral Workings (Offshore Installations) Act 1971 which empowered the Minister of State for Energy to make such regulations as considered appropriate to secure a safe working environment on installations exploiting mineral deposits. Strangely, those persons who advised the government appear to have worked in isolation from discussions which were simultaneously in progress on other employment safety matters. The Holland-Martin Report in 1969 dealt with safety in fishing, another industry where the sea poses particular hazards and it specifically recommended joint union-management safety committees on vessels.[11] The Robens Report 1972 was the basis for a major amendment in United Kingdom safety legislation which reached the statute book as the Health and Safety at Work Act 1974.[12]

The philosophy underlying the Robens Report and the subsequent legislation was that persuasion was preferable to compulsion and that consequently the principle of voluntarism in the achievement of safe working conditions was to apply. This philosophy was, nevertheless, tempered by the principle that no government department was to be responsible for accident prevention within the industry for which it had to account to Parliament. Consequently there was established a unified supervising authority, the Health and Safety Commission (HSC), with an executive arm, the Health and Safety Executive (HSE). The HSC is tripartite in nature with its membership composed of representatives from industry, trade unions, and the government.

In most onshore industries there were already accident prevention committees with representation from employees, who were usually union members. Trade unions also negotiated with employers when they believed that their members needed protection from any hazards specific to the industry or to any particular forms of employment within an otherwise *safe* industry. In

1977 the Safety Representatives and Safety Committee Regulations gave to trade unions recognized by employers the right to appoint representatives. They were empowered to demand the creation of safety committees where none existed, but by this time it was too late for the trade unions to apply these regulations to the oil and gas industry. As stated earlier, the oil employers had no intention of negotiating with the trade unions and since the Regulations specifically referred to trade unions recognized by employers, the Regulations could not be used by the unions. Moreover, the Department of Energy, in contradiction to the philosophy of the Robens Report, continued to use the powers given to it under the Mineral Workings (Offshore Installations) Act of 1971 to control accident prevention on oil installations. "Offshore safety was thus insulated from the Robens reconstruction."[13] As trade unions complained over these years, the responsibility for ensuring a safe working environment aboard offshore installations was delegated to the government department which had as one of its principal objectives the uninterrupted flow of oil (and therefore of tax revenue) from the mineral deposits of the United Kingdom continental shelf.

As the oil and gas industry expanded offshore there was a corresponding and unacceptable growth in fatalities, especially among divers.[14] In contrast to the Gulf of Mexico, where divers had simply followed the reservoirs offshore into shallow water and the climate was benign, the North Sea was deep and the weather often hostile. This led the government to appoint in 1978 a Committee of Enquiry under Dr. J. H. Burgoyne, which reported two years later. The Burgoyne Report concluded that "the government shall discharge its responsibility for offshore safety as a single agency" and recommended that the Department of Energy should "continue its policy to employ an Inspectorate consisting of well-qualified and industrially experienced individuals."[13] This was a bitter disappointment for the trade unions which had hoped that Burgoyne would recommend that offshore safety be transferred to the HSE and the two trade union representatives on the Committee of Inquiry issued a six-page note of dissent stating their preference for the HSE to be the responsible agency. The single agency therefore remained the Petroleum Engineering Division of the Department of Energy which had entered into an agreement with the HSE in 1978 to act in a proxy role for the HSE offshore.

The British trade unions had realized by 1980 that despite the *Memorandum of Understanding on Trade Union Access to Offshore Installations* their efforts at recruiting offshore oil workers had been almost a complete failure. An alternative strategy was therefore needed and they decided that their strongest argument for obtaining recognition from the employers was their interest in safe working environments. Each trade union has built up a considerable body of expertise on the particular hazards common to the industries wherein their members are employed. Moreover, this wealth of knowledge has been recognized by trade union participation, as of right, on public institutions concerned with accident prevention, not least the HSC.

Their case for recognition by the oil employers on the grounds that they could make a positive contribution to the industry through their wide knowledge of safety was pursued throughout the 1980s. In the opinion of many within and without the industry, this objective appeared to have been reached when Lord Cullen carried out his inquiry into the *Piper Alpha* disaster and made his report. Trade union officers had given evidence at the inquiry and Lord Cullen stated that union representatives could be of benefit in making the work of safety committees effective. The subsequent legislation saw the removal of the PED as the responsible agency for accident prevention and its replacement by the new Offshore Safety Division (OSD) of the HSE in 1991, but there was no requirement for companies to appoint union representatives on safety committees.

The huge sum of £2.6 billion (nearly 4 billion dollars) has been spent by the oil and gas industry on accident prevention since 1990. Companies have made every effort to provide for their employees a working environment that is as free as possible from all hazards known in their operation. In conversation with the author, the head of industrial relations in one of the largest oil companies commented, "Whereas previously the company that generally sought to meet the minimum requirements of the law as it then stood, it now regards the legal obligations on the employer merely as the minimum acceptable base upon which the company will always attempt to improve." For the trade unions this is small comfort. The Offshore Installations (Safety Representatives and Safety Committees) Regulations 1989 require employee representatives, as distinct from trade union representatives, on platform safety committees. Although many of these representatives may well be members of a trade union it is their immediate colleagues for whom they speak and not their trade union. The trade unions have still no direct voice on the accident prevention measures which an employer wishes to discuss and/or implement.

Two pieces of research call into question the whole rationale of the trade union point of view. Peter Kidger argues that since statutory participation by trade unions on safety committees has been restricted to workplaces onshore, there has been no opportunity to study the experience of committees where the employee representation is not union influenced other than on platforms offshore since 1989. He even goes so far as to suggest that "the system operating on North Sea oil installations provides a useful model which could be drawn upon for application onshore."[16] Kidger's argument is based on the

Robens' principle that collective bargaining has no place in discussions on accident prevention and that in their joint consultative approach the oil companies are interpreting correctly the philosophy of the Health and Safety at Work Act. A study carried out by Malcolm Spaven and others for the HSE concluded that

> *Support for increased involvement of trade unions in the work of Safety Representatives is considerable among offshore workers. However there is no clear majority for a system of Safety Representatives, and such a system, if widely applied, would present difficulties for the representational rights of non-members of trade unions.*[6]

Currently the trade unions continue to assert their moral right to represent offshore employees and claim that since employee representatives on safety committees are unprotected by trade unions, they can be intimidated from expression of opinion, despite the provisions of the Offshore Safety Representatives Act 1992 and the Trade Union Reform Employment Rights Act 1993 which extended the same rights to all employees offshore. Legal redress for dismissal can be sought through the Industrial Tribunal, but this is only *after* dismissal and even if the applicant is successful reinstatement does not necessarily follow.[17] All employees offshore have the right to telephone the OSD direct if there is a safety matter which is exercising their concern but, again, unions believe that fear of losing one's job makes this an unrealistic privilege. The oil companies have over the past two years been following a policy to which the acronym CRINE has been given; it stands for Cost Reduction Initiative in the New Era and is an attempt to reduce unnecessary expenditure at a time when there is plenty of oil available worldwide. (Over 10 years ago oil was priced at just above $30 per barrel. It is currently just under $17.) The trade unions consider that it is unlikely that accident prevention measures can escape some trimming of the expenditure which companies are hoping to reduce and that this can result in accident rates beginning to rise.[17] The oil companies remain, as they always have been, interested in what the unions may say but unwilling to accept them as equal partners in the formation of policy on accident prevention.

Industrial Relations in Norwegian Waters

Norway enjoys immense reserves of oil and gas under her continental shelf. The revenues which have accrued to this small nation of under four million people from the exploitation of these resources have resulted in her citizens having among the highest *per capita* incomes in the world. Her current and assured future prosperity arises not simply from having a lengthy coastline along the North Sea, but from the manner in which she has managed this fortunate inheritance.

In 1935 the Norwegian Federation of Trade Unions (Landsorganisasjønen i Norge, usually referred to as LO) and the Norwegian Employers Association (Næringslivets Hovedorganisasjon, usually referred to as NHO) signed the Basic Agreement (Hovedavtalen) whereby freedom of association was guaranteed to trade unions who in turn contracted to settle all industrial disputes through national institutions established for that purpose. At regular intervals since 1935 the Basic Agreement has been revised and updated with the full support of the government. Thus during any contract period there is an obligation upon employers as well as employees to resolve disputes through negotiation or by referral to the Labor Court. By 1960, Norway had become a societal-corporatist state with cooperation between government, national organizations such as trade union federations and employer associations widely accepted as the appropriate method whereby the kingdom's interest was best served. It was this sense of management of business operations in Norway which the oil majors initially failed to recognize when oil was discovered under Norway's continental shelf.

Exploration drilling had begun in 1966 and the companies were almost all American since Norway had no indigenous expertise in the industry. Norwegians were employed at the lower skill levels and were subject to *hire and fire*, as labor requirements dictated. Any suggestion of a collective agreement between a company and a representative body of employees was brushed aside. Eventually Norwegians as a whole came to understand that this new industry was operating an industrial relations policy utterly alien to the accepted practice of their nation and they demanded action from their government.[18]

On account of both trade union and government decisions, 1977 is the watershed year of Norway's oil and gas industry as far as industrial relations are concerned. The Storthing (The Norwegian parliament) passed the Working Environment Act and LO formed a new trade union for oil workers, the Norwegian Oil and Petrochemical Workers' Union (Norsk Olje-og Petrochemisk Fagforbund, usually referred to as NOPEF). Another union, the Federation of Oil Workers (Oljearbeidernes Fellessamengslutning, usually referred to as OFS), had already grown out of an association of employees on the Phillips Petroleum Company Norway (or PPCoN) installations. The company first recognized the association in 1973, no doubt expecting that it would be what in America is called a *sweetheart* union, an innocuous staff association which an employer can manipulate with ease. It has remained outside LO, is more militant than NOPEF and claims a membership of about 6,000.

Originally it attracted only workers directly employed by the operators, but it now consists of four divisions: operators, drillers, caterers and employees on mobile units. It has developed in the last few years very strong links with OILC in Aberdeen. NOPEF and OFS are rival unions and managements must work with both.

The Working Environment Act 1977 was the government's response to national feeling, almost outrage, that foreign companies were denying to Norwegian workers those rights to representation and conditions of employment that were common across the rest of the nation. The following two quotations outline the main provisions of the law with which all employers, offshore as well as onshore, must comply.

> *Solution of an enterprise's working environment problems shall be reached through close cooperation between management and employees. A number of the act's provisions expressly stipulate cooperation in questions, concerning, for example, the organization of work, planning systems, building work etc. By virtue of the Working Environment Act formal institutions / bodies shall be established to ensure that the employees can exercise influence in working issues.*

> *In every enterprise one or more protection officers shall be elected (whose duty will be) to take care of the employees' interests concerning the working environment and to see that the work can be carried out in a thoroughly safe and sound manner.[19]*

The reaction of the oil companies was expressed as follows: "There is nothing we can do, we just accept what we are being told to do by the government and unions—it is very expensive,—but if that is the way they want it, they can get it."[20] This remains the case today. Whatever an organization's or an individual manager's opinion may be on the place of trade unions in the operation of a commercial undertaking, if that undertaking is based within Norwegian territory the trade unions must be allowed to carry out the functions which the law has guaranteed to them.

There was not immediate harmonization of conditions of employment onshore and offshore, partially on account of the conflict between OFS and NOPEF over the right to organize employees and partially on account of the good sense of the Norwegians in allowing the oil companies time to adjust to a method of labor control which was new to them. The Working Environment Act also empowered the government to introduce additional regulations as were deemed relevant. For example, the act stated that all enterprises which regularly employed at least fifty persons had to set up working environment committees with equal membership between employers and employees. In addition, safety delegates (a better translation that "protection officers" as given in the quotation above) had to be elected and they were empowered to require operations to cease if they considered them to be dangerous. Then a few years later it was made compulsory for employers to permit trade unions with 50% membership on an installation to appoint worker representatives onto the working environment committees. By the mid-1980s there had been further changes favoring trade unions when, following another Basic Agreement, all enterprises with over one hundred employees had to have a works committee with equal representation from management and employees. Oil companies had joined NHO in 1981 and were bound to comply but with the usual Norwegian sense of balance it was agreed that on offshore installations works committees and working environment committees could be amalgamated as single bodies.

Thus in Norway the oil companies have been driven to recognize trade unions for collective bargaining and other representational purposes and where membership of working environment committees are involved they have often to accept the nominees of the trade unions. On the other hand they are now operating within and not without the national industrial relations system and consequently their human resource management is accepted in a far more positive light than it once was. Readers who seek more detailed accounts of industrial relations on the Norwegian continental shelf should consult Andersen, 1984 and 1988.[21,22]

Conclusion

Fundamentally the labor process in the Norwegian oil industry is typical of the national pattern while in the identical British industry the process is atypical, but the different labor processes seem to have no economic consequences.[23] Norwegian and British workers appear to be equally satisfied with safety on their installations.[24] Trade union appointed safety delegates did not prevent the *Alexander Kielland* tragedy and it seems unlikely that British trade union appointees to a safety committee could have prevented *Piper Alpha*. Managerial cultures differ but there is no conclusive evidence of greater levels of stress among one or the other workforce who share the common problems of employment on isolated installations in the North Sea.[25]

The British trade unions envy the success of their Norwegian counterparts and see it as almost *politically correct* that traditional collective bargaining should be the method of establishing pay and conditions of work offshore as it is onshore. It can be argued equally well that in the United Kingdom a new labor process is being developed offshore where direct communications between managers and workers eliminate the need for unions in the achievement and control of safe working environments. The success of voluntarism offshore with elected representatives as distinct from union appointees suggests that it could be just as successful onshore but has never been fully implemented on account of the trade unions' statutory right to participation.

Industrial relations on the United Kingdom continental shelf exhibits a special form of voluntarism in that it emerges outside the collective bargaining which is common onshore in Great Britain and is almost the standard practice across all Norwegian industry. Moreover, the labor process offshore is becoming more complex on both the Norwegian and the British continental shelves as operators reduce the number of their own direct employees in favor of increased proportions of contract employees. Separation of the bulk of the necessary human resource from direct employment is now standard practice offshore in both Britain and Norway with consequences which are more predictable for Norway than for Britain. There is no indication that there will be any change in terms and conditions of employment on Norway's continental shelf and so the industrial relations scene will remain much as it has been over the last five years.

For the United Kingdom prediction and conclusions are more difficult. The OILC is currently pursuing a merger with the National Union of Mineworkers to form a union of workers in energy but this is unlikely to come to fruition. There is also the possibility that trade unions may seek to advance their claims for recognition offshore through their existing bases among the contractors onshore. There is no evidence to persuade one to believe that this strategy will be any more successful than previous trade union attempts to attract membership which will be in any way significant. Indeed, quite the contrary view has greater support and some recent research has shown that involvement of offshore workers by and with their managements has become part of the culture of the industry.[26] If there is any retreat among the oil producers on the United Kingdom continental shelf from their present policy towards recognition of trade unions it will be a small one and based upon their own terms.

Endnotes

a Almost all oil installations in the North Sea are in the Scottish part of the United Kingdom continental shelf and, consequently, the law of Scotland and not of England applies. Legislation affecting employment offshore is, however, common to both legal systems. Where prosecutions occur, the case for the Crown is led by the Procurator Fiscal, whose role is similar to that of the District Attorney in the U.S., except that he is appointed and not elected.

b   On July 21, 1976 the United Kingdom government extended the Employment
    Protection Act 1975 to include offshore employment and simultaneously the
    UKOOA agreed that oil producers "would ensure that trade union officials, on
    request, are granted reasonable access for recruitment purposes to all their off-
    shore installations".

c   Offshore Installations (Safety Representatives and Safety Committees)
    Regulations 1989. 21(i).

d   The other four sub-committees are Training, Contractors' Liaison, Aberdeen;
    Contractors' Liaison, London; and Pay and Benefits.

e   Offshore Contractors' Council Annual Review 1994.

f   Fraser, S. October 22, 1995. Safety Hopes Buried at Sea. Scotland on Sunday.

g   Appeals from Disciplinary Action exercised by OIM or other Company Manager
    against Contractors' Personnel by their Employers. Recommendations to
    Members by UKOOA Council 1978.

h   ibid.

References

1. Clegg, H. *The Changing System of Industrial Relations in Great Britain.* Blackwell:
    Oxford, 1979.
2. Foster, J. and Woolfson, C. *Trade Unionism and Health and Safety Rights in Britain's
    Offshore Oil Industry.* International Centre for Trade Union Rights, London, 1992.
3. Herman, E. S. *Corporate Control: Corporate Power.* Cambridge, 1981.
4. Marchington, M. Joint Consultation in Practice in K. Sisson (Ed) *Personnel
    Management in Britain* Oxford: Blackwell, 1989.
5. McLoughlin, I. and Gourlay, S. *Enterprise without Unions.* Open University Press:
    Buckingham, 1994.
6. Spaven, M., Ras, H., Morrison, A. and Wright,C. *The Effectiveness of Offshore Safety
    Representatives and Safety Committees.* University of Aberdeen OTO Series No. 93
    012. Sudbury: HSE Books, 1993.
7. Cullen, The Hon. Lord. *The Public Inquiry into the Piper Alpha Disaster. Vols. I & II.*
    London: HMSO. Command Paper 1310, 1990.
8. Green, R. L. *Collaborative Relationships between Producers and Contractors in the United
    Kingdom Oil and Gas Industry.* Paper presented at the British Academy of
    Management Research Conference, Lancaster, September, 1994.
9. Offshore Information Centre, Aberdeen. *The Crisis in Offshore Trade Unionism.*,
    1991.
10. Adams, J. R. *Report of the Inquiry into the Collapse of the Drilling Rig Sea Gem.*
    Command Paper 3409. London: HMSO, 1967.
11. Holland-Martin, D. *The Final Report of the Committee of Inquiry into Trawler Safety.*
    Command Paper 4114. London: HMSO, 1969.
12. Robens, The Right Hon. Lord. *Health and Safety at Work: Report of the Committee
    1970-1972.* Command Paper 5034. London: HMSO, 1972.
13. Offshore Information Centre, Aberdeen "*Striking Out*", 1991.
14. Warner, J. & Park, F. *Requiem for a Diver.* Glasgow: Brown, Son and Ferguson,
    1990.

15. Burgoyne, J. N. *Offshore Safety: Report of the Committee*. Command Paper 7866. London: HMSO, 1980.

16. Kidger, P. *Should Union Appointed or Elected Safety Representatives be the Model for the United Kingdom?*. University of Salford Working Paper No 9003, 1993.

17. Woolfson, C. & Beck, M. *Seven Years after Piper Alpha: Safety Claims and the New Safety Case Regime*. University of Glasgow, 1995.

18. Karlsen, K. *"The nature of this new industry took the unions by surprise". v. The Norwegian Experience*. Paper presented at the "Workforce Involvement and Health and Safety Offshore", Conference and published by the Scottish Trades Union Congress, Glasgow, 1993.

19. The Royal Norwegian Ministry of Foreign Affairs. *Industrial Democracy in Norway*. UDA 167/83 ENG. Oslo, 1983.

20. Quale, T. V. (1986) *Safety and Offshore Working Conditions : the Quality of Work Life in the North Sea*. Oxford:Oxford University Press, 1986.

21. Andersen, S. V. *Conflict over Labor Relations in the Norwegian Petroleum Sector*. Institute of Energy Report, 3/84, Norwegian School of Management, Oslo, 1984.

22. Andersen, S. V. *British and Norwegian Offshore Relations*. Avebury: Aldershot, 1988.

23. Gourlay, D. H. F. (1996) *Labour Processes in the Norwegian and British Sectors of the North Sea Oil and Gas Industry*. Paper presented at the Fourteenth Annual International Labour Process Conference, Aston University, Birmingham, 1996.

24. Fleming, M., Rundmo, T., Mearns, K., Flin, R. and Gordon, R. A *Comparative Study of Risk Perception on the United Kingdom and Norwegian Continental Shelves*. Paper presented at "Work and Wellbeing in Europe" Conference at Nottingham University, England, December 1995.

25. Mearns, K., Flin, R., Rundmo, T., Fleming, M., and Gordon, R. "A Comparative Study of Organizational Factors and Safety in the United Kingdom and Norwegian Offshore Oil Industries". (In prep.).

26. Royle, D. J. C. *Workforce Involvement in the United Kingdom Offshore Oil and Gas Industry*. Paper presented at the Society of Petroleum Engineers Offshore Europe 1995 Conference and Exhibition, Aberdeen, 1995.

27. United Kingdom Offshore Operators Association *Employment Practices Committee Information Booklet*, 1988.

Chapter 12

Lessons From Offshore Aviation: Toward an Integrated Human Performance System

Glyn David

Introduction

This chapter provides an overview of the development of human factors appreciation in a technology-based commercial environment that demands high levels of technical and procedural performance of its human operators. It is hoped that this chapter will provide some insight of support helicopter flying. Offshore installation managers also will gain an additional perspective on the importance of integrating human factors awareness and knowledge, not only with standard operating procedures, but most importantly, at all levels of training and with everyday operational practices.

Like the modern OIM, the modern aircraft commander is a resource manager. His or her duties include the efficient commercial operation of complex machinery while interacting with and managing the human resources that constitute the essential operating crew. The captain is responsible also for liaison with and coordination of supporting agencies and contractors—such as engineering, refuelling, handling agents, caterers, flight dispatch or operations, and air traffic services. Such routine is the duty of any industrial manager, and resolution of minor managerial crises, which seem to occur with relentless regularity, is an area of expected and assessed competence. However, the nature of both the aviation and oil and gas industries provide an additional managerial dimension with the possibility of life-threatening emergencies. An ability to cope with not only routine operations but potentially disastrous abnormal circumstances is a requirement for the OIM and aircraft commander alike.

As in the oil and gas industry, aircraft accident investigation has caused emphasis to be placed on the importance of human performance and training—or its lack—as a determinant of safety. Fairly recent developments have brought into question the validity of some of the training and standard operating procedures which were established through traditional understanding and attitudes. Today, commercial and air transport operators world-wide, including helicopter operations in offshore support, apply Crew Resource Management (CRM) training as a means of reducing the problems posed by failures in human performance.

CRM training attempts to improve safety and efficiency initially by raising awareness of human factors issues that are demonstrably significant to the industry. Then the training incorporates this awareness in ongoing procedures and practices. This process has not always been comfortable. Established attitudes towards what is necessary for proficiency may be entrenched—especially in highly professional cultures where attitudes tend to be conservative and self-protecting. An examination of the evolution of CRM training in aviation shows the lessons which have been learned, the derived and developed constituents of effective training, and the practices developed. Consequently these lessons may provide valuable insight and experience that can be transferred between industries placing similarly high demands and responsibilities on their resource managers.

Offshore Support Operations

Personnel transfers using helicopters are now common throughout the world, including the Gulf of Mexico, Brunei, Thailand, Vietnam, Nigeria, China, Australia, Burma, Norway, Denmark, the United Kingdom, Holland, and South Africa. Statistics on the volume of traffic and safety vary with the operating locale. An example, from 1989 to 1993 in the United Kingdom sector of the North Sea a total of 10,629,291 passengers were carried on some 1,433,100 oil and gas industry related flight sectors. Fourteen passenger fatalities were suffered in the two fatal aircraft accidents which occurred during the period—a fatality rate of approximately 0.0001%.[1] The industry considers an acceptable fatality rate to be zero, and so improvement is sought constantly. Yet, for a relatively young industry, large scale civil helicopter transportation has an enviable safety record, and in some ways this is remarkable given the operating environment.

Offshore helicopter operations take place without many of the aviation operating system advantages enjoyed by fixed-wing airline operators. The environment itself degrades the level of air traffic control services available, and rarely are any radar services available during the descent, landing, take-off or initial climb portions of a flight to and from an installation. Collision avoidance and aircraft separation are achieved instead through a variety of methods ranging from satellite tracking of aircraft to strict compliance with procedures and communication initiatives taken in individual cases.

Throughout the world, helicopter commanders often find themselves acting with large degrees of autonomy. Flights may terminate in a landing on a moving helideck at night, sometimes in climatic conditions which approach the limits for operation and always in a complex machine that produces high levels of fatiguing noise and vibration. There seems little doubt that high stresses are imposed by the task demands placed on offshore helicopter crews, regardless of the local operating environment. Continuing training and assessment is required to arm aircrew with the technical and procedural competencies necessary to safely conduct operations in both normal and abnormal situations.

There is an old saying in aviation that successful landings are the result of good approaches. Considerable training effort goes into ensuring that pilots are well versed in emergency procedures. Simulated emergencies (single and double engine failures, electrical failures, hydraulics failures, fuel system problems, navigation system errors, various mechanical problems, instrumentation failures, and radio failures) are practiced on a regular basis so as to provide aircrew with the tools for the successful resolution of technical problems. More difficult to train for, and often more significant, are those abnormal situations which arise from the mismanagement of otherwise routine operations—through simple human failings such as a desire to get the job done, fatigue, poor communication between crew members, and peer pressure. Of the three instances where helicopters have ditched in the United Kingdom sector of the northern North Sea since 1990, two were cases where there was no physical problem with the aircraft. Rather, they illuminated failings of the aircrew to make correct routine decisions—possibly exacerbated by problems of fatigue and perception.[2,3]

For many years, aviation has produced operating regulations and procedures which, had they been applied and adhered to, would have prevented many of the accidents that occurred. Yet having speed limits does not prevent speed-related automobile accidents. Only in recent years have we been able to identify and realize a need to address the underlying causes of human failure in aviation. This realization has been slow to develop for two main reasons. First, our perception of aircraft accident causes was that external factors such as mechanical failure or adverse weather conditions were more important determinants of safety than human performance. This perception was rooted in the problems associated with early aircraft (such as reliability, flimsiness, and level of equipment). Second, our reliance on procedures and discipline—to which adherence would identifiably have prevented incidents—remained a seductively convincing answer to the need to provide human performance.

Only over time have we realized that procedures and regulations alone do not constitute a safety system unless there is an accompanying appreciation of the reasons that actual practice often diverges from stated procedures. We should also understand that these root causes must be addressed through education and training rather than discipline.

The development of aviation safety (and training to achieve it) rests essentially on the interplay of three factors—operator practices (particularly the flight crew themselves), accident and incident analysis, and regulatory requirement. This is exemplified during the industry's development of human factors awareness and the emergence of CRM training. While we recognize that an understanding of human error is essential to the effective training of offshore support helicopter crews, we must turn to the more general world of commercial aviation to view that development.

The Development of Human Factors Awareness

The Early Years—Developing the Right Stuff

In 1903 the Wright brothers launched powered aviation with a flight of just over 120 feet. Initially disbelieved (the report was carried in only two newspapers, one of which was the Beekeeper's Journal), their efforts were celebrated eventually as an astounding feat. This was unsurprising in an era when each flight brought the probability of engine failure, or even structural failure of an airframe component (such as the wings!) because the aerodynamic forces involved were poorly understood or the loads imposed exceeded the construction technology available.

The development of aircraft technology was accelerated considerably during World War I, along with pilot selection and training—though the quality of the later was of dubious value in many instances. (The British used a man's horse-riding ability as a selection criterion, while the French judged a candidate's tolerance of stress by noting how he reacted to a pistol being discharged close to his head without warning!)

These initial attempts may seem laughable or tragic by today's standards, but they are indicative of the attitudes toward the qualities it was felt a pilot should possess: attitudes which crystallized into a stereotype during the 1920s and 1930s. This was a period of great expansion in aviation. The early experimenters and eccentrics were joined by a new breed of adventurers and innovators, and an image was set of the pilot as a stalwart, self-reliant individual, braving the skies with white scarf trailing in the slipstream. The image persists today; it remains a major career attractant. Indeed, throughout World War II and on into the jet era, the qualities embodied in this stereotypical pilot seemed appropriate to the task. Traditionally, the selection, training, and assessment of the ongoing proficiency of pilots has focused on their ability to perform autonomously. This was to the extent that in multi-crew evaluation other crew members were forbidden to assist or correct errors made by the pilot under assessment.[4] The *right stuff* was a combination of technical knowledge, physical skill and the attitudes and behavioral characteristics of the stereotype. The hypothesis was simple: if everyone on the team is good at what they do individually, you have a good team.

Lessons in Maturity - The Jet Transport Age

The 1950s saw the beginning of a new era in commercial aviation - the age of the airliner. Massively stimulated by the funding and motivation provided by the Second World War, aviation technology reached new heights. Improvements in engineering knowledge, materials technologies, fuels and oils, aerodynamics understanding, meteorology, radio communications, and navigation facilities combined to produce levels of safety previously unseen. The introduction of a new generation of reliable turbojet transport aircraft, such as the Boeing 707 and the DeHavilland Comet, heralded the development of intercontinental transport which was faster, safer, and within the reach of more people than ever before.

The airliners grew larger and the number of passengers multiplied, yet as the volume of air traffic increased, accidents became less frequent—though this highlighted those accidents which still occurred. The crash of a modern airliner (with upwards of 200–300 people on board) is unlikely to be described as an accident. Rather, perhaps understandably, it will be reported as a catastrophe or disaster on every newspaper's front page and the television news on every channel. Despite and partly because of their rarity, aircraft accidents are extremely high profile events, and their causes attract the attention of those passengers and other clients that determine the continued survival of the industry.

The changes in technology and understanding which allowed the modern era of air transport also provided the tools for accurate accident investigation. Aircraft which had suffered quite major destruction could be assessed component by component to discover which had been operational at the time of the crash, and which had played a part in its cause. Flight Data Recorders and Cockpit Voice Recorders (FDR and CVR—the famous *black boxes*) were designed to be as crash-proof as possible, and could be recovered to supply precise evidence of the systems and flight path of the aircraft and the actions of the crew. With such evidence available, a recurrent pattern emerged in accident investigation reports by the 1970s—that the primary cause of aircraft accidents was *pilot error*. In most cases it was decided crews were not fulfilling properly their assigned roles on the flight deck. Moreover, these errors would not have occurred if the correct operating techniques and procedures had been applied or adhered to. Recommendations reiterating or emphasizing such procedures and techniques were made after a number of accidents during which crews apparently had failed in their duties.

Pilot training and assessment were advanced and professionally conducted by this time, and the airlines and regulatory authorities felt that adequate operating procedures were in effect already. Yet experienced pilots, who performed well in training and met the required standards, continued to make fatal errors. Captains were not making decisions which were their responsibility; copilots were allowing captains' errors they had noticed to go unannounced. Workloads were not shared, so that one pilot attempted to do everything, or everyone attempted to do the same job simultaneously, to the detriment of other tasks. Concerns voiced by a crew member were ignored by others. The mere fact that there were guidelines and regulations delineating the specific roles and areas of responsibility of crew members did not seem to be providing an answer.[5]

The phenomenon led to the institution of a number of independent studies to analyze the problem further. Study of *pilot error* was not new but had concentrated traditionally on the interface between the human and the machine.[6,7] This new phenomenon appeared to be concerned with how pilots interacted with each other when on the flight deck, and how they attempted to accomplish their tasks—both individually and as members of a crew—on a routine basis rather than during proficiency checks. In the United States, studies were undertaken at the National Aeronautics and Space Administration's (NASA) Ames Research Center, in particular. Pilots were interviewed about normal operations and on *pilot error* accidents, and the causes of some 62 jet transport accidents which occurred between 1968 and 1976 were analyzed in detail[8]. Also at NASA, a flight simulator study—the first of its kind—was conducted on pilot performance and vigilance.[9]

The research was in agreement that the crux of the matter appeared that crews were not acting as teams, and a number of specific problem areas were identified. These included leadership, management of available resources (both within and outside of the cockpit), task delegation and coordination, situation awareness, interpersonal communication, and assertiveness. Furthermore, although the modern environment required multiple crew members to operate aircraft of the size and complexity now in existence, little or no training was given in crew operation as opposed to individual operation. In general, additional crew members were treated almost as redundant back-ups to the pilot in command (an observation supported by earlier researchers, e.g.[10]). Grounded as it was in traditional attitudes to the *right stuff*, training emphasis remained centered on autonomous technical proficiency.

In Europe, analysis of accident investigation reports led Elwyn Edwards to develop what he called the SHEL model of system design and operation.[11] This referred to software (manuals, regulations, and other documents used), *hardware* (the physical resources), *environment* (the external world in which the system operated) and *liveware* (the humans who operated the system). He later refined his work by scrutinizing the liveware element to define a new concept— the Trans-cockpit Authority Gradient (TAG). This referred to the optimum relationship between the captain and crew, where maximum team efficiency would be achieved if the captain's authority was neither over—nor under emphasized.[12]

In 1979 the results of NASA's various projects were reviewed at a meeting at the Ames Research Center—attended by representatives of the academic research community, accident investigators, regulatory authorities, numerous airlines from around the world and other interested parties. In many ways, this was a milestone event in the evolution of CRM training. There had been a growing awareness that the apparent escalation in *pilot error* accidents was rooted somehow in problems of crew coordination and management. However, there was little in the training traditions or ethos of the industry to provide a framework to address the problem. For example, in 1974 Pan American Airlines had introduced the evaluation of crew performance in proficiency evaluation. This had been an important step in human factors training, but while crews were expected to act as teams, no formal instruction or guidance was provided. The NASA meeting provided a forum for discussion, and the research results gave form to concepts and language which were to be used as a foundation upon which to build future training systems, regulatory interventions and as causal indicators in accident investigations.

Crew Resource Management

Individual Pilot Performance

Prior to the recognition of a need for crew-based training, emphasis on the individual had not been limited to pilot training and assessment. The study of human factors in aviation was concerned with individual pilot performance, which centered on the physiological and psychological effects of the flight environment. Knowledge of aeromedical phenomena was of limited use in air-crew training (such as in preparing pilots for problems associated with high altitude flight). However, its impact was felt mainly in

- regulations (e.g. allowable duty times based on the effects of fatigue and sleep deprivation or the provision of equipment such as oxygen above certain altitudes)
- aircraft design (e.g. the design and arrangement of cockpit instru-mentation based on human visual and perception limitations)
- medical regulations (e.g. minimum standards of eyesight, hearing, and cardiovascular health based on the known effects and require-ments of flight).

Such knowledge provided, and continues to provide, essential informa-tion on the liveware element in the aviation system (in the terms of Edwards' SHEL model). In the meantime, from the research and accident analysis a new field for aviation human factors—group dynamics and performance—appeared pertinent to safety. Within the boundary of this new area, individual factors were significant mainly in their effect on interaction with other crew members. Individual factors such as personality traits, leadership styles, atti-tudes towards other crew members or rules and procedures, communications styles, and individual decision making skills would influence group relation-ships and performance. Traditionally not the concern of aviation medicine, the study of crew factors has formed almost a separate category of human fac-tors study in aviation, drawing on social psychology rather than medicine and individual psychology. Recently though, there has been a greater emphasis on the importance of promoting an awareness of any human factors which might have an impact on flight safety. This emphasis demands an integration of all the areas of human factor study, at least during the formulation and presenta-tion of training.

Training Development

Since the pioneering efforts of the 1970s there has been a proliferation of training courses and programs designed to address
1)   human factor problems identified as causal in aircraft accidents
2)   those that have been viewed as operationally and/or commercially worthwhile to alleviate.

With accident reports indicating an apparent lack of managerial skills on the flight deck and little awareness of the elements of successful teamwork, ini-

tial training development centered on existing management training principles. These early efforts were often in the form of some sort of generic management course bought *off-the-shelf* and to some degree adapted to suit the aviation environment and its terminology. As a result, the inaugural programs varied greatly in content, validity, and methods of delivery. Individual airlines concentrated their efforts on those areas which appeared most applicable to themselves. Training recipients varied among organizations—some operators
trained the whole flight deck crew, others trained the pilots, and a few operators elected to train only the captains.

Probably the most comprehensive of the early efforts was provided by
United Airlines. Following the 1979 NASA/industry workshop, they developed, in conjunction with the Air Line Pilots Association and management
training consultants, a program they called Command, Leadership and
Resource Management (CLR). This was a structured and long-term training
initiative. Beginning with a multi-day seminar designed to introduce the
human factor issues deemed relevant to aircrew, the training went on to review
periodically the concepts introduced so as to build on and reinforce the initial
awareness promoted. These classroom presentations, which were highly interactive, were reinforced further through flight simulator exercises designed to
incorporate this new human factors training into the technical training pilots
had received traditionally. United Airlines' CLR program provided a template
which was followed by others as human factors training developed, becoming
known as Cockpit Resource Management or Flight Deck Management training.

The level of understanding of human factors issues achieved by those
responsible for the formulation and delivery of training improved with time.
This was a result of their own education in human factors awareness, with further research results becoming available, and with feedback from accident and
incident reports and from the aircrew receiving the training. As awareness
grew of those issues which were relevant and valuable, the initial concentration
on crew coordination and interaction solely on the flight deck became considered too narrow a view. Training emphasis broadened to encompass anything
which might contribute to the safe and efficient conduct of a flight, more in
line with the systems approach used by Edwards.

While there remain considerable variations among aircraft operators, it
is becoming more common for human factors awareness training (now Crew
Resource Management) to be given to a broader spread of people involved in
flight operations. These can include cabin staff, flight dispatch or operations,
engineers, aircraft handlers, and management. Moreover, the more compre-

hensive CRM training programs do not confine themselves to applied management concepts. Based on the principle that the most effective resource managers will have a thorough knowledge of the strengths and weaknesses of their resources (including themselves) CRM training embraces all areas of human performance in aviation. It attempts to build from an awareness of performance at the medical and individual levels to promote a greater understanding of group performance—both within the group and in its interaction with its environment.

Enhanced Accident Investigation

Even as progress in the technical sphere promoted accurate physical investigation of aircraft accidents, so awareness of the relevance of human factors has provided the means and language to scrutinize the phenomenon of *pilot error*. Prior to detailed research into *pilot error* accidents, investigators were forced to conclude merely that all too often a pilot had failed in his duties. Other than reiterating those duties, little could be suggested as corrective action.

With increasing understanding of the human factors that determine and contribute to safe flight operations, particular attention could be given to human performance considerations in accident investigation. Human factors are now an integral part of accident investigation. By drawing on particular instances, recommendations can be made concerning the importance of specific human performance elements in both failure and providing successful conclusions to incidents.

In 1971 a Convair 340/440 aircraft, operated by Allegheny Airlines, crashed during an instrument approach.[13] The investigation into this accident exemplifies the reaction of investigators to *pilot error*. When an aircraft flies an instrument approach (i.e. without reference to the outside world) there is a minimum height to which it might be flown. To descend below this height safely the crew must be able to do so using outside cues (i.e. they must have sufficient visual references, such as the runway or its approach lights). At the time of the accident the weather conditions were such that when the aircraft reached its minimum descent altitude on instruments, the crew could not acquire the visual cues necessary to continue. Rather than breaking off the approach, the captain elected to continue the descent regardless, ignoring the advisory prompt of the first officer that the minimum height had been reached yet the aircraft was still descending. The United States National Transportation Safety Board (NTSB) determined that these decisions were the probable cause of the accident, but: "The Board was unable to determine what motivated the captain to disregard prescribed operating procedures and altitude restrictions, and finds it difficult to reconcile the actions he exhibited during the conduct of this flight."[13]

NTSB investigators noted also that the copilot might have played a preventative role in the accident, but it was unable to decide how to deal with the thorny matter of questioning the captain's authority without eroding that authority otherwise. Eventually, the only recommendation was to emphasize the importance of applying correct operating procedures.

On the December 28, 1978, United Airlines Flight 173 crashed near Portland International Airport.[14] It had run out of fuel after circling in the vicinity of the airport while the crew attempted to deal with an undercarriage problem. The actions of the crew during this incident had important elements in common with the Allegheny Airlines accident some six years previously. The copilot and flight engineer were both aware of the worsening fuel state, and attempted to communicate their concerns to the captain. However, when the captain failed to respond to their concerns they remained compliant with his authority. By now advances had been made in deeper analysis of pilot behavior on the flight deck. The NTSB was able to use the research and growing awareness of such issues to provide a more constructive assessment than they had in the earlier accident. The NTSB noted that, ". . . this accident exemplifies a recurring problem—a breakdown in cockpit management and teamwork."[14] Moreover, they were able to recommend that, "...flightcrews are indoctrinated in principles of flight deck resource management, with particular emphasis on participative management for captains and assertiveness training for other cockpit crewmembers." (NTSB Recommendation No. AAR-79-47.)[14]

The focus and direction of the NTSB's deliberations over the human performance problems exhibited in the Portland accident are in striking contrast with their earlier attempts, particularly that they were able to offer a training solution rather than discipline. Since the Portland accident report, investigative bodies around the world have been able to incorporate a wide range of human factor considerations in their analyses (sometimes using consultants, but often with their own human factors units). This provides invaluable feedback for those responsible for the formulation of both training and regulatory efforts to prevent future occurrences.

Regulatory Change

Regulations pertaining to human factors in aircrew training more often than not have lagged behind the formation of the courses themselves, and even the recommendations made by investigative bodies following accidents.

Recently the various national regulatory authorities have attempted to take more of a lead—e.g. through the validation of training, the production of suggested syllabi, publications dealing with specific areas of human performance (such as decision making or stress management). However, even where they have mandated that CRM training take place, they have remained unwilling to commit themselves to prescriptive measures regarding the precise content or conduct of that training.

As in many professional systems, aviation training regulations set the standards of competence judged necessary for qualification, the nature of the qualifying evaluation and the training regime which must be undertaken prior to assessment. With regard to technical or procedural competence, aircrew must attend prescribed training and then pass an assessment of their abilities in a given area. The training itself is subject also to evaluation. Its content is stipulated by the regulatory authorities, and instructors must pass an examination of their competence to train. In the area of CRM, however, regulators have found it difficult to decide the precise constituents of effective training programs, and impossible to define the exact competency standards or evaluative methods to be applied. Qualifying standards, in particular, should be clearly defined and rest on reliable, accurate and consistent assessment criteria whose application achieves the desired goal, yet many central aspects of CRM (such as leadership or assertiveness) appear to defy absolute measurement. It is relatively straightforward to assess, for example, a pilot's ability to fly an aircraft on instruments from point A to point B. Whether he achieves the qualifying standard can be decided using objective indicators and ranges—such as maintaining the correct altitude (plus or minus 100 feet), the correct speed (plus or minus 10 knots), and the correct heading (plus or minus five degrees). On the other hand, if the same pilot is to be tested for his leadership abilities, it is difficult to conceive of an objective standard to be met—let alone the range of allowable performance, and indicators which are accurate, reliable and consistent—denying the institution of regulations designed to set the standard and conduct of proficiency assessment.

Mounting evidence from accident reports led the airlines to institute training ahead of any regulatory requirement to do so. With only subjective criteria available as assessment tools, initially little could be done by the authorities responsible for training regulation in evaluation or validation of the various training programs. As research results became available, and accident reports and training more focused, clearer identification of the relevant issues became possible. In the United States, the Federal Aviation Administration (FAA) began to issue guidelines and encourage certain directions in CRM training. Although it remained unprepared to legislate specific requirements, the FAA issued a number of Advisory Circulars to the industry. For example, in 1989 an Advisory Circular was published outlining the FAA's recommendations for CRM training overall.[15] This suggested three phases of training, which had been developed from the best available research and considered practice. An introductory seminar was recommended to introduce CRM concepts, to be followed by flight simulator exercises dedicated to practicing CRM skills in the work environment. The third phase was recurrent classroom or seminar review and reinforcement of the concepts learned. Also the FAA has issued publications dealing with specific CRM-related topics following its own or other reputable research into areas decided of importance, such as decision making and flight simulator training.[16,17]

Different national authorities have taken different stances in their responses to CRM training. In the United Kingdom the regulatory stance has had a different tenor. An examination in Human Performance and Limitations became part of the licensing requirement for pilots as of January 1, 1992. In 1993 the United Kingdom Civil Aviation Authority (CAA) mandated CRM training for all commercial and air transport pilots, and a suggested model syllabus was presented.[18] The requirement for CRM training was extended in 1995 to include cabin crew or flight attendants and any other person who formed part of the flight crew.[19] At the same time, regulations were introduced which instructed recurrent training to take place through the use of flight simulators, or via classroom or seminar presentation sessions if flight simulators were not available, and that CRM skills should become an integral part of all aircrew training and debriefing.

Having mandated training, the CAA has had to respond to the concomitant responsibility of quality control. In order for specific elements of CRM training to qualify aircrew for continued exercise of their professional privileges, the training itself must gain approval. This is achieved on inspection, as with other forms of training, yet no clearly stated standard is set; a program being recognized on the subjective approval of individual inspectors. Furthermore, the rationale for introducing regulated CRM training has been to improve flight safety by inculcating an awareness of human factors and suggesting or requiring the continued practice of CRM skills. Meanwhile, neither trainers nor trainees are required to demonstrate their having achieved or maintained a stated minimum standard of competency. Given the problems associated with setting such standards (as discussed earlier) subjective assessment remains the only available method, and the CAA have stated that CRM training shall be "non-assessable" unless "a crew or crew member demonstrates a clear inability to manage the situation or safely handle the aeroplane/helicopter."[19]

As we have noted, the FAA has yet to mandate CRM training. Nevertheless, they have instituted a highly structured system of research to provide, among other things,

- an assessment of CRM training techniques integrated with technical training
- tools for evaluating CRM skills and behaviors
- proficiency standards to be met as qualifying criteria for aircrew in performing integrated technical and CRM tasks.

This initiative—called the Advanced Qualification Program (AQP)—currently is a voluntary program undertaken with the cooperation of industry and conducted on a non-jeopardy basis for data gathering. Individual tasks associated with the operation of specific aircraft types are scrutinized so that both the technical and CRM-related skills necessary for their safe and efficient execution may be identified. These now identified integrated skills can then provide a basis for the content of future aircrew training and an associated valid standard for competency assessment.

The approaches taken by both the FAA and the CAA differ in certain respects, yet they show a clear recognition of the importance of human factors as a determinant of safety, and a growing commitment to training to provide enhanced performance. The United Kingdom regulations, though resting on largely subjective assessment criteria, provide a formal system for ensuring that aircrew are trained in any and all human factors issues which may have an impact on safe flight operations. The FAA's AQP, on the other hand, is designed to provide,

> . . . all the necessary ingredients to permit the systematic development of flight standards for CRM and to determine empirically the reliability and validity of such standards. Of particular significance to that endeavor, AQP also provides the opportunity to reassess the specification of all flight standards and to incorporate CRM considerations into that process.[20]

Both approaches have strengths and weaknesses. The United Kingdom method retains flexibility and acknowledges the uncertainty inherent in prescribing rules for managing people but allows subjective standards (albeit based on the considerable experience of the inspectors). The U.S. system promises exact criteria for safe and efficient task performance. However, the likelihood of identifying all the potential combinations of technical task demands (complicated further by the possible variations in human crew composition) seems a monumental endeavor.

Aviation training regulations will continue to evolve. For the OIM and other industry managers the details of that evolution may be of little interest—unless they are involved in training design and implementation. Undoubtedly, national and international regulations have an impact on the development (or degradation) of safety systems. The most significant points of note from the aviation industry common to all attempts to assume regulatory responsibility for CRM training are

- an appreciation of a requirement for increased awareness of the human influence over safety
- emphasis on the importance of technical and resource management skills being exercised in concert
- operationally specific training designed to promote an integrated operational system.

CRM and the Offshore Installation Manager

Industry Parallels and Divergence

The roles of the OIM and the professional aircraft commander have many similarities. Common to both is a requirement to operate efficiently (in both routine and abnormal situations) utilizing high degrees of technical and procedural knowledge while managing also the human resources available. The natures of both industries are such that the executive decision-maker must act often beyond the bounds of normal managerial expectations and training. In his report following the *Piper Alpha* disaster in 1988, Lord Cullen noted:

> *The post of OIM calls for decisions which may make the difference between life and death of personnel on board. The remoteness of installations, the requirement for installations to be self-contained in the means of dealing with a rapidly developing incident, the need to obtain, verify and consider data communicated to him from various sources for immediate decision on which the lives of those on board depend demands a level of command ability which is not a feature of normal managerial posts.[21]*

This *level of command ability* has long been a qualifying requirement for aircraft commanders. Any and all problems which arise or might arise must be dealt with locally and successfully, and nowhere are these responsibilities more obvious than in the often testing environment of offshore support helicopter flying, with its associated command autonomy.

Inherent in operating any complex machinery containing many different, independent and/or interdependent systems is a likelihood of minor malfunctions. For either the OIM or the helicopter commander, following a predetermined procedure is often the safest and simplest way of resolving a problem, especially during routine operations or when dealing with simple malfunctions or emergencies.

For example, a helicopter takes off from an offshore installation and its undercarriage fails to retract, with no other associated problem. A simple procedure exists, which might be (dependant on the aircraft type)

1) continue the flight
2) expect that airspeed will be reduced by five knots at any given power setting because of drag
3) expect that fuel consumption will increase by six percent to overcome the drag and
4) replan fuel required and flight times.

For the OIM an equivalent simple problem might be that on inspection a lifeboat is found to have an engine defect which puts it out of commission. A typical procedure might be

1) reallocate personnel to other lifeboats
2) ensure personnel are informed of new check points and lifeboat number
3) ensure administrative personnel are informed (roster checkers, coxswains, etc.)
4) arrange repairs to defective lifeboat.

Yet problems are not always simple, or may occur in combinations, and the resources available to diagnose and deal with them may vary. In our aviation example above, the undercarriage may have failed to retract because of a hydraulic system problem—which will have consequences for other equipment supplied by the system. There may be a hydraulic leak with an attendant risk of fire. The nearest land-based diversion may be close or some distance away. The weather may be a factor. There may be procedures applicable to all of these problems, but the task of the aircraft commander is now risk analysis and assessment, and management of procedures and resources. The aircraft commander must ask the following:

- What are the priority problems?
- What are the time scales involved?
- Which procedure should be applied first?
- Are some procedures rendered invalid because of the combination of circumstances?
- What assistance can be gained from (a) the crew? (b) the passengers? (c) air traffic services? (d) company engineering? (e) the offshore installation?

- What is the most effective way of controlling and coordinating these resources?
- IIow sure are we of the accuracy of information?
- How can the rate at which information is being received be increased or reduced to render it more manageable?

Such resource management and command and control questions will be as familiar to the experienced OIM as they are to the experienced pilot.

Inasmuch as there are commonalties in the roles of aircrew and offshore managers, equally there are both apparent and real differences. In particular, the OIM may be utilizing considerably larger numbers of people than an aircraft commander. The command and control of groups of specialists, each of which may be granted independent decision-making responsibilities, presents communication and executive control problems which would not normally be encountered by aircrew. For example, these include the dispatch of fire teams and engineering inspection/repair teams in response to a process equipment failure which has caused the outbreak of a number of minor fires on different decks aboard a drilling rig. Also, while aircrew are expected to respond effectively to any situation for the duration of a flight, the OIM faces the same responsibility 24 hours a day for two weeks, or longer. Nevertheless, I would contend that these, and many other differences in the tasks of the OIM and aircrew, are largely differences in scale rather than kind. Indeed, the differences which exist often demand an equal if not greater emphasis on the mechanisms and limitations of human performance in effective offshore resource management as in aviation.

Command Competence - The Role of Training

The operational command systems in place in the aviation and oil and gas industries rely heavily on operating manuals, rules and procedures. The effectiveness of these procedures in dealing with both the routine and the unexpected will be enhanced greatly if incorporated within them is a realistic awareness of human factors. The aviation system has discovered, often by tragic experience, that while it may appear reasonable to expect professional aircrew to adhere to established rules, often they do not. Accident analysis and research have indicated that discipline and apparently reasonable expectations of performance are sometimes overcome by human factor limitations and behaviors. These factors can include stress, fatigue, a desire to conform, perceptual failures, communication difficulties, and attitudinal problems (especially complacency, machismo, resignation). Procedures can be improved considerably if they include safety checks based on an acknowledgement of such limitations.

Operating procedures may be enhanced by an awareness of the limitations of human performance in the operating system. However, the existence of well-founded procedures alone is not sufficient to ensure safe and efficient operation. Training in human factors, initially at a foundation level and later amalgamated with all operational training and assessment, is essential to enhanced normal operations, the avoidance of abnormal situations, and often the successful resolution of emergencies. In aviation, the task of initial training is to equip prospective aircrew with the knowledge, skills, and attitudes necessary to do the job. Yet knowledge can be forgotten if it is not reviewed, skills can dull when they are not practiced, and complacency may creep in over time. As mentioned earlier, much time and effort is expended in aviation on integrated continuation training and evaluation so as to maintain or improve aircrew performance.

A constant reference to reality is central to CRM training. In helicopter support operations, especially with their attendant environmental demands, training cannot be based on *what we ought to do* or what we are *supposed to do.* Effective training must recognize actual practice and why it exists in order to promote more effective behaviors as necessary. For example, using flight simulators as a means of learning and practicing procedures by rote is generally considered outmoded and non-productive. Instead, normal operations are simulated, perhaps with minor problems introduced, so that human factors limitations can be recognized, awareness levels raised, and skills developed that are founded on everyday behavior. CRM training has caused a shift in emphasis in aviation training. Simulator trips and check flights are no longer expected to be sweat boxes for testing procedures, and periodic assessment is viewed rightly as a training tool, rather than training used as an assessment tool.

A suggestion is that offshore managers would benefit likewise from the integration of human factors awareness in all forms of training, and that training should be recurrent. Mention is sometimes made of considering some form of leadership or command training such as exists in most military systems.[21] These often have elements which might be useful in preparing OIM's for emergency response tasks, but such training is organizationally, operationally and culturally specific, forming only a part of the overall training picture. The utility of OIMs attending courses that are not designed for them is questionable. This kind of piecemeal training is unlikely to prove either time- or cost-effective in comparison to properly designed industry specific training. The lessons learned through years of experience in aviation can be applied in very similar ways in OIM and emergency response team training. Not only are the task demands of a common nature but similar training facilities exist.

Operationally specific CRM-type training can be conducted in control room simulators as in flight simulators. The training and assessment tools developed in aviation are easily adaptable to offshore control room scenarios and team composition. Training can be tailored to the specific task demands of different operations. Such training can make allowance for organizational constraints and identities, and cater for the national and cultural differences which may exist in an offshore facility's crew composition.

Today, aviation training requires a commitment to an emphasis on improved performance and how to achieve it rather than proficiency evaluation based on operating rules. This has been achieved through the integration of human factors awareness with technical and procedural training. The consequent development of human resource management skills has enhanced aircrew competence in

- improved communication
- decision-making
- tolerance of behavior
- teamwork
- situation awareness and risk perception
- realization of physical limitation
- understanding the effects of national and cultural differences in crew composition

This can only serve to improve the safe conduct of helicopter operations, whatever the national operating arena.

Aviation is moving toward an integrated human performance system, where reality and expectation are balanced to promote safety and efficiency. Such balance is based on competencies achieved through training in and awareness of the strengths and failings of the most important resource in any system—the people themselves. This experience may be useful to a wide range of industries, in particular one so closely allied as the management of offshore oil and gas facilities.

References
1. CAA Safety Data Department. *Offshore Helicopter Operations Statistical Report For 1994*. London: CAA, 1995: 10.
2. Air Accidents Investigation Branch. *Report on the accident to Sikorsky S61N, G-BEWL at Brent Spar, East Shetland Basin, on 25 July 1990* (Aircraft Accident Report 2/91). London: HMSO, 1991.
3. Air Accidents Investigation Branch. *Report on the accident to AS332L Super Puma, G-TIGH, near the Cormorant 'A' platform, East Shetland Basin, on 14 March 1992* (Aircraft Accident Report 2/93). London: HMSO, 1993.

4.   Helmreich, R.L. & Fouchee, H.C. Why crew resource management? Empirical and theoretical bases of human factors training in aviation. In E.L. Weiner, B.G. Kanki & R.L. Helmreich (Eds.), *Cockpit Resource Management*. San Diego: Academic Press, 1993: 3-45.

5.   Kayten, P.J. The accident investigators perspective. In E.L. Wiener, B.G. Kanki & R.L. Helmreich (Eds.), *Cockpit Resource Management*. San Diego: Academic Press, 1993: 283-314.

6.   Fitts, P.M. & Jones, R.E. *Analysis of 270 "pilot error" experiences in reading and interpreting aircraft instruments* (Report TSEAA-694-12A). Wright-Patterson Air Force Base, OH: Aeromedical Laboratory, 1947.

7.   Davis, D.R. *Pilot error: Some laboratory experiments*. London: HMSO, 1948.

8.   Cooper, G.E., White, M.D. & Lauber, J.K. (Eds.) *Resource management on the flightdeck: Proceedings of a NASA/Industry workshop* (NASA CP-2120). Moffat Field, CA: NASA-Ames Research Center, 1980.

9.   Ruffell Smith, H.P. *A simulator study of the interaction of pilot workload with errors, vigilance, and decisions.* (Tech. Memorandum 78482). Moffat Field, CA: NASA - Ames Research Center, 1979.

10.   Gann, E.K. *Fate is the Hunter*. New York: Simon and Shuster, 1961.

11.   Edwards, E. Man and machine: Systems for safety. In *Proceedings of British Airline Pilots Association Technical Symposium*. London: British Airline Pilots Association, 1972: 21-36.

12.   Edwards, E. *Stress and the airline pilot*. Paper presented at British Airline Pilots Association Medical Symposium. London, 1975.

13.   National Transportation Safety Board. *Aircraft Accident Report: Allegeny Airlines, Inc., Allison Prop Jet Convair 340/440, N5832, New Haven, Connecticut, 7June 1971* (NTSB-AAR-72-20). Washington DC: NTSB, 1972.

14.   National Transportation Safety Board. *Aircraft Accident Report: United Airlines Inc., McDonnell Douglas DC-8-61, N8082U, Portland, Oregon, December 28, 1978* (NTSB-AAR-79-7). Washington DC: NTSB, 1979.

15.   Federal Aviation Administration. *Cockpit resource management training* (Advisory Circular No. 120-51). Washington, DC: FAA, 1989.

16.   Federal Aviation Administration. *Aeronautical Decision Making* (Advisory Circular No. 60-22). Washington, DC: FAA, 1991.

17.   Federal Aviation Administration. *Line oriented flight training* (Advisory Circular AC-120-35A). Washington, DC: FAA, 1978.

18.   Civil Aviation Authority. *Crew Resource Management.* (United Kingdom Aeronautical Information Circular 143/1993). Civil Aviation Authority (AIS 1c), London/Heathrow Airport: CAA, 1993.

19.   Civil Aviation Authority. *Crew Resource Management Training.* (United Kingdom Aeronautical Information Circular 37/1995). Civil Aviation Authority (AIS 1c), London/Heathrow Airport: CAA, 1995.

20.   Birnbach, R.A. & Longridge, T.M. The regulatory perspective. In E.L. Weiner, B.G. Kanki & R.L. Helmreich (Eds.), *Cockpit Resource Management*. San Diego: Academic Press, 1993: 263-281.

21.   Cullen, D. The Hon. Lord. *The Public Inquiry into the Piper Alpha Disaster Vols. I & II* CM 1310. London: HMSO, 1990.

Chapter 13

Women in the Offshore Workforce
Kathryn Mearns and Trudy Wagstaff

Introduction

This chapter provides an overview of the role of women in the offshore oil and gas industry. The question may be raised as to why women should be selected for such specialist attention. The reason is not to promote the feminist cause or even to make a special case for women being employed offshore. Rather, this chapter has been written with the era of equal opportunities in mind, in the recognition that many women who are qualified as scientists, engineers or technologists may wish to fulfill their careers in this most international of industries. Also it should be remembered that most of this book is written with men in mind—selecting, training, managing and motivating them. Furthermore, it largely considers how men view risk and safety, how men experience stress, and what medical problems men suffer. Although perhaps it is not politically correct to flag this point given the western world's emphasis on equal opportunities for all, there can be no question that women are different, both physically and psychologically. This is not to say that they are less capable; indeed, in many cases they may be more so. It is just to say that they are different. For example, women tend to be more cautious and less likely to take risks than men. They also may experience more stress in certain situations, (e.g. the second shift of cooking, cleaning and child-care when their paid work is done) or cope with it differently, (e.g. women's predisposition to discuss problems more openly).

The chapter therefore includes a brief review of research on women who are working in the offshore oil industry, either in the normally male dominated professions of geology, engineering and drilling or in the more traditional female roles of cleaning, cooking, and caring. These studies have been conducted in the United Kingdom, Norway, and Canada, but as far as the authors know, no other such studies have been conducted elsewhere in the world.[1-3] The chapter also reports the background, aims, and results of a pilot study examining the attitudes and experiences of women engineers, scientists and technologists in the United Kingdom offshore oil industry.[4] This study concludes that more information is required to establish why women are still under-represented in traditionally male professions offshore and whether attitudes to the hiring of women have changed over the years, since over a decade ago the United Kingdom oil industry was presented as a microcosm of discriminatory practices.[1]

Finally, the chapter takes into consideration another, largely ignored part of women's role in offshore life, namely the support they provide for their husbands and partners. While at home, the offshore worker may expect a period of rest and recuperation with the family, although the family will probably have their own commitments to fulfill. Depending on how this situation is managed, it could be ripe for tensions and frustrations. Little research has been conducted on this clearly sensitive subject (certainly not since the early 1980s). It is hoped that this chapter will highlight this topic as a potentially fruitful avenue for further investigation, especially since the quality of home and work life are intricately linked and provide special problems for workers engaged in Long Distance Commuting (LDC).[5]

History of Female Participation in the European Offshore Oil Industry

The European offshore oil industry developed during the mid 1960s, though women do not appear to have joined the offshore work force until the late 1970s and early 1980s. Consequently, female participation remains low to this day although detailed factual data are lacking. In 1983, two sociologists, Robert Moore and Peter Wybrow were commissioned by the British Equal Opportunities Commission to investigate discriminatory practices in the North Sea oil industry.[1] These researchers experienced problems in finding statistics for women working on the United Kingdom Continental Shelf; however, they concluded from a survey of passengers traveling to offshore installations from Aberdeen heliport, that the best estimate would be less than 0.5% (based on a total United Kingdom offshore population of 21-22,000 in 1981-82). They believed that at the time about 25 women were working offshore on a regular normal shift basis as geologists, petroleum engineers, structural engineers, and administrative assistants. The researchers also observed that a few more women went offshore for brief, occasional visits as part of their work. Moore and Wybrow's report for the Equal Opportunities Commission concluded that there was evidence of widespread discrimination against women employed in the United Kingdom sector of the North Sea oil industry and since no research has been carried out in the intervening period, it is difficult to ascertain whether the alleged discriminatory practices are still prevalent. Even figures for the percentage of women in the United Kingdom offshore work force are lacking, although data from a recent survey of 3611 offshore medicals taken in

1995 showed that 3.5% were taken by women.[6] However, it should be stressed that at present no formal figures are available and research on women working in the United Kingdom offshore environment is conspicuous by its absence.

The position in Norway is somewhat different. Of all the nations involved in hydrocarbon exploration and extraction, Norway would appear to be ahead of its time in terms of encouraging women to go into offshore employment and conducting research on the subject. In 1985, Hellesoy reported that 16.9% of the work force on the Norwegian Statfjord Field were female, with 76 of the 77 women in this sample being employed as caterers (the other woman was a nurse).[7] This sample would appear to be unrepresentative (perhaps due to one catering company with a large female contingent) since Moore & Wybrow report that in 1983 there were 588 female workers in a total Norwegian offshore population of 15,340 (i.e. 3.8%). These figures were obtained from the Norwegian Work Directorate (Arbeidsdirektorat). Again, the majority worked in catering, as nurses, medics, or in administrative functions with few employed in traditionally *male* occupations such as drilling, engineering and geology. More recent figures from Norway indicate that women now make up 9.5% of its offshore workforce, the majority working for oil companies (907 women out of a total of 5882 employees) and in catering (616 out of a total of 1071).[8]

Compared to the progress of women working offshore in the United Kingdom sector of the North Sea, this represents a veritable explosion and is due to a number of cultural, legislative and demographic factors. Despite legislation in Norway and the United Kingdom which aims to protect women against job discrimination on the grounds of sex, only Norway seems to have actively encouraged the recruitment of women in offshore occupations for both cultural and political reasons. For example, since the 1980s the Norwegian government and the powerful Norwegian trade unions have had a deliberate policy to replace foreign workers with native Norwegians. Given the small population of Norway, this has probably led to the recruitment of more women in offshore occupations, especially in catering where they have replaced a largely foreign workforce.

Another important factor has been the 1978 Norwegian Equal Status Legislation which aims to ensure equality of treatment between the sexes and influence attitudes towards sex roles. The Norwegian Equal Status Act (ESA) 1978 promoted the status of women in employment and, unlike the British Sex Discrimination Act 1974 and Equal Pay Act 1975, covered offshore installations. This position was rectified in Britain by the Sex Discrimination and Equal Pay (Offshore Employment) Order, which became effective November

1987. The ESA, however, makes reference to inappropriate hygiene facilities or accommodation as inadmissible reasons for failing to employ women. This message was enforced by the Norwegian Minister of Oil and Energy in 1980 when he issued a letter to all offshore operators insisting on the implementation of the ESA, and by the provision of equal status grants which contribute to the cost of the first six months of employment.

Despite the current United Kingdom legislation, discriminatory practices still appear to be widespread throughout British industry in general.[9] Therefore perhaps it is unfair to single out the offshore oil and gas industry for special attention, but its traditions and culture make it an interesting medium through which to study the phenomenon. The number of women working in traditional female roles offshore is indicative of a continuation of the sexual division of labor where women are seen as caregivers. Research from Norway and Canada indicates that women employed offshore also take on roles as unpaid caregivers by listening to male workers' domestic concerns, providing psychological support, creating a homey atmosphere and improving standards of hygiene and cleanliness.[2,3] It is suggested that women overcompensate in this role for daring to impinge on the male environment. As one offshore installation manager put, ". . . the first thing that hits you when you get out of the chopper when there are women on the rig is the smell of aftershave." (*Offshore Engineer* editorial in June 1985). But is this somewhat cynical observation a reflection of the true feelings and attitudes of male workers to women offshore?

The following section provides some insights into how the predominantly male offshore workforce perceives the presence of women in their midst.

The Attitudes of Male Workers to Women Offshore

A survey by the Norwegian researcher Hanne Heen found that male Norwegian workers generally commented favorably on having women offshore, especially if they occupied traditional female roles.[2] It was felt that having both sexes on board *normalized* the atmosphere, facilitating both the platform community and the adjustment required on returning home. In addition, having women on board broadened the range of social interactions, thus reducing boredom and monotony. Heen reports, however, that due to their heightened profile women offshore can consequently become targets for gossip and rumor. Their relationship with the men remains precarious giving added meaning to the phrase *never mixing work with pleasure*. Since there is little scope for personal relationships to develop, loneliness can be a problem for women workers although this is obviously dependent on the size of the female community on the installation.

Moore has pointed out that the British and Norwegian offshore work cultures may be intrinsically different.[10] He observed that British offshore workers create a characteristic *pub culture* in which off duty workers play cards and dominoes and take part in organized activities. By contrast, the Norwegian worker is characterized as "sitting in his cabin thinking of home." This representation is probably an exaggeration, although Heen noted a tendency to withdraw or become *lonesome* among Norwegian men offshore and Solheim noted that their social interaction tended to be fairly passive and stereotyped.[11] In any occupation or walk of life, British culture does not lend itself to enabling women to become "one of the boys". Indeed many women may not want to be integrated in such a way, but they may nevertheless be excluded if they are seen to threaten the male group solidarity. A quote from Moore and Wybrow's study serves to illustrate this point,

> *Male geology students live in a male world. They move into employment in a male environment—and in the oil industry they are joined by graduate engineers with similar educational experience, by groups of male workers with a culture stressing physical prowess, a strong competitive ethic and a myth of man against the environment standing at the frontiers of technology. They may be joined offshore by men with experience in the merchant marine or the armed services, or men drawn from skilled industrial trades from which women are still largely excluded. . . . Men create a world-wide network of friends and contacts in a highly mobile industry. . . .[1]*

The Norwegian studies suggest that although women may be fully integrated into the social element of the Norwegian offshore community, they are less likely to be quite so fully integrated into the work culture. Although there has been little research done to fully substantiate such a view, it would be interesting to discover whether women working in the United Kingdom sector are fully integrated into the social community and the work environment on offshore installations.

But how do women actually feel about working in the traditionally male-dominated oil industry and, more specifically, about working offshore? In 1994, a pilot study was carried out to investigate how a small sample of women scientists, engineers and technicians felt about working in such an atypical occupation.[1] The study was a preliminary phase in a forthcoming project which aims to measure how many women are working in the United Kingdom offshore oil industry and what their experiences have been. The study will also survey current hiring practices and attitudes of companies operating on the United Kingdom Continental Shelf with regard to the employment of women offshore and the career aspirations of young female graduates in engineering and geology from two Scottish universities.

The following section reveals how some women have managed their work and home commitments in an uncompromising man's world.

Applying Science in a Man's World

In order to record the attitudes and experiences of women employed in science, engineering and technology (SET) in the offshore oil industry, an interview schedule was designed covering the following:

- Demographic details, e.g. age, education and marital status.
- Job and career details, e.g. job title, length of time in the oil industry, periods offshore and long-term aims and objectives
- Work/home interface, e.g. support from home, balancing home/work, leisure pursuits

In particular, we were interested in determining (1) what factors had led these women to choose a non-traditional career and who had been the greatest influences in their lives (e.g. parents, teachers, boyfriends, etc.); (2) how they managed to balance the demands of the public and private domains of their lives and (3) how their careers had developed, what types of problems had they encountered and how they saw their careers progressing.

Six women were interviewed: two geologists, one electrical engineer, one production engineer, one drilling engineer, and one technician. They ranged in age from 23 to 39 and had one to 14 years experience in the industry. Two of the women were single, three were married (although only one had children) and one was divorced (with children). Their home backgrounds varied considerably, but all the women were educated to university level and they all had mothers who worked, (although it was not ascertained whether the mothers had worked when these women were children).

When asked who were the main influences in their lives regarding choice of education and career, one women mentioned her father, another the senior manager who recruited her into her first job, and a third mentioned a senior woman colleague. Otherwise, these women seemed to be largely self-motivated with a desire for interesting jobs with good pay and an opportunity for travel. These factors were considered to be the positive aspects of working in their chosen careers. The women mentioned that their work was exciting and challenging; there were feelings of power associated with the job, "having a lot of money behind you" and "doing real things with that money which make a difference" was how one woman put it. There was also a feeling of satisfaction about being accepted to some degree in a male-dominated industry.

The picture was not altogether rosy, though. Being a woman was perceived as a disadvantage and a negative aspect of working in the oil and gas industry. For example, it was perceived that being a woman led to problems of credibility and career advancement. One woman mentioned that these problems with credibility had actually got worse as she had got older because "all the older women in the office were other people's secretaries". She pointed out that when she had started out on her career she had just been one of a number of graduates (both male and female), who were all *green* and no one person stood out. There was also a feeling that men sometimes felt uncomfortable with a woman around and did not know what to say or do. Some of the women reported occasionally feeling ostracized and alienated by the conversations of their male peers.

Although, in general, these women felt that men seemed to accept their choice of career, peers seemed to be most threatened by a woman in the group because these women were seen as competitors for jobs and advancement. Presumably, because these women had succeeded in a male-dominated environment it is a valid assumption that they were exceptionally good at their jobs and therefore very much a threat to others in the same position. Younger and older men did not seem to perceive these women as so much of a threat and those women who had a lot of experience in the industry felt they got along well with younger and older men. Nevertheless, some of the women interviewed felt that despite their ability and relative seniority, they had been passed over for promotion and advancement. They felt that the oil industry was still very much a *man's world* and that many companies merely paid lip service to ideas of equal opportunities and the recruitment and advancement of women.

The women surveyed in this study also reported what they termed *hassle* from male colleagues, mostly in the form of irritating comments and lack of respect. Some of these comments were reported as upsetting and unsettling, but the women felt that they had to put a brave face on it and pretend not to care. In many cases, the women felt that their male colleagues would stick up for them if the bantering got out of hand, but only if the men were part of a group and not on their own. They also felt that their working environment was often a competitive and uncompromising man's environment which was not welcoming to women.

When asked about how other women perceived their careers, their reactions appeared to depend on educational level. Young, uneducated women whose aspirations were perceived to lie in finding a husband, settling down and having a home and family, were reported as being envious of the fact that these women "went offshore with all these guys." However, the interviewees reported that some of the younger women were heartened by what could be achieved and they felt that they were role models for these girls. Women in the same position were few and far between, but female peers were reported as supportive and there was a feeling that they all got on well together.

Husbands and partners were also reported as generally supportive. They were also educated to university level and had an understanding of their partner's desire for a career and the demands of work commitments. Only one woman reported that her ex-partner had problems with her working offshore, mainly because she was away for such long periods at a time.

Child care caused few problems. These women were well-paid and could afford nannies and private nurseries. They reported that they felt good about working when their children were small, although both the women who had families would have liked to spend more time with their children. They emphasized that they tried not to let work demands interfere with their leisure time nor become trapped in the long hours culture of the oil industry. They worked as efficiently and proficiently as possible and did not bother with the social activities that many of their male colleagues engaged in. The women interviewed felt that they managed to balance the public and private domains of their life, although those with children had little time for leisure pursuits or an active social life.

When asked about working offshore no real problems were reported. Five of the women interviewed had worked offshore for various lengths of time and all had enjoyed it, despite the isolation they sometimes felt. One woman commented that she found the offshore environment very *sterile* and not very homelike, although the men did not seem to notice this or find it a problem. In general, the problems experienced while working offshore were no different from the problems experienced onshore.

In conclusion, the women surveyed were generally highly-motivated in their jobs and enjoyed the opportunities and rewards that their chosen careers afforded them. However, there was still the feeling that they were outside the male group culture of their peers and that they were discriminated against when it came to career advancement or when facing redundancy. Some of the women interviewed had learned to cope with these problems and make progress, but others were disillusioned with the oil industry. It is sobering to note that of the six women interviewed, three of them were in the process of leaving the industry. The reasons were mainly because the prognosis was not good for their future careers developing within the industry. The oil and gas industry is still very much a man's world, but perhaps by noting and learning from the experiences of these women, those within the industry can be persuaded to stay and new graduates can be encouraged to view it as a valid career option.

Women Offshore—The '90s Onward

It is apparent that very few women occupy non-traditional jobs offshore, either professional, skilled or in senior management. There have been no women Offshore Installation Managers in the United Kingdom sector, although women have occupied this position in Norway on both the Frigg and Ekofisk fields.[5] The situation in the United Kingdom sector is largely unknown although reports from in-house oil company magazines and the press indicate that the number of women professionals may be slowly increasing in the offshore oil industry. Those women who do want viable careers within the industry have usually experienced both the discriminatory practices and the fiercely male work culture when they become competitors for advancement and challenge male domination. Many male workers may be reluctant to accept women as equal workers, although they may recognize and accept female ambition and desire for a career.[12] They may appreciate it even less if it occurs in their *own backyard*. This attitude can be summarized by the following statement from a British male offshore worker, "I've never taken orders from a woman in my life and I don't intend to start now."[1]

In 1993, the British Government addressed the issue of attracting more women into science, engineering and technology (SET), and put together an advisory committee to examine why women fail to realize their potential in these fields.[13] A vast research literature exists mainly addressing the issue from a sociological perspective. Many of the reasons for the lack of women in SET have strong social and cultural antecedents. Factors which inhibit young girls from seeking careers in science, engineering and technology include intimidation by male peers which can reduce the quality of their experience with science subjects, and the attitudes of both teachers and career advisors who tend to try to steer girls into more stereotyped female occupations.[1,14,15] The result is that despite the fact that women now make up approximately 45% of the United Kingdom workforce, they tend to be concentrated in a narrow range of occupations which are basically extensions of their roles as housewives and mothers. As we have seen, the situation is no different in the offshore oil and gas industry where relatively few women are employed in traditionally male occupations like engineering and geology.

Although many oil companies maintain that it is not their policy to discriminate against women, 10 years ago most referred to difficulties in providing suitable accommodation and the undesirability of sending women offshore alone, as explanations for their reluctance to recruit equally.[1] Such excuses are untenable when installations in the Norwegian sector operate smoothly and with minimum adaptation for women. What must be considered is whether women are genuinely interested in careers offshore, but are finding several barriers of entry to their desired profession, or whether the industry has no real attraction to the majority of women, thereby explaining the low female participation rate.

Although the offshore life may not appeal to many, some women are interested in working offshore. From a financial perspective, offshore work attracts higher wages than comparable onshore work. A period of work offshore may also be necessary for promotion and career development within a company, for example, in the field of geology. The lifestyle may also be attractive. By renouncing the role of traditional family responsibilities and re-scheduling family care, the woman may enjoy two or three weeks of concentrated free time at home after completing a hitch offshore. The evidence seems to suggest that on return, the women resume their caring and mothering roles as some form of compensation for their absences, depriving them of the free time enjoyed by the majority of men. However, there also may be advantages to women in this method of working. Ruth Carter and Glynis Kirkup note in their case studies of women engineers, that it was important for successful women in this profession to keep their working lives (public domain) and their domestic and family responsibilities (private domain) as two very separate entities. Only in this way could they cope with the demands and rigors of both. However, despite their best intentions, getting away from work while at home was not always easy. The offshore environment provides an ideal way of keeping the public and private domains of life separate, which could be of advantage to many women, providing that they have adequate child care and domestic arrangements while they are away. A quote from a female Norwegian radio operator on the Draugen platform serves to illustrate this point. "Working offshore works well for women with small children but it does mean that your partner has to take more responsibility in the home for the 14 days you're away. It works brilliantly for us."[16]

One of Norske Shell's key objectives is to increase the number of female employees. However, the fact remains that when questioned, companies frequently claim a distinct lack of female applicants. For example, Norske Shell reports that only 5% of the large number of applicants for jobs in the Operations Department were women. However, 22% of the permanent staff at their Kristiansund office are women and although most of them were recruited into traditional female jobs, the company has taken on female engineers, a female account manager and a female head of recruitment. Similarly, only 2% of those who applied for jobs on the Draugen platform were women, but they make up 13% of the new recruits and occupy positions such as production manager, computer operator, electrician, administrative assistant, radio operator, and nurse. In conclusion, the majority of women working offshore are still employed in traditional women's work. All that makes them non-traditional is their location.

Home And Away—The Offshore Worker's Dilemma

The foregoing sections have considered the situation regarding the experiences of women who are actually working in the offshore oil industry and to some extent the attitudes of the men with whom they share this inhospitable working environment. As noted above there is a distinct absence of information in this area but there is even less information available about the experiences of the partners and children who are left at home onshore. In terms of problems with domestic relationships, the worlds of work and home are not distinct and separate entities. The feelings that an offshore worker's family may have about the work and its impact on their lives, is in part determined by the worker's moods and behavior when he or she is at home. It is the family who has to cope with the presence and then the absence of the father (or mother), however, it is the workers who carry their home-related tensions back to work with them at the end of their rest periods. Domestic relationships may not fail only in assisting with work-related stressors, but may actually exacerbate and contribute to them. Valerie Sutherland and Cary Cooper in their study of occupational stress in the offshore oil industry report that, "the clearest and most unambiguous variables affecting mental problems during the work period are: problems when leaving home; dissatisfaction over the duration of the onshore period; and how seriously a possible illness or injury was experienced."[17]

Some argue that many of these tensions will diminish over time as the worker and his/her family adjust to the offshore routine. However, it would appear that many spouses feel it is impossible to adapt and the best one can do is learn to cope.[3,12] There is also the argument that those who have a problem will opt out of offshore employment (or the relationship) and those that survive do so as a result of a self-selection process. This indeed may be the case in the mature offshore development which now characterizes North Sea operations.

The little work that has been done on the effects of offshore worker's absence has provided a useful insight into the ways in which women have coped with family and domestic responsibilities and paid work outside the home in these periods of absence. Research into this area began in the mid 1970s when Dr. Ken Morrice, a consultant psychiatrist in Aberdeen, noted that an increasing number of his female patients displayed symptoms of anxiety and depression. These women shared the common factor that they were the wives of offshore workers. Morrice concluded that these women were experiencing such problems as a result of their husband's pattern of presence and absence, a condition which he referred to as "Intermittent Husband Absence". Later studies of offshore oil workers wives have drawn on Morrice's findings. Taylor, Morrice, Clark and McCann having investigated this condition noted that the women most likely to be prone to these problems were novices, i.e. wives who had pre-school children and lacked previous experience of husband absence.[18]

Studies of offshore workers' wives have highlighted both the advantages and disadvantages of having a spouse who is intermittently absent. Conflicts may arise in relation to the allocation of household tasks and family responsibilities during the husband's period onshore. Often these conflicts are a result of the spouses' differing expectations of how this time will be spent. Whereas the husband may perceive his time at home to be a holiday, and a chance to be with his wife and children, his wife may also want a break from some of the household chores and care of the children for which she has had sole responsibility in her husband's absence. "The male offshore worker's view of *being home* may thus be very different from the wife's needs for *having him home.*"[19]

As Jorun Solheim has pointed out, the returning husband's belief that his wife should be present around the home most of the time that he is onshore can be seen as a result of the heightened expectations of family life produced by the isolation from the home and family during the time spent offshore.[11] It may also be due to the husband's feeling of isolation from his community, which contrasts with the wife's need to retain her links with her social network who are instrumental in enabling her to cope during her time alone. For both spouses the time they spend together is a period of readaptation. The offshore worker lives in two cultures which are very different from each other, while his wife moves between a single and a married life involving changes in behavior. As Solheim explains these different social realities, "his offshore life, her single life at home, and the joint life of togetherness" need to fit together which can prove difficult with such a short space of time to readjust before the next period of absence.[11]

The pattern of offshore employment provides an opportunity for a radical change in the organization of the household and in particular the domestic division of labor, allowing for greater female independence and increased male involvement in the home. However, as David Clark and Rex Taylor have argued, this largely has not happened.[19] Women still retain the bulk of domestic and caring work even when they are in full time employment outside the home.

One of the advantages of having a husband who works offshore is that it allows a couple an allocated amount of time to spend together, and in this way is preferential to having a husband who is working onshore which really only leaves a few hours in the evening and weekends free to spend together. As Clark and Taylor also have pointed out, the space which is created by the husband's period offshore allows both spouses time to reflect on their relationship and place into perspective any difficulties they have experienced or conflicts that have arisen.[19]

As mentioned earlier it is important for the wife to have a social network, for emotional support and to help remove any feelings of social isolation. One British organization dedicated to providing this kind of support is the Offshore Women's Link Support (OWLS). Their prime objective is, "the relief of distress for family members and friends of offshore workers who have fallen victim to tragedies, accidents or any other situation in their work or domestic life."[20] The Central Offshore Wives Group (CSOWG) was set up in 1988 by a small group of offshore wives who began fund-raising for the Chinook helicopter and *Piper Alpha* Disaster appeals. It was soon realized that these women shared similar experiences, fears and uncertainties; thus OWLS was born in 1991 to offer support and friendship to anyone who has family members working in the offshore oil industry worldwide.[21] OWLS runs a telephone helpline and organizes educational days for wives to visit survival and fire-fighting centers and heliports to give them an insight and understanding of the environment in which their husbands are employed. This experience also helps reduce the stress that many wives have as a result of their husbands' working offshore in a setting which is hard to relate to without firsthand experience. OWLS has been successful in making the oil industry more aware of the problems faced by women who are *home alone*, leading to a relationship based on cooperation. For example, OWLS has been invited along to meetings and training sessions on Emergency Response and Aftermath.[22]

In conclusion, it would appear that insufficient research has been directed at understanding the issues surrounding the work/home interface for long distance commuters in general and offshore workers in particular.[5] It has been noted earlier in this chapter that the work/home interface provides a major source of stress for the offshore workforce. Management therefore has a responsibility to understand and manage this aspect of offshore workers' lives. Without understanding and appropriate management support such stresses and strains may impact workers' performance offshore.

References

1. Moore, R. & Wybrow, P. *Women in the North Sea Oil Industry: A Report for the Equal Opportunities Commission.* Manchester: Equal Opportunities Commission, 1984.

2. Mearns, K., & Flin, R. Applying science in a man's world: Women in science, engineering, and technology in the offshore oil industry. In M.R. Masson & D. Simonton (Eds.) *Women in Higher Education: Past, Present, and Future.* Aberdeen: Aberdeen University Press, 1996: 65-71.

3. Heen, H. Making out in a man's world: Norwegian women workers offshore. In J. Lewis, M. Porter & M. Shrimpton (Eds.) *Women, Work and Family in the British, Canadian and Norwegian Offshore Oilfields.* London: The Macmillan Press Ltd., 1988: 62-82.

4. Anger, D., Cake, G., & Fuchs, R. Women on the rigs in the Newfoundland offshore oil industry. In J. Lewis, M. Porter & M. Shrimpton (Eds.) *Women, Work and Family in the British, Canadian and Norwegian Offshore Oilfields.* London: The Macmillan Press Ltd., 1988: 83-101.

5. International Labour Office *Workers in Remote Areas. The Petroleum, Mining and Forestry Industries.* Draft Working Paper. Occupational Safety and Health Branch., June, 1955.

6. Wagstaff, T., Mearns, K., & Flin, R. *Women working in the offshore oil industry.* Aberdeen: The Robert Gordon University, (in preparation).

7. Hellesoy, O.H. (ed.) *Work Environment Statfjord Field. Work Environment, Health and Safety on a North Sea Oil Platform.* Oslo: Universitetsforlaget, 1985.

8. Graven, A. *Sysselsettingen ved oljeaktivitetene* (Employment within oil activity). Report 1992-1. Oslo: Norwegian Department of Employment, 1995.

9. Carter, R, & Kirkup, G. *Women in Engineering; A Good Place To Be?* Basingstoke: Macmillan Education Ltd., 1990.

10. Moore, R. The effects of offshore oil on onshore women. In, Women & Oil, International Conference on Women and Offshore Oil, September 5-7, St. Johns, Newfoundland, 1985: 106-143.

11. Solheim, J. Offshore commuting and family adaptation in the local community. In, Women & Oil, International Conference on Women and Offshore Oil, September 5-7, St. Johns, Newfoundland, 1985: 313-322.

12. Newell, S. The Superwoman syndrome. *Work, Employment and Society,* 7, 1993: 275-289.

13. Office of Science and Technology *Rising Tide: Report on Women in Science, Engineering and Technology*. London: HMSO, 1993.

14. Kelly, A. The construction of masculine science; *British Journal of Sociology of Education, 6*, 1985: 133-146.

15. Stanworth, M. Gender and *Schooling: A Study of Sexual Divisions in the Classroom.* London: Hutchinson, 1983.

16. Norske Shell Draugen—*Meeting the Challenge.* Stavanger: Norske Shell, 1993.

17. Sutherland, V. J. & Cooper, C. L.*Man and Accidents Offshore: An Examination of the Costs of Stress among Workers on Oil and Gas Rigs.* Colchester, Essex: Llyod's List, Dietsmann (International) NV, 1986.

18. Taylor, R., Morrice, K., Clark, D., & McCann, K.The psycho-social consequences of intermittent husband absence: An epidemiological study. *Social Science and Medicine, 20,* 1985: 877-885.

19. Clarke, D. & Taylor, R. Partings and reunions: Marriage and offshore employment in the British North Sea. In J. Lewis, M. Porter & M. Shrimpton (Eds.) *Women, Work and Family in the British, Canadian and Norwegian Offshore Oilfields. London*: Macmillan, 1988: 112-139.

20. Offshore Womens Link Support (OWLS) Report. PO Box 80, Falkirk, Scotland, FK2 0ZX., October, 1993.

21. Offshore Womens Link Support (OWLS) Report. PO Box 80, Falkirk, Scotland, FK2 0ZX, June, 1993.

22. Offshore Womens Link Support (OWLS) Report. PO Box 80, Falkirk, Scotland, FK2 0ZX, October, 1995.

Index

112, 117 chronic, 57, 60, 67 emergency, 40 offshore survival training, 32 definition, 66 effects on performance, 34 fear of flying, 30, 33, 34, 74 litigation, 66 management, 79 mental/physical health, 70, 78 OIM, 71 post-traumatic stress disorder (PTSD), 34, 66 PTSD, 66 supervisors, 57, 60, 71 symptoms, 72, 77

Substance abuse, 35

Supervision, 154, 163, 178, 190, 191-192 job satisfaction, 58 leadership style, 56, 59 motivation, 57 onshore, 57 performance, 58 personality, 58 safety, 60 stress, 57, 60, 71 training, 57, 60

Synergy, 156

T

Team Building, 51, 62

Teamwork, 108, 115, 121, 136, 141-144

Three Mile Island, 168

THERP, 169

Time pressure, 154

Topside medical cover, 28, 29

Training, 57, 60, 154, 163, 167

Triggering events, 159, 165, 173

TRIPOD, 165-167

U

Unsafe acts, 158

USA Offshore Safety Age, 177, 178 Behaviour Modification, 178-179 Experience, 177, 178 Gulf of Mexico, 177 Training, 177, 178

V

Values, 143

VERITEC, 151

Violations, 162, 164, 173

Visitors (medical fitness requirement), 27, 30

W

Water supply (contamination of), 33

Well Control (training), 20-21

Wives of offshore workers, 250-251

Wireline team, 135

WOAD, 151

Women caregivers, 242 hiring of, 240 offshore installation managers, 247 stress, 239, 251 traditional female roles, 239, 241-242 traditionally male professions, 239, 241, 244, 247

Work/Home interface, 244, 252

Work environment, 105, 111-115 overload, 157 patterns, 49, 50, 73, 118 pressure, 59 rotation patterns, 106, 108, 118, 121

Worlds of Risk, 184

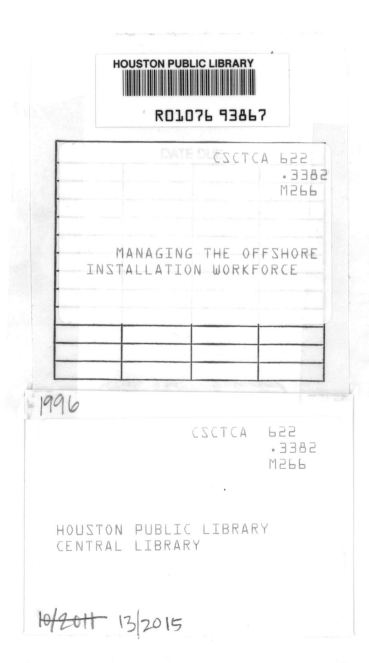